W9-DDW-576

F.V.

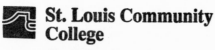
St. Louis Community College

Forest Park
Florissant Valley
Meramec

Instructional Resources
St. Louis, Missouri

Cultures of Color
in America

Cultures of Color in America

A GUIDE TO FAMILY, RELIGION, AND HEALTH

Sybil M. Lassiter

Greenwood Press
Westport, Connecticut • London

Library of Congress Cataloging-in-Publication Data

Lassiter, Sybil M.
    Cultures of color in America : a guide to family, religion, and
health / Sybil M. Lassiter.
        p. cm.
    Includes bibliographical references (p.) and index.
    ISBN 0–313–30070–4 (alk. paper)
    1. Minorities—United States. 2. Ethnology—United States.
3. United States—Race relations. 4. United States—Ethnic
relations. I. Title.
E184.A1L33 1998
305.8'00973—dc21   97–24550

British Library Cataloguing in Publication Data is available.

Library of Congress Catalog Card Number: 97–24550
ISBN: 0–313–30070–4

First published in 1998

Greenwood Press, 88 Post Road West, Westport, CT 06881
An imprint of Greenwood Publishing Group, Inc.

Printed in the United States of America

The paper used in this book complies with the
Permanent Paper Standard issued by the National
Information Standards Organization (Z39.48–1984).

10 9 8 7 6 5 4 3 2 1

Dedicated to the fond memory of my loving parents,

Lillian and Aubrey,

and to my dear children,

Vivien, Courtney, and Yasmine

Contents

Acknowledgments

I would like to thank all the librarians at East Tennessee State University's Sherrod Library and the Medical Library. Also, I sincerely appreciate the vital support of my family, friends, and colleagues. The compilation of the manuscript was enhanced by my many interviewees and reviewers, listed individually as follows:

Africans:
- Reverend G.W. Goah (Liberia), Outreach Asst., Johnson City Senior Center, Tennessee.
- Linda Nwosu (Nigeria), Coordinator, College of Medicine, East Tennessee State University.

African Americans:
- Dr. Dorothy Drinkard-Hawkshawe (Professor of History), Director of African American Studies, East Tennesse State University.
- Vivien P. Mott, C.S.W., M.S.W., B.S.S.W., Medical/School Social Worker, Roosevelt Schools, New York.

Asian Americans:
- Dr. Thomas T. S. Huang (China), Professor and Chair, Department of Chemistry, East Tennessee State University.

Haitian Americans:
- Students of the Haitian Students Organization at Baruch College, City University of New York.

Native Americans:

- Dr. Michael Abram, Director of Cherokee Heritage Museum, Smoky Mountains, North Carolina.

- Richard Crowe, Cherokee Goodwill Ambassador, Qualla Boundary Reservation, Smoky Mountains, North Carolina.

- Dr. John R. Finger, Professor of History, University of Tennessee, Knoxville, Tennesse.

- John W. Greene, Cherokee Archaeologist and Author, Smoky Mountains, North Carolina.

Puerto Rican Americans:

- Sister Alicia Alvarado, Catholic nun, Missouri.

- America Moreno, Social Worker, California.

West Indian Americans:

- Vincent P. James, Retired Businessman, Florida.

Introduction

According to the 1990 census report, one in every four Americans is a person of color. By the turn of the century, more than one-third of the U.S. population will be persons of color (Harris, 1988–1989).

Births, deaths, and migrations are officially categorized by race (or skin color), and these categories are major factors in housing, employment, and education. Yet classification by self-identity has become complicated. The "established" four racial categories apparently do not describe the changing population of the United States. In the 1990 census, almost 10 million people selected the "Other, Not Specified" race category. These individuals identified themselves as belonging to 300 races, 600 Native American tribes, 70 Hispanic groups, and 75 combinations of multicultural ancestry. With the "Spanish Origin" category eliminated from the 1990 census, most immigrants from Latin America classified themselves as other than black or white (U.S. Bureau of the Census, 1990).

Some immigrants from Asia, Latin America, and the Caribbean have different concepts of racial identity. Some Mexicans may perceive a racial continuum from white to red, whereas some Puerto Ricans may view a range from white to black. Further, some Puerto Ricans perceive a continuum related more to culture than to skin color. Likewise, some Asians perceive a continuum based more on social and political factors than on color. In addition, some Caribbean immigrants view a continuum based more on socioeconomic status than on color alone. Then there is an unknown number of individuals who ascribe to a culture of color and endorse the black-white continuum but are "passing" for white.

Classification is further complicated by the assimilation process. Some ethnic groups are assimilating not only culturally but also physically, through intermarriage. For example, about 40% of Japanese and more than 50% of Native Americans are interracially mixed. There is a tendency for children of mixed races (if one parent is white) to be classed as white. However, when one parent is African American, the children are classified as African American or Black, regardless of skin color.

Historically immigration has had a profound impact on the racial composition of the United States, but present and future cultural/racial groups will render more diversity to the overall population than did immigrants in the past. It is predicted that nonwhite groups will account for 45% of the total population by the year 2050, if the current demographic and racial trends continue (McDaniel, 1995). Consequently, many Americans are showing increasing interest in the lifestyles of different cultures among them. As cultural diversity awareness is expanding, the topic is currently included in the curricula of several institutions of learning.

This book was written as a source of basic information about some of the cultures that constitute the increasing number of Americans of color. From the number of references used to compile each chapter, it is apparent that volumes could be written about each culture and its inherent variations. The book is not encyclopedic. The chapters present an overview of selected cultural groups in order to enhance the reader's understanding of diverse lifestyles and to offer motivation for further study.

Each chapter deals with one cultural group with respect to its history, immigration, population in the United States, language, family customs, nutritional preferences, religious practices, health beliefs and practices, common diseases, and ideas about death and dying. Unlike my previous book, *Multicultural Clients*, intended for health professionals and social workers, this book, *Cultures of Color in America*, is more appropriate for general audiences, including young people of about junior high age and older.

Objective information for the book was obtained from extensive research sources, including the Internet. Subjective information is incorporated into each chapter from individuals of the culture who served as interviewees and/or reviewers and from some professors who teach the specific cultural study. Individuals associated with a chapter are identified in the Acknowledgments.

I am aware that all individuals of the selected cultures may not necessarily describe themselves as people of color. However, the book focuses on some cultures that incorporate a significant number of nonwhite individuals or "persons of color." The book makes every effort to avoid stereotyping by frequently using the words "some individuals" when discussing a culture. The book emphasizes the fact that as many differences exist within cultures as between cultures and that individuals on comparable socioeconomic levels across cultures often display similar values and lifestyles regardless of their ascribed culture or color. Thus, factors other than ascribed culture, color, or race may influence behavior patterns.

Acknowledging and understanding the differences that exist among and between our American cultures might help overcome some fears and prejudices, yet maintain an appreciation for the joy and vitality that evolve from pride of heritage. Once we understand the differences, it might then be appropriate to identify and emphasize our similarities.

REFERENCES

Harris, L. (1988–1989). The world our students will enter. *College Board Review*, 150, 23.

McDaniel, A. (1995, Winter). The dynamic racial composition of the United States. *Daedalus*, 124(1), 179–99.

U.S. Bureau of the Census. (1990). *Statistical abstracts of the United States*. Washington, D.C.: U.S. Government Printing Office.

1

Africans

Africa is the second-largest continent (Asia is the largest). Africa occupies over 11 million square miles, or 20% of the earth's land surface and is 5,000 miles long and 4,500 miles wide. The continent contains an enormous supply of potential riches, including 30% of the world's uranium, 50% of the world's gold, 40% of its platinum, and the bulk of the world's diamonds, plus a large supply of other valuable minerals. The name "Africa" may have come from the Latin word *aprica* (sunny) or the Greek word *aphrike* (without cold).

Africa is situated in the Eastern Hemisphere, south of Europe between the Atlantic and Indian Oceans and is bounded on the north by the Mediterranean Sea. Before the Suez Canal was built in 1869, the Isthmus of Suez joined Africa and Asia. The Suez Canal and the Red Sea now form the northeast boundary between Africa and Asia. Africa is composed of 53 nations, including South Africa, Botswana, Mozambique, and Zimbabwe in the south; Egypt, Ethiopia, Kenya, and Sudan in the east; Morocco, Algeria, Tunisia, and Libya in the north; and Liberia, Senegal, Ghana, and Nigeria in the west. Sudan has the largest land area, but Nigeria has the largest population (Mazrui, 1986; Nobles, 1980; Oliver, 1991).

CLIMATE

Africa is a tropical continent; the equator divides it almost in half. Although the extreme southern portion may have a cold season, it is relatively mild when compared to the winters of other continents. Because Africa is in the South Temperate Zone, opposite that of the United States, southern Africa may experience snow during the U.S. summer. Africa's climate varies widely, from temperate in the high plateaus to tropical along the coastal plains, to hot and dry in the desert, to hot and humid in the central rain forests. Climatic extremes are exemplified by floods and drought.

In northern Africa, the Sahara, covering one quarter of the continent (an area as large as the U.S. mainland), is the world's largest desert. The Kalahari Desert, lying at the far south of the continent, is the world's seventh largest. Mount Kilimanjaro in Tanzania is the highest point in Africa; although it is located on the equator, its peaks remain snow-capped year round (Lamb, 1982; Lewin, 1990; Mazrui, 1986).

PEOPLE

The variety of African ethnic groups are as diverse as the land itself. African peoples are multicolored, with a majority of black Africans inhabiting areas south of the Sahara and largely brown Africans residing north of the desert. Several ethnic groups, including Arabs, Jews, Europeans, Asians, Americans, and indigenous Africans make up the African population. Africans are further divided into about 6,000 tribes. The African Diaspora consists of over 100 million descendants of African slaves who are currently dispersed throughout the world. This chapter will focus on indigenous Africans in the United States who may or may not be American citizens. African Americans will be discussed in a subsequent chapter (Lewin, 1990; Mazrui, 1986).

According to the 1990 census, there are approximately 400,000 Africans in the United States, constituting 1.9% of the American population. The largest number of Africans is from Egypt, and the second largest is from Nigeria. The African population in the United States has doubled in the past ten years (U.S. Bureau of the Census, 1990).

HISTORY

In the Beginning

Archaeology indicates that man originated in Africa. The Garden of Eden, from which our ancestors emerged, is located in the highland interior of East Africa. The remains of the first human ancestors, called *australo-pithecines*, were found between Ethiopia and the Transvaal. It is believed that these ancestors lived about 4 million years ago. Fossils indicative of the earliest occurrence of fully modern man, *homo sapiens*, who lived about 200,000 years ago, have been found in South Africa. Thus theory has it that earliest man originated in eastern and southern Africa (Oliver, 1991).

Early indigenous Africans survived by gathering fruits and berries, fishing, and hunting small game. Over the centuries, the people progressed from hunting and gathering to deliberate food production by herding goats and cultivating oil palm and other vegetables. Food production became highly developed in northeastern Africa along the six hundred miles of the fertile Nile Valley. Here the temperate weather pattern offered a full range of southwest Asian foodstuffs such as wheat, barley, lettuce, radishes, dates, and olives, as well as domesticated animals such as sheep, goats, pigs, and cattle.

The successful development of a prosperous society in Egypt about 6000 B.C. was based on environmental factors such as the climate and the surrounding mountains that limited the intrusion of other populations. The Nile (the longest river in the world) was readily navigable, making Egypt easy to govern and police and facilitating the transport of food, security officers, and tax collectors. In the late fourth century B.C., Egypt was conquered by the Greeks, who later fell to Rome. As trade with the interior developed in the Greco-Roman era, Jewish merchants spread first into the high plains of Algeria and Morocco and later by camel caravans through the deserts to southern Africa. Jewish settlements are documented by the remains of synagogues and cemeteries bearing Hebrew inscriptions (Oliver, 1991; Mazrui, 1986).

Colonization

Colonization began when European countries entered Africa and divided the continent into sections that ignored established ethnic divisions. By 1920, every part of Africa except Ethiopia, Liberia, and the Union of South Africa was under European rule or claimed by a European country. All outsiders sought to exploit and convert the Africans. However, by 1993 all African countries had become independent nations (Lamb, 1982; Mazrui, 1986; Oliver, 1991; Tutu, 1994).

The Slave Trade

During African warfare and raiding, captives were taken who became slaves. These slaves were of all colors and races. Egypt used many slaves as house servants, builders, farmers, and soldiers. Although the slave trade may have begun in the north, the trans-Saharan slave trade led to a growing circulation of people, cultures, and ideas throughout Africa.

Intercontinental slave trading had its earliest beginnings during the Muslim era, in medieval times, when slaves were transported from Africa to Asia. In the middle of the fifteenth century, the Portuguese slave traders became the first European slave traders to arrive in Africa. About a century later they were joined by the British, French, and Dutch, who increased the slave trade from 1,000 to 6,000 per year. Shortly after Columbus discovered the New World, there arose a great demand for slaves to work on its plantations. The forced migration of some 11 to 12 million Africans to the

New World was far more significant than the introduction of slavery to any other part of the world. The first slaves arrived in Jamestown in 1619, at least 70% of whom came from the Mande (West) and the Bantu (Central) African groups (Holloway & Vass, 1993; Oliver, 1991).

Racism became an important factor in New World slavery. Black Americans were the only ethnic group in America whose identity was based on the color of their skin. Other groups were referred to as Irish Americans, Jewish Americans, Italian Americans, Oriental/Asian Americans, and so on, but American blacks have always been identified by a racial characteristic—their skin color (as Negro, colored, or black). America began the process of dis-Africanization of personal identity, initially by changing the African names of the slaves to those decided on by their masters. Re-Africanization has been evolving, as evidenced by the many individuals of African ancestry now assuming African names and referring to themselves as "African Americans" (Mazrui, 1986). A list of some typical African names is presented at the end of this chapter.

AFRICAN NATIONS

The following section briefly discusses selected African nations from areas representing northern, eastern, southern, western, and central Africa. The nations are Morocco, Ethiopia, South Africa, Liberia, and Nigeria, respectively.

Morocco

The Kingdom of Morocco, occupying about 172,000 square miles, is located in northern Africa. The country is bordered by Algeria on the southeast, Western Sahara on the southwest, and the Atlantic Ocean and the Mediterranean on the north. The Kingdom of Morocco is a constitutional monarchy with a legislature of 333 elected deputies. Currently, King Hassan II (ruling since 1961) is the sovereign head of state. He approves legislation, appoints the prime minister, and has the right to dissolve Parliament. The capital of Morocco is Rabat. The well-known and most densely populated city is Casablanca.

Arabic, the official language of Morocco, is spoken by 75% of the population. The other 25% speak Berber, French, or Spanish. Islam is the state religion. Ninety-eight percent of Moroccans are Sunni Muslims, and 2% are Christians, mainly Roman Catholics. Morocco also has a large Jewish population (Hunter, 1996; Mazrui, 1986).

Ethiopia

Ethiopia, occupying about 472,000 square miles, is located in eastern Africa. Ethiopia is bordered on the northeast by Erithrea, on the east by Djibouti and Somalia, on the south by Kenya, and on the west by Sudan. Ethiopia is unique in that it was never officially colonized, but remained a multiethnic and independent political entity until the Italian invasion in 1935. The Italians were in turn defeated by the Allied forces in 1941, and Emperor Haile Selassie returned as ruler. In 1987, a provisional military government elected Lt.-Col. Mengistu Haile Marian president of the New People's Democratic Republic. Ethiopia then established a democratic charter that guaranteed freedom of expression and the right to self-determination for all ethnic groups. In 1991 an 87-member Council of Representatives unanimously elected Meles Zenawi president.

Haile Selassie, the last emperor of Ethiopia, ruled from 1930 to 1974 and became known as the "enlightened reformer." He expanded the army and the police force, strengthened the ministerial system, expanded the modern school system, established strong alliances with foreign powers, and initiated the first constitution in 1931. He was overthrown and imprisoned by a military committee in 1974. He died in 1975. Haile Selassie is currently the proclaimed God and spiritual leader of the Rastafarians, a Jamaican religious group (Olcansky & Berry, 1993; Wubneh & Abate, 1988).

There are about 68 ethnic groups in Ethiopia, who speak about 286 languages. The official language is Amharic, although Oromo-speakers represent the largest group. Muslims comprise about 45% of the population, and Christians about 40%, while about 12% practice traditional religions (Hunter, 1996; Wubneh & Abate, 1988).

South Africa

The Republic of South Africa, occupying 471,000 square miles, is located in southern Africa. It is bordered by Namibia, Botswana, and Zimbabwe on the north, by Mozambique and Swaziland on the northeast, by the Indian Ocean on the east, and by the South Atlantic on the south and west.

The Union of South Africa, formed in 1910, became a republic in 1961, when the government embarked on a formal policy of social and political racial segregation or apartheid. In a system unique to the modern world, less than 4.5 million whites (Afrikaners) controlled 24 million nonwhites (Blacks, Coloreds, and Indians) under the apartheid system.

The African National Congress (ANC) was organized in 1920 to protest the unfair treatment of blacks in South Africa. In 1960, after the massacre of 69 Africans at a demonstration protesting apartheid in Sharpeville, the government outlawed the ANC and arrested the key leaders, including Nelson Mandela. By the mid-1960s the government had subdued all efforts to end apartheid. Nelson Mandela, a prominent African attorney, had articulated the aspirations of blacks and was prepared to pay the price for his convictions. During Mandela's imprisonment, Desmond Tutu, Archbishop of Capetown, through his speeches to public groups and interactions with government officials served as a constant source of hope and strength for black South Africans.

Finally, in 1989, after international pressures and much local bloodshed, the government considered removing its restrictions of apartheid and announced its willingness to consider the rights of black South Africans. In 1990, the government lifted the ban on the African National Congress (ANC) and released its leader. After 27 years in prison, Mandela emerged as a national hero. A Government of National Unity took office in 1994 and elected Nelson Mandela president of the Republic of South Africa (Hunter, 1996; Lamb, 1982; Mazrui, 1986; Tutu, 1994).

There are eleven official languages in South Africa, including English, Setswana, Afrikaans, Zulu, and Xhosa. The use of each of these is constitutional and may be adopted by any of the provinces as its official language. A significant number of South Africans are bilingual, speaking Afrikaan and English. In keeping with South Africa's ethnic diversity, several religions coexist. The majority of South Africans are Christians: Roman Catholics, Methodists, Lutherans, Presbyterians, Baptists, Anglicans, Seventh Day Adventists, Pentecostals, and Mormons, to name some. Non-Christian religions include those of the Hindus, Muslims, Jews, and Buddhists (Hunter, 1996).

Liberia

The Republic of Liberia, occupying 43,000 square miles, is located in western Africa. It borders the North Atlantic, between Sierra Leone and the Ivory Coast. Liberia, never officially colonized, is the second-oldest black Republic (after Haiti) in the world. The independent nation of Liberia, established by freed slaves from the United States and the West Indies, became a republic in 1847. The name "Liberia" means "land of the free." The capital was named Monrovia, in honor of U.S. president James Monroe. Its founders and ancestors are known as Americo-Liberians.

The Americo-Liberian minority, currently constituting 5% of the Liberian population, became the elite, who established a society based on American models. They emphasized education and proper attire as essential to success and erected schools in their communities. Indigenous tribes are the majority, making up 95% of the people of Liberia. These tribes include the Mande, Kpelle, Bassa, Gio, Kru, Mano, Gola, Gbandi, and Bella, each of which speaks a different tribal language or dialect. Seventy percent of

Liberian people practice traditional religions, 20% are Muslims, and 10% are Christians.

Because Liberia is richly endowed with water, mineral resources, forests, and a climate favorable to agriculture, the nation has long been a producer and exporter of basic products. However, since 1990, civil war has destroyed much of Liberia's economy. Today political instability threatens prospects for economic reconstruction and the repatriation of some 750,000 Liberian refugees who have fled to neighboring countries (Goah, 1995; Hunter, 1996).

Nigeria

The Federal Republic of Nigeria, the most populous country in Africa, occupies 356,669 square miles and is located in central-west Africa. Nigeria is bordered by Niger on the north, Chad and Cameroon on the east, the Gulf of Guinea on the south, and Benin on the west.

Nigeria became a federation in 1954, achieved independence in 1960, and became a republic in 1963. The nation's complex history has included colonial rule, followed by independence, then interethnic and interregional competition, military coups, a civil war, an oil boom that produced corrupt government and individual triflers, severe droughts, and finally a debt crisis that caused a major recession and lowered standards of living. Recently the nation has experienced unstable presidential elections. Under such circumstances, the people turned to the familiar—ethnicity, kin, and local governments. Efforts to demilitarize and democratize the country motivated the development of two parties, the Social Democratic Party (SDP) and the National Republican Convention (NRC). These parties control the local districts under the auspices of elected governors.

Nigeria has about 250 ethnic groups. The largest are the Hausa-Fulani, Yoruba, Ibo, Kamuri, Tiv, Edo, Nupe, Ibibio, and Ijaw, who constitute 80% of the population. Nigeria's official language is English. Similar to that in many nations of Africa, Nigeria's ethnic diversity is reflected in a variety of coexisting religions. Approximately 48% are Muslims, 34% Christians—17% Protestants, 17% Roman Catholics—and others, comprising about 18%, practice traditional indigenous religions (Hunter, 1996; Metz, 1992).

LANGUAGE

Africa's spectrum of languages has made Africa the most linguistically complex continent in the world and consequently has created significant communication problems. Language barriers and tribalism serve as major obstacles to the African people's development of a true sense of unity. The 6,000 tribes of Africa speak at least 1,000 different languages and dialects.

Imagine, if you will, a hypothetical situation in the United States whereby the people of Washington, New York, Dallas, Chicago, and Los Angeles all spoke different languages and were thereby unable to communicate. Problems with respect to national unity would certainly be evident.

Most African nations recognize a European official language, usually that spoken by the controlling country during colonization. In addition, many nations have a "national" language, which generally represents the largest indigenous ethnic group. Of the indigenous languages, Arabic is the most frequently spoken in northern Africa. South of the Sahara, languages such as Hausa, Kiswahili, Wolof, and Somali are popular.

Swahili (also known as Kiswahili) is the most widespread indigenous language of Africa. African politicians often speak at least three languages: English, Swahili, and a tribal tongue. Swahili is a Bantu language, influenced by other languages such as Arabic, Persian, Hindi, Portuguese, Indian, and English. A knowledge of Swahili, which has been spoken since the thirteenth century, facilitates the understanding of other African Bantu languages, including Kiganda, Kikambu, Kishona, and Kiduala. Although there are many dialects of Swahili, the dialect of the coastal regions is considered standard Swahili, examples of which are presented at the end of this chapter (U.S. Bureau of the Census, 1990; Goah, 1995; Lamb, 1982; Lewin, 1990; Mazrui, 1986; Zawawi, 1972).

FAMILY

Traditional African Families

African family concepts are rooted in traditional African practices. Because of the intense cohesiveness of the African family, the conjugal unit (husband and wife) often functions within and shares most activities with the original extended family. This family philosophy, based on communality and the survival of the entire kinship unit or tribe, is embodied in the philosophy of Africentricity.

Africentricity

Africentricity derives from a sense of regional communality, supported by the following beliefs: (1) people are synonymous with the normal rhythms of nature, and (2) a collective consciousness manifests in the survival of the entire ethnic unit. Communal behavior is basic to the survival of all living forms of nature. Traditionally, many indigenous Africans have believed that because the community (or tribe) created the individual, each person exists in relationship to that group. Consequently the extended family has been the most common family structure, and the individual's identity has been linked to tribe affiliation. Many Africans who are now living in America maintain their tribe affiliations in Africa.

Therefore, unlike Eurocentricity or Western orientation, which emphasizes the primacy of the individual, Africentricity posits survival of the entire unit/family/tribe. Whereas Eurocentricity is intellectual, Africentricity is intuitive and holistic. Whereas Eurocentricity is based on individualism, Africentricity is based on collectivism (Akbar, 1984; Mpofu, 1994; Nobles, 1980).

Family Roles

The traditional male role in rural Africa included hunting, clearing land, and building dwellings. Women were responsible for such duties as fetching water, gathering wood for the fires, harvesting crops, selling food, and raising children. Women were the major resources of rural development, and their positions were essentially autonomous and rarely subservient. Some indigenous African cultures were often matrilineal and/or matriarchal. Female religious figures are more likely to emerge from indigenous groups than from Islamics or Christians in Africa (Mazrui, 1986; Romero, 1988).

Traditionally, the African conjugal (marital) relationship has been generally subordinate to the consanguinal (bloodline) relationship. This is not to imply that the conjugal bond was unimportant, but only that it did not take precedence over the consanguinal union. Because the stability of the extended family was not dependent on conjugal unions, divorce did not disrupt the extended family unit. Although the consanguinal relationship took precedence over the conjugal unit, divorce was rare in the traditional African extended family. Marriage was a very stable institution because each partner derived great satisfaction from the experience of playing an important role in a total family unit (Foster, 1983; Romero, 1988).

Some traditional marriages in Africa have been polygamous. The number of wives a man can have is usually determined by his ability to support them. Some have believed that the polygamous relationship served as a solution to the problem of a shortage of men due to the more dangerous male lifestyle as hunter and warrior. In some areas the polygamous relationship has been considered highly prestigious for the man (Semaj, 1982; Romero, 1988).

Traditional marriages were usually arranged by the kinship system. Girls married very young to avoid out-of-wedlock pregnancies, which often prevented them from completing schooling past puberty. Their husbands were generally much older, on the assumption that an older man would be better able to support a family financially. The major purpose of the traditional marriage was less for companionship than for the production of many children to help in the fields and later become the caretakers of their elderly parents (Romero, 1988).

Children

In several traditional African kinship systems, a child would call several women "mother." These women included the birth mother (with a special attachment) and the wives of the father's brothers and paternal cousins as well as all other wives of the father (in a polygamous unit). In addition, the child would refer to the mother's sisters and cousins as "mother" and likewise recognize the father and his brothers as "father." Consequently, all children of these related adults would be called brothers and sisters. Birth parents would be primarily responsible for the care and discipline of their child; but because the child recognizes several additional mothers and fathers, these other family members must also assume responsibility for the child's welfare (Foster, 1983; Lamb, 1982).

Traditionally "rites of passage" (coming-of-age) rituals and ceremonies have been performed to prepare the adolescent child for the transition into adulthood. In some African cultures clitorectomy has been one such ritual performed on young girls. Poet Mariama L. Barrie (1996) reveals her personal experiences during and after clitorectomy (genital mutilation) at the age of ten, in her native Sierra Leone. Ms. Barrie states that advocates of female mutilation (mostly male) hold to the traditional belief that an uncircumcised woman is impure and unclean and thereby unfit to marry, bear children, and attain respect in old age. Barrie claims that, although some died after the procedure, there are over 100 million women who are living victims of this practice. As a result of clitorectomy, these women have experienced agonizing pain, septicemia, tetanus, and/or persistent chronic vaginal and uterine infections. She decided to write the article, "Wounds That Never Heal" to present the truth about her experience and to emphasize the fact that this practice still continues in some areas of Africa. Barrie, a young woman now residing in New York, is currently active in the international campaign to end female genital mutilation.

Elders

Traditionally, African elders have been respected and honored. Grandparents often care for their grandchildren, and elders reflect family history and traditions. Also, many elders have been held in high esteem because they served as family advisors and judges, using the wisdom acquired from many years of experience. The older the elder, the more he or she is respected for being wise enough to have lived so long. Finally, an elder will soon become an ancestor whose spirit will protect the family. Traditional African families have always assumed responsibility for the care of their elders (Lamb, 1982; Metz, 1992; Romero, 1988).

Modern African Families

As have individuals of most indigenous cultures, Africans have acculturated to many Western family practices and lifestyles. Currently, in the
United States, Africans are frequently found in nuclear family groups, generally residing in African American communities. Despite cultural disruptions through migration, many Africans have preserved kinship
relationships and maintained some African traditional practices. The following section describes a traditional African wedding of today.

A Nigerian Wedding

This author was privileged to interview a colleague, Linda Nwosu, coordinator in the College of Medicine at East Tennessee State University.
Linda Nwosu was preparing to leave for Nigeria to participate in the weddings of her two daughters to Nigerian men (July 1996). Her husband had
preceded her and was in Nigeria helping with the preparations. Linda
Nwosu was born in this country, and her husband is an indigenous Nigerian of the Yoruba tribe. The Nwosu family resides in Tennessee.

Mrs. Nwosu describes the Nigerian wedding as a "process, not just an
event." The process begins with a series of visits by the intended groom
and his family to the family of the prospective bride. During the first visit,
the intended groom asks for permission to marry the young lady, and the
bride-to-be indicates her approval to both families by sealing the visit with
a toast of wine. Couples usually select each other prior to the visit. On the
final visit (*Igba Nkwa*), the groom-to-be brings gifts and wine to the prospective bride's family; now she leaves her family and goes with him to his
family's ancestral village in Nigeria.

Unlike the practice of some eastern cultures, the Yoruba groom gives a
dowry (*Igbo*) to the bride's family, who has designated the amount. In
addition to the dowry, the groom's family must present several gifts to the
bride's family. These gifts include a goat that will be slaughtered for the
wedding feast. The goat has been traditionally believed to insure a good
marriage. The groom's family determines the location of the ceremony and
pays most of the wedding expenses. The groom's tribe prescribes the couple's wedding attire, and tribal laws determine the ceremony protocol. The
Yoruba tribe is a patrilineal society, although other tribes, such as some in
Ghana, are matrilineal. Finally, after weeks of intense planning, visits, and
preparation, the elaborate wedding ceremony and reception take place, on
a weekend day within a strict limit of six hours (usually noon to six). The
strict time limit is related to the success of the marriage. Several family
members participate in the ceremony, including the mother of the bride,
here Linda Nwosu, who performs a ritual dance. After the wedding, the
couple will retreat to the home of the new husband's father. The names of
the children will be determined by the elders of the tribe (Nwosu, 1996).

NUTRITION

African nutritional patterns have been influenced by a philosophy of unity with nature. Fresh fruits and raw vegetables are favorite foods because of the belief that enzymes are alive in raw foods. Muslims do not eat pork. Several Africans prefer a vegetarian diet (Afrika, 1989).

Favorite fruits include apricots, avocados, bananas, breadfruit, kiwis, carambolas, cassava melons, cherimoyas, coconuts, dates, figs, mangos, papayas, and guavas. Favorite vegetables include beets, red cabbage, yams (or sweet potatoes), white potatoes, celery, spinach, lettuce, yellow squash, cauliflower, carrots, okra, and corn. Other nutrients are corn meal, barley meal, whole wheat flour, rolled oats, nuts, honey, rice, and brewer's yeast.

For vegetarians, there are a variety of African meatless dishes. For example, chickpea okra fry combines vegetables and dried peas or beans. Since fish and shellfish are plentiful in African waters, with Nigerian waters alone offering over 200 varieties, fish dishes are popular.

Other favorite dishes include Egyptian collard greens, Tanzanian fish curry, sweet potato pudding, and soups such as plantain and corn soup, groundnut soup, and spicy squash soup. Fu Fu, still prepared in the traditional manner, consists of boiled vegetables that are pounded until smooth and sticky, forming "finger food" that is then scooped up (may be dipped in a stew) and eaten from a communal bowl. Favorite desserts include tropical fruit pancakes and papaya and mango with mango cream, which use the plentiful fruits of Africa. Many African meals end with a bowl of fresh fruit (Nash, 1996).

RELIGION

Religion has played a vital role in the lives of most Africans because it explains one's culture and one's relationship to nature and humans. Religion also determines one's role in the community and society and how one copes with misfortune, illness, and death. A variety of traditional indigenous religions coexist with the many Christian and Islamic faiths in Africa. Similar to Christianity and Islam, traditional African religions believe in a Supreme Being (God or Creator). The Akan-Ashanti refer to God as *Onyame*. The Bantu's god is called *Nzambi*. For the Mende, God is *Ngewo*; and to the Gola, *Daya* The Supreme Being, generally considered to be omniscient and omnipotent, is the creator of all life and embodies the qualities of kindness, justice, and mercy. Unlike Jehovah, the African God is not to be feared and does not require prayer offerings. Belief has it that evil comes from sources other than God (Creel, 1990).

Some traditional indigenous African religions have not perceived the Supreme Being as a centralized force. God is not usually viewed as being in the form of a man or as abiding in heaven or seated on a throne. Man was not created in the image of God, but the universe and all life forces are manifestations of God. Traditional belief holds that all nature acts as expressions of God: the sunrise as God's smile, the floods and droughts as God's wrath, and the thunder and lightning as divine interactions (Creel, 1990).

Below the level of the Supreme Being, lesser deities serve as intermediaries. These deities prescribe certain methods of worship, ceremonial dances, dress codes, foods, and special days to honor. Voodoo (*Vodu*) is a religion based on a highly organized hierarchy of deities. Women (queens) have usually conducted the rituals of voodooism. Voodoo generally represents the positive religious rites, while "hoodoo" connotes the mystic and magical aspect used for negative purposes. Presently, voodoo is also practiced in Haiti and several areas of the United States, most predominantly in New Orleans (Mulira, 1990).

Some traditional Nigerians have held that religious practices and supernatural forces strongly influence human situations. Access to resources such as agriculture and house rights, political office, and social relations are defined by religious beliefs and protected by souls of ancestors. Two groups of spirits, those of ancestors and those of place (e.g., trees, rocks, animals), mandate loyalty to the authority of elders and to traditional practices. Thus everyday misfortunes such as illness, political rivalries, inheritance disputes, and marital problems can be explained within a religious framework. Protection against misfortune can be enhanced by wearing certain jewelry such as charms and amulets and by using medicinal products from practitioners. This jewelry may also be helpful in protecting one from sorcery and witchcraft associated with evil people (Metz, 1992).

Many African belief systems have adopted symbols that identify humans with other animals and objects and are often called animistic religions. These belief systems establish a sense of continuity between man and nature that tends to blur the distinction between man and the environment, between the living and the dead, between the divine and the human, and between the natural and the supernatural (Mazrui, 1986).

Divination

In addition to belief in a Supreme Being, many traditional Africans have held a belief in divination. Divination, *ohulagula*, has been a specific act performed by specialists called diviners. Some diviners function as healers, who make diagnoses and treat illness with the assistance of supernatural forces. Other diviners function as protectors, believed to protect people from witchcraft and sorcery. Some tribes have believed that the ancestors guide human action through divination and that divination is one of the tools that God gives humans to help them cope with the problems of life.

Traditionally, to become a diviner the individual must have overcome some tragic life experience such as a severe death-defying illness. Diviners must excel in intelligence, imagination, fluency in tribal language, and knowledge of traditions. In addition they must be able to mediate between the living and the dead. In many societies the diviners must also undergo extensive training by elder diviners (Peek, 1991).

Life and Death

Belief in the afterlife has been integral to traditional African religions. The future world is not viewed with fear or as a place of rewards and punishments, as in the Christian sense. Rather, death is a journey into the spirit kingdom, where there is no sickness, disease, or poverty. This concept is expressed by the Ba Kongo in their description of the four stages of the life cycle. Observing the sun in its course around the world, the stages of life are as follows: sunrise is birth, or the beginning; ascendancy is maturity; sunset represents death and transformation; and midnight is the passage into another world and eventual rebirth. Thus, life is viewed as a circular continuum symbolized by the four moments of the sun. Death is not the end of life but rather a door (*mwelo*) between two worlds (Creel, 1990).

HEALTH

Health Beliefs

Africans generally believe in holism: Mind, body, and spirit are inseparable. Good health is defined as harmony with nature, whereas illness is a state of disharmony or "dis-ease." Disharmony could have many causes, such as demons or bad spirits of the living or souls of the dead. Traditionally, since good and evil have been perceived as natural forces, one must maintain harmony between these two forces in order to remain healthy.

Because of the holistic nature of the body, belief has held that any part of the body can indicate illness in another part. Thus changes in the skin such as color, texture, rashes, and hair-growth pattern, as well as abnormalities of the tongue, ears, eyes, fingers, and hair, can indicate disease even of internal organs. Consequently, a good healer should be able quickly to diagnose an illness by observation of the appropriate body surfaces. It is noteworthy that modern medical science has acknowledged "clubbed fingers" as symptomatic of chronic oxygen deprivation, frequently observed in clients with congenital heart disease and chronic pulmonary disease There has been no scientific explanation for this phenomenon (Asante, 1987; Sherman & Fields, 1982).

Health Practices

Traditional belief has it that metals, as a part of the mineral world, are a form of living energy. They are capable of emitting, conducting, and absorbing energy and thus have an effect on the human body. Traditional Africans have worn metals as jewelry for adornment as well as for curative and protective effects. Some metal bracelets are worn because it is believed that the metal will change color in the presence of abnormal body conditions and thereby alert the wearer to seek treatment. Examples of metals believed to stimulate body processes are gold for metabolism; copper for blood, liver, pancreas, eye, ear, and emotions; and silver for adrenal, thyroid, and brain processes.

Similar to several other cultures, African traditionalists have believed that crystals also are able to prevent and treat illness because they stimulate mental and spiritual energies. Since crystals or gems are crystallized plants, some Africans believe they possess the energies of the plants.

In addition, colors have been thought to produce a holistic healing effect on the body. The use of many colors can be observed in African clothing and art. Colors rubbed on the face are thought to be protective as well as therapeutic. In ancient Egypt, colors on the eyelids (later called eye makeup by the Europeans) indicated that a woman was fertile. Colors observed on the skin might indicate distressed organs (e.g., red for heart and small intestine disorders, blue-gray for liver and gallbladder disturbances, etc.) (Afrika, 1989).

Musical sounds have been considered a form of energy that has a healing effect on the body organs. Healers use various musical modes to heal and relax the body. Today, scientific practitioners utilize music for both its relaxing and its therapeutic effects.

Herbal Medicines

Traditional healers have been proficient in the therapeutic use of roots and herbs. The use of herbal medicine is based on traditional knowledge about the healing effects of plants. The effectiveness of remedies such as *Desmodium adscendens* for the treatment of asthma and *Bridelia ferruginea* to control sugar levels in diabetes has been confirmed by the Center for Scientific Research in Ghana. Laboratory experiments have yielded evidence that twigs of the *Diospyros* species, which have long been chewed by East Africans, cleanse the teeth and prevent mouth infections. These twigs were found to contain antifungal and antibacterial substances. Derivatives of the plant *Catharanthus roseus* (red periwinkle, old main, church flower) have been used to treat diabetes, leukemia, Hodgkin's disease, and other forms of cancer (Morris, 1987).

The following are other herbal remedies for selected health problems:

- Appetite: ginseng, calamus, goldenseal
- Arthritis: yucca, parsley, alfalfa
- Gas: bay leaves, cayenne, cascara, chamomile
- Corns/Calluses: garlic powder (in socks)
- Backache: uva ursi, nettle, tansy
- Coughs: flaxseed, red sage, ginseng, myrrh
- Heart disease: sorrel, bloodroot, peppermint

- Headache: chamomile, holy thistle, rhubarb
- Hypertension: black cohosh, ginseng, garlic (Afrika, 1989)

Sickle Cell Anemia

Sickle cell disease is a term used to describe a group of hemoglobin (red blood cell) disorders. In the event of body trauma such as lack of oxygen, dehydration, or infection, the disease causes red blood cells to become abnormally shaped, resembling sickles (sickling). These cells clump together, obstructing circulation to body areas and causing various problems, including severe pain. This event is called sickle cell crisis.

Sickle cell disease, caused by the inheritance of an abnormal hemoglobin gene, is most prevalent in populations of African descent. The gene is also found, less frequently, in persons of Mediterranean ancestry (southern Italians, Sicilians, and Greeks), in Saudi Arabia, and in India. Because the sickle cell gene apparently renders an individual immune to malaria, the highest frequencies of sickle cell disease have been found in the malaria belt of equatorial Africa. Among persons of African ancestry in the United States, one in 500 has sickle cell disease, and 8–10% carry the trait. In certain areas of western Africa, like Ghana and Nigeria, prevalence of the sickle cell trait may reach 25–30%.

Sickle cell disease was once considered a disease of childhood because 50% of its victims died before the age of 20. In the United States, recent advances have been made in treating the disease. The median age of death for a male with sickle cell disease is now 42, and for a female, 48. Although not unaffected by symptoms, some individuals with the condition are living into their 70s. Treatment for sickle cell disease includes transfusions, bone marrow transplants, and new antisickling drugs such as HU (hydroxyurea), Butyrate (arginine butyrate), and Bencyclane (Gribbons, Zahr, & Opas, 1995; Kocak et al., 1996; Steinberg et al., 1995).

AFRICAN HERITAGE

Cultural exchanges between cultures are usually mutual and simultaneous. Therefore, while the African slaves acculturated into the Western way of life, they also affected American culture. Because the house slaves lived and worked in closer contact with their masters' families, they usually abandoned African traditional practices to a greater extent than did the more removed and communal field slaves. Obviously, the strongest African cultural influences are found in areas where Africans and their descendants are a majority of the population. These areas include the South in general, especially South Carolina and Mississippi. Likewise, the West Indies and Latin America demonstrate strong African cultural influences.

Santeria, meaning "worship of the saints," is a Cuban religion that combines Roman Catholic principles and African Yoruba tribal beliefs and practices. Santeria is one of a series of Yoruba-based religious forms found in the Caribbean, Central and South America, and the United States. Some examples of other Yoruba religions are *shango* in Trinidad and Grenada, *xango* and *candomble* in Brazil, *kele* in St. Lucia, and *voodoo* in Haiti and New Orleans.

Although many African churches encourage active audience interaction and clapping as a communal response, the Pentecostal church presents a dynamic demonstration of traditional practices. Pentecostal services often include possession trances, fainting, ritual dancing, drumming, and ecstatic speech, thought to be the language of angels or spirits. Often the pastor, during an emotional sermon, uses unknown speech patterns, referred to as "speaking in tongues." A prescribed dress code is required for certain services.

The persistence of Africanisms is found in traditional art forms. Folklore includes songs such as "Stagolee," "John Henry," and Uncle Remus's songs and sayings. The famous Brer Rabbit, Brer Fox, and Sis Nanny-goat stories are Wolof folk tales introduced to America by the Hausa, Fula, and Mandingo tribes. Distinct Kongo influences are noted in Cuban dance forms like the rumba, mambo, conga, and samba. The banjo, although seldom played by African descendants, was originally introduced to America by African slaves. The rhythms of jazz, the blues, and gospel are notably of African origin. Jazz playing fosters a communal, cooperative gathering of musicians. Likewise, the blues and gospel evoke a communal effect by encouraging audience participation. These music practices manifest typical characteristics of Africentricity.

Foods throughout North and South America have reflected influences of Africa, as exemplified by the gumbos of New Orleans, the feijoadas of Brazil, and the jerks of Jamaica. Also, sweet potatoes, hot peppers, peanuts, sesame seeds (benne), okra, black-eyed peas, and watermelons were originally cultivated in Africa (Nash, 1996).

Other forms of Africanism in America include the popularity of kente cloth, originally woven by Ashanti weavers. African hairstyles, from the "Afro" to braids, have been adopted by Americans of various cultures. Traditional gestures are frequently observed among African Americans. The most common gesture is a pose with both hands on the hips. In northern Congo, this akimbo stance means that the person is ready to accept the challenge of a situation. In the United States, standing with both hands on the hips is recognized as the African American woman's classic challenge pose (Brandon, 1990; Philips, 1990; Robinson, 1990; Thompson, 1990).

Kwanzaa

Kwanzaa, a time of celebration, reflection, and feasting, is America's fastest-growing holiday. Neither political nor religious, Kwanzaa is a seven-day observation of cultural unity, celebrated between Christmas and New Year's Day. The holiday was created in the United States by Dr. Maulana Karenga, a black-nationalist scholar and professor at California State University, in order to motivate a sense of community after the 1965 Watts riots. Originally Kwanzaa was primarily observed by African American family and community groups, but today it is celebrated in public schools and museums, in advertising, and on television.

The foundation of Kwanzaa is the *Nguzo Saba*, which means "Seven Principles" in Swahili. These seven basic principles are: (1) *Umojo*, or unity; (2) *Kujichagulia*, or self-determination; (3) *Ujima*, or collective work and responsibility; (4) *Ujamaa*, or collective economics; (5) *Nia*, or purpose in building the community; (6) *Kuumba*, or creativity; and (7) *Imani*, or faith in our teachers and leaders. Each of these principles is discussed on one night of Kwanzaa. On the sixth night, there is a feast (*karamu*) followed by a ritual that reaffirms the continuity of the living, the dead, and the unborn (Crowley, 1994).

CONCLUSION

African people are of different races, cultures, and languages. They have experienced a unique and tragic past, and yet today many live in the midst of civil unrest, violence, and poverty. In spite of their many problems, the African people have made major cultural contributions to the world. Our prayer today is that soon they may see a peaceful, united, and prosperous homeland.

AFRICAN NAMES
Days of the Week with Corresponding Names

Day	Male Name	Female Name
Monday	Cudjoe	Juba
Tuesday	Cubbenah	Beneba
Wednesday	Quaco	Cuba
Thursday	Quao	Abba
Friday	Cuffee	Phibba
Saturday	Quamin	Mimba
Sunday	Quashee	Quasheba

More African Names (Holloway & Vass, 1993)

Male Names	Female Names
Ankey	Abey
Banjoe	Binah
Cully	Camba
Goma	Embro
Tokey	Fortimer
Stepney	Mabia
Zick	Sibbey

SWAHILI

Selected English-Swahili Translations (Zawawi, 1972)

English	Swahili
Hello	Hujambo
How are you?	Uhali gani?
What is your name?	Jina lako nani?
Do you understand me?	Unanifahamu?
Why?	Kwa nini?
Where?	Wapi?
How long? (time)	Muda gani?
Help me	Nisaidie
I am hungry	Nina njaa
I am thirsty	Nina kiu
I am cold	Ninaona baridi
I am sick	Ninaumwa
Yes	Ndiyo
No	Hapana
Thanks	Ahsante sana
Good	Vizuri
Bad	Vibaya
My relatives	Jamaa zangu

REFERENCES

Afrika, L. O. (1989). *African holistic health*. Silver Springs, Md.: Adesegun, Johnson, and Koran.

Akbar, N. (1984). Africentric social sciences for human liberation. *Journal of Black Studies*, 14(4), 395–414.

Asante, M. K. (1987). *The Afrocentric idea*. Philadelphia: Temple University Press.

Barrie, M. L. (1996, March). Wounds that never heal. *Essence*, 26(11), 54.

Brandon, G. (1990). Sacrificial practices in Santeria, an African-Cuban religion in the United States. In J. E. Holloway (Ed.), *Africanisms in American culture* (pp. 119–47). Bloomington and Indianapolis: Indiana University Press.

Creel, M. W. (1990). Gullah attitudes toward life and death. In J. E. Holloway (Ed.), *Africanisms in American culture* (pp. 69–97). Bloomington and Indianapolis: Indiana University Press.

Crowley, C. H. (1994 November/December). Out of Africa. *Cooking Light*, pp. 120–24.

Foster, H. J. (1983). African patterns in the Afro-American family. *Journal of Black Studies*, 14(2), 201–32.

Goah, J. G. W. (1995). An historical analysis of educational policy and its development and shortcomings in Liberia, West Africa. Unpublished master's thesis, East Tennessee State University, Johnson City.

Gribbons, D., Zahr, L. K., & Opas, S. R. (1995). Nursing management of children with sickle cell disease: An update. *Journal of Pediatric Nursing*, 10(4), 232–42.

Holloway, J. E., & Vass, W. K. (1993). *The African heritage of American English*. Bloomington: Indiana University Press.

Hunter, B. (1996). *The Statesman's Year-Book: Statistical and historical annual of the states of the world for the year 1995–1996* (132nd ed.). New York: St. Martin's Press.

Kocak, R., Baslamisli, F., Guvenc, B., Tamer, L., Aikimbaev, K. S., & Isbir, T. (1996). Bencyclane as an anti-sickling agent. *British Journal of Haematology*, 92(2), 329–31.

Lamb, D. (1982). *The Africans*. New York: Random House.

Lewin, A. (1990). *Africa is not a country: It's a continent*. Milltown, N.J.: Clarendon.

Mazrui, A. A. (1986). *The Africans: A triple heritage*. Boston: Little, Brown.

Metz, H. C. (1992). *Nigeria: A country study*. Washington, D.C.: Federal Reserve Division, Library of Congress.

Mpofu, E. (1994). Exploring the self-concept in an African culture. *Journal of Genetic Psychology*, 155(3), 341–53.

Mulira, J. G. (1990). The case of Voodoo in New Orleans. In J. E. Holloway (Ed.), *Africanisms in American culture* (pp. 34–68). Bloomington and Indianapolis: Indiana University Press.

Nash, J. (1996, February). Taste of Africa. *Essence*, 26(10), 101–3.

Nobles, W. (1980). African philosophy: Foundations for black psychology. In R. Jones (Ed.), *Black psychology*. New York: Harper and Row.

Nwosu, L. (1996, July). Nigerian weddings. Personal interview at College of Medicine, East Tennessee State University.

Olcansky, T. P., & Berry, L. (1993). *Ethiopia: A country study*. Washington, D.C.: Federal Research Division, Library of Congress.

Oliver, R. (1991). *The African experience: Major themes in African history from earliest times to the present*. New York: Icon Editions, an imprint of HarperCollins Publishers.

Peek, P. M. (1991). *African divination systems: Ways of knowing*. Bloomington: Indiana University Press.

Philips, J. E. (1990). The African heritage of white America. In J. E. Holloway (Ed.), *Africanisms in American culture* (pp. 225–39). Bloomington and Indianapolis: Indiana University Press.

Robinson, B. J. (1990). Africanism in the study of folklore. In J. E. Holloway (Ed.), *Africanisms in American culture* (pp. 211–24). Bloomington and Indianapolis: Indiana University Press.

Romero, P. W. (1988). *Life histories of African women*. Atlantic Highlands, N.J.: Ashfield Press.

Semaj, L. T. (1982, August). Polygamy reconsidered: Causes and consequences of declining sex ratio in Afro-American society. *Journal of Black Psychology*, 28–43.

Sherman, J. L. Jr., & Fields, S. K. (1982). *Guide to patient evaluation* (4th ed.). Garden City, N.Y.: Medical Examination Publishing Co.

Steinberg, M. H., Ballas, S. K., Brunson, C. Y., & Bookchin, R. (1995). Sickle cell anemia in septuagenarians. *Blood*, 86(10), 3997–98.

Thompson, R. F. (1990). Kongo influences on African-American artistic culture. In J. E. Holloway (Ed.), *Africanisms in American culture* (pp. 148–84). Bloomington and Indianapolis: Indiana University Press.

Tutu, D. (1994). *The rainbow people of God: The making of a peaceful revolution.* New York: Doubleday.

U.S. Bureau of the Census (1990). *Statistical abstract of the United States.* Washington, D.C.: U.S. Government Printing Office.

Wubneh, M., & Abate, Y. (1988). *Ethiopia: Transition and development in the Horn of Africa.* Boulder, Colo.: Westview Press.

Zawawi, S. W. (1972). *Say it in Swahili.* New York: Dover Publications.

2

African Americans

In the United States, African Americans are generally dark-complexioned (not always) individuals who identify with either African, Caribbean, black American, or black Native American cultures in conjunction with aspects of mainstream culture. African Americans may be categorized into two groups, "natives" and "immigrants." Natives include African Americans whose ancestors arrived in this country before slavery and individuals whose ancestors were brought here as slaves. Immigrants are African Americans who migrated post-slavery from Africa and the Caribbean; but their children, if born in the United States, are natives. African Americans are further divided into affluent and non-affluent groups.

Diversities exist among African Americans with respect to geographic origin, age, family and religious values, level of acculturation, intermarriage, and socioeconomic status (based on education and occupation). Since behavior patterns are not universal within any one culture, African Americans of diverse cultures and socioeconomic levels should not be expected to have the same values and needs or to behave alike. Diversity in the African American community, may be partially responsible for their lack of unity (Davis, 1993).

In the past many terms have been used to refer to North American peoples of African descent. The list includes derogatory terms, along with descriptors that have been accepted as appropriate such as "African" and "Negro" (slavery period, 1619–1865), "colored" (segregation period, 1865–1954), and "black" or "Afro-American" (desegregation era, 1954-1988). However, most of these descriptors have primarily reflected white society's perception at various stages. Many African Americans were referring to themselves as Afro-Americans and "people of color" as early as the

1800s (Douglass, 1845; Du Bois, 1903). Popular early civil rights groups included the Afro-American League (1882–1891) and the Afro-American Council (1898–1903) (Drinkard-Hawkshawe, 1974). During the civil rights movement of the 1960s, the concepts of black pride and black power influenced the social consciousness of peoples of African descent. "Black is beautiful" and "I'm Black and I'm proud" became popular expressions, hence "black" became the preferred term of reference. In the late 1980s, Jessie Jackson, along with other well-known political figures, made a point of using "African American" in preference to other terms (Houk, 1993).

Currently the term "African American" is accepted as an improvement over "black," since black is a color, not a culture, and African culture is not inextricably linked to dark-complexioned peoples. Considering the descriptors associated with Italian Americans, German Americans, and so forth, the ancestral birthplace of Americans of African descent is Africa, not "Afro." Consequently, "African American" is currently the preferred term to describe people of North America who are of African ancestry. Although the term is preferred, some disagree that it is appropriate; the word "black" is also used frequently to refer to African Americans (Davis, 1993; Houk, 1993; Lassiter, 1994).

African Americans comprise 12% of the American population, constituting the nation's largest minority group (U.S. Bureau of the Census, 1990). African Americans experience the highest rate of discrimination of all the minorities in America. The rejection of blackness by mainstream society, viewed as an aspect of social power, has had negative effects on the African American population (McDaniel, 1995).

Until recent decades, the majority of African Americans lived in the South. Although since 1940 many African Americans have migrated to the North, East, and West, the South remains the homeland for over half of this population, with 59% of its elderly living in the thirteen southern states (Maryland, Virginia, North Carolina, South Carolina, Georgia, Florida, Alabama, Mississippi, Tennessee, Kentucky, Louisiana, Arkansas, and Texas) (U.S. Bureau of the Census, 1990).

HISTORICAL HIGHLIGHTS

Since the history of African Americans or any culture can encompass volumes, this brief discussion will highlight some areas of African American history generally omitted from textbooks and the media. The discussion will include pre-Columbian African Americans, black Indians, African Americans of the Northwest, and an overview of post-Columbian periods.

Pre-Columbus

In the early sixteenth century, the Spanish first encountered black populations in isolated groups, as well as among various nations, like the

Charruas of Brazil, the Caribs in the Gulf of Mexico, and the Jamassi of Florida. Because these African descendants were generally encountered in areas washed by a Pacific current or an equatorial Atlantic current, the Europeans believed that black pirates from Ethiopia might have established settlements in the New World after their ships wrecked (De Quatrefages, 1905).

Historical records in Cairo indicate that an African king, Abubakari, sailed from West Africa across the Atlantic with a well stocked fleet of ships in 1311. Although none of the ships returned to Africa, American archaeologists have found artifacts such as statues, masks, and paintings in the Andes mountains and Mexican valleys that show cultural similarities to Western Africans and Mexicans, dated about that time. Also, archaeologists have discovered skeletons with crania resembling African Americans in pre-Columbian earth layers in Texas and Mexico, and established that African Mandingo traders had traveled to Mexico and other areas since 1310. In addition, Negroid terra-cotta and stone heads, from as early as 800 to 700 B.C., were found in parts of Mexico and Central America.

Figures of Negroid gods found among several Indian tribes depicted people with close curled hair, goatees, and beards (uncommon to the hairless Indian chin) and heavy ear pendants (popular among West Africans). These figures included the Aztec god Tezcatlipoca and the Mexican gods Naualpilli, god of jewels, and Ek-chu-ah, god of traveling merchants. Many of these artifacts may be viewed in the National Museum, Mexico City (Sertima, 1976).

It may be difficult for many to perceive African American figures venerated as gods by some Native Americans, because since the era of slavery individuals of African ancestry have been represented as inferior beings whose universal humiliation began with the arrival of Columbus. Then, African cultural and technological achievements were erased from the consciousness of history (Sertima, 1976).

An early prevailing misconception was that European transoceanic ships of the fifteenth century were superior to previously made primitive ships. Thus it was assumed that primitive ships ended up in the New World only by accident and that these small numbers probably had no significant influence on the existing populations. But in fact, the navigational knowledge of Columbus and the Spaniards in the fifteenth century was elementary when compared to that of some earlier civilizations. For example, the system of latitudinal and longitudinal coordinates was used in China as early as 100 B.C. Also, the shipping expertise of ancient Egypt is well known. During the third dynasty, the black Egyptian Pharaoh, Sneferu, built 63 seafaring ships measuring 100 to 170 feet, over a period of two years (Bailey, 1973). In 1970, the Norwegian writer and explorer Thor Heyerdahl performed a test run proving that the ancient Egyptian papyrus reed boats were indeed capable of successfully crossing the Atlantic from Africa to America (Heyerdahl, 1971).

Mandingo Africans, accustomed to long journeys over unchartered expanses, compared the desert to the ocean and referred to the Sahara as the "sandy sea." Mandingo traders employed efficient nautical instruments, astronomical computations, and guides using the sun, moon, and stars to pilot them across the deserts as well as the oceans. Consequently, although some pre-Columbian ships to the New World may have arrived accidentally, it is possible and probable that other landings were intentional (Sertima, 1976).

Black Indians

The previous discussion established that Africans settled with some early Native American tribes before slavery. The early colonists first enslaved Indians and then, later, Africans to relieve the severe labor shortage. The first 20 Africans were brought to Jamestown in 1619. The status of these Africans has been a subject of debate. However, most agree that they were servants. Franklin (1974) contends that they were indentured servants. Nevertheless the system of black servitude gave way to black slavery, which was sanctioned by law.

The colonists preferred African slaves, because of the great distance from their homeland, over the Indians who, when they escaped to their nearby villages, would return with armed tribe members seeking revenge. Between 1622 and 1632, full-scale battles between the colonists and the Native Americans occurred in Virginia, where the Indians usually murdered the whites but spared many Africans. Consequently, in an attempt to discourage unions between the two groups, the colonists tried to indoctrinate the Native Americans with the European concept of black slavery.

The Seminoles and some other tribes rejected the concept of slavery. Thus, many runaway slaves were taken in by several Native American tribes who willingly accepted other people into their villages. The Seminoles were particularly prone to admitting different people into their tribes. The Native Americans then refused to deliver these fugitives to slavehunters. Africans and Native Americans found that they shared common values, such as the belief in economic cooperation instead of competition, and that skills, friendship, and trust were more important than skin color. Racial mixing between Native Americans and Africans in Mexico became so common that slavehunters could no longer rely on color to differentiate between freemen and slaves. By 1650, Mexico alone had a mixed African and Native American population of 100,000.

Not all runaway slaves lived among the Seminoles; some established independent villages known as "Maroon" settlements with names such as

"God Knows Me and None Else" and "Disturb Me If You Dare." Both Seminoles and maroons united against the slavehunters. Maroon cultures evolved from a combination of African and Native American experiences as well as elements of European customs. In maroon communities, women were prominent and were often assigned leadership roles by men. Because they were outnumbered by the men, women were protected and often allowed to have more than one husband.

Escaped slaves living as maroons became Florida's first settlers. Jungles, reptiles, and tropical diseases discouraged most intruders and slavehunters. Africans, familiar with tropical jungles, were generally immune to malaria and European diseases such as smallpox. Unfortunately, many Native Americans died of these diseases (especially smallpox). As a consequence, their population was severely reduced after the Europeans arrived. The Native American population of 80 million in 1492 was reduced to 10 million a century later, while the 10,000 Africans in the Americas in 1527 increased to 90,000 by the end of the century.

Several Seminole and maroon wars with the colonists erupted. The government was determined to crush their communities and to break the alliance between Africans and Native Americans. However, many of these communities survived. By the eighteenth century, many maroon and Seminole settlements had become successful independent agricultural communities. During the nineteenth century, when the U.S. Army faced serious problems with Texas and the Union was threatened, black Seminole fighters and scouts volunteered to assist the government. Although these Seminoles were excellent fighters and a major asset to the army, they were often mistreated by other soldiers and by disgruntled Confederate veterans who were still armed and resentful. Yet the Seminole fighters were courageous and undaunted. Some were later awarded the Congressional Medal of Honor. Even today the valor of the remaining members of the black Seminole nation goes unrecognized by the outside world. Their descendants reside on both sides of the Rio Grande near Eagle Pass, the scene of their greatest victories and disasters.

Currently it is estimated that about one-third of African Americans have Native American ancestry, with a higher level of Indian ancestry in Latin America. Well-known historical African–Native Americans include Crispus Attucks, who was the first to die in the Boston Massacre; Paul Cuffee, a wealthy Dartmouth merchant concerned with protecting blacks from discrimination in the United States and who became the first black man to sponsor a migration of blacks to Africa, in 1815; Frederick Douglass, who became the leading voice for black emancipation during the Civil War era; and Langston Hughes, a creative writer of poetry, plays, novels, and newspaper columns, who became the popular voice of Harlem, New York's African American community (Katz, 1986).

African Americans of the Old Northwest

The old Northwest territory consisted of five states: Ohio, Illinois, Indiana, Michigan, and Wisconsin.

After the government's relocation of most Native American nations, large numbers of black and white settlers moved into Ohio, Illinois, and Indiana from 1810 though the 1820s and into Michigan and Wisconsin from 1830 through the 1840s. By 1830, over half of the Old Northwest's black population resided in the state of Ohio. Some white settlers had moved to the Northwest to escape the atrocious slavery atmosphere, but most whites wished either to continue slavery or to maintain the subordinate status of free blacks or to avoid all contact with people of color—whereas most blacks had relocated to the Northwest in search of liberty and the rights of citizens. Obviously, the political motives of the blacks and whites differed immensely.

Some African Americans had migrated from other free states, and some were former slaves who had purchased their freedom or were emancipated, but the majority were fugitives from slavery in the South. However, in the Northwest, they had to contend with legal discrimination, poverty, and the ever-present danger of recapture. Racial prejudice and segregation were present in the free states as well as the Northwest territories. Black children could not attend public schools in Indiana, Wisconsin, or Michigan. Segregation existed in all public facilities such as hospitals, orphanages, and transportation, although all northwestern blacks paid taxes to help support these facilities. Yet residence in the Northwest permitted African Americans to resist some mistreatment that could not be avoided by slaves.

Both free blacks and fugitives lived in constant fear of the slavehunters, who often kidnapped free blacks as well as runaways. Black children were most vulnerable. Being weaker, children were frequently kidnapped and sold by the slavehunters. An apprenticeship system supposedly initiated to teach trades to black children was often used to separate black children from their families. The children were then sent to distant areas for long periods of time. One sixteen-year old, named Jacob, was apprenticed for 90 years (Cashin, 1995).

Although the Northwest Ordinance of 1787 (article 6) outlawed the introduction of slavery into the Northwest, there was no enforcement provision, so some slave owners retained their slaves. The Fugitive Slave Act of 1850 stated that runaways living in free states were not subject to legal protection such as jury trials. The act also provided rewards for federal marshals who returned fugitives to slavery. Because the act gave slave owners so much power to recapture fugitive slaves, it became unsafe for slaves to remain in the United States after 1850. Consequently, between 1850 and 1860, over 20,000 African Americans migrated from the Northwest to Canada (Cashin, 1995). Further discussion of the Northwest African Americans will continue in the later section on the Family (Cashin, 1995; Piersen, 1988).

Post-Columbus Overview

The post-Columbian history of African Americans in the part of America that became the United States can be divided into three periods: slavery (1619–1865), postslavery and segregation (1865–1954), and desegregation (1954-present). The formal status of African Americans has evolved from "nonhuman and/or property" during the slavery era to "sub-human," as aliens who were not entitled to citizenship and voting rights, during the segregation period to "human" during desegregation (Davis, 1993, p. 24; Franklin, 1974, p. 341). As a consequence, the black marginality that began during slavery and thrived with racism and segregation has greatly affected the lifestyles of African Americans (Davis, 1993).

During the Civil War, Negroes served in every theater of action as Union or Confederate soldiers. Congress awarded many medals and commendations to the brave colored soldiers. More than 38,000 Negro soldiers lost their lives. This high rate of mortality was estimated to be 40% greater than that for the white troops (Franklin, 1974). The surrender of the Confederate Army and the end of the Civil War in 1865 marked a victory for the abolitionists but the beginning of increased racial tensions between blacks and whites. Many emancipated slaves were left homeless and unemployed. Those freedmen who were able to obtain work from Southerners, often disgruntled about the outcome of the war and the new status of their former slaves, were frequently not paid (Du Bois, 1903; Franklin, 1974).

To help relieve some of the problems of the freedmen, the government established the Freedmen's Bureau in the War Department (1865–1870). The bureau, also known as the Bureau of Refugees, Freedmen, and Abandoned Lands, placed officials in each of the Southern states to aid the refugees and freedmen. The Freedmen's Bureau furnished supplies and medical services, established schools, supervised contracts between freedman and their employers, and authorized recognition of freedmen in the courts of law. In addition, the bureau resettled some people who had been displaced during the war, and distributed land to some freedmen. Notably, the bureau achieved its greatest success in education. In cooperation with philanthropic and religious organizations in the North, the bureau established and supported many institutions of learning. These institutions include Howard University, Hampton Institute, St. Augustine's College, Fisk University, Atlanta University, and Johnson C. Smith University. Religious groups were also active in establishing schools on all levels. Although the bureau was successful in many endeavors to improve the life of freedmen, it failed to create an atmosphere of goodwill between ex-masters and freedmen. In fact, the Bureau operated in an atmosphere of intense hostility from many Southern whites. The bureau also failed to provide (as promised) land to all freedmen. The "forty acres and a mule" that was to be a gift from the government had not materialized. Yet some freedmen became successful landowners. Within a year, freedmen in Florida owned land covering 160,690 acres; and by 1874, Negroes of Georgia owned more than 350,000 acres of land (Du Bois, 1903; Franklin, 1974).

During the segregation area, several all-black towns like Allensworth, California; Boley, Oklahoma; Nicodemus, Kansas; and Mount Bayou, Mississippi, sprang up throughout the United States. These segregated towns provided African Americans the opportunity to establish an alternative economy for themselves, elect their own public officials, and educate themselves within their communities. Self-employment in their own small businesses with a captive black market was a successful means of economic advancement. Today, several African Americans have been successful in business enterprises such as banking, insurance, manufacturing, and entertainment.

During the desegregation era, the interest in black community business declined because reduced discrimination provided opportunities for African Americans in mainstream employment. However, many unskilled workers were unemployable. Today, some community leaders are considering the advantages of black community business in which individuals who are unable to attend college may acquire work skills. Some believe that the reestablishment of black-owned businesses could be a method of revitalizing decaying cities. Politicians argue that providing jobs in these community businesses would be preferable to supporting the poor in economically depressed areas. With the remarkable growth of the black middle class, with available capital, an increase in black-owned businesses could be a viable future option (Davis, 1993).

A commentary on African American culture by Dr. Thomas Sowell of Stanford University (1995) contends that a major part of what we call African American culture today did not originate with Africans but was introduced to the slaves by British colonists in the South. For example, "Black English" actually originated with Englishmen who migrated from southern and western England to colonial Virginia centuries ago. Expressions including "I be" and "you be," "dis" and "dat" (this and that), "chitlins" (pork intestines), "yaller" (yellow), and "ax" (ask) were common in those parts of England. Also, phrases that became southern dialect were commonly used by rich, poor, educated, and illiterate alike in southern and western England and Virginia.

Many of the original colonists who settled in the South came from areas of England that were less economically and socially developed than other parts of Britain. Migrants from the violent "no-man's lands" between England and Scotland transported their lawless behaviors (from family feuding to lynching) to the American South. According to Sowell, because many ancestral behavior patterns were brought to the South from Britain, illiteracy and lawlessness were more common among white Southerners than among the Puritans of Massachusetts or the Quakers of Pennsylvania.

As social advances, prosperity, and education spread throughout the South, several of the negative Southern aspects disintegrated notably in the white population. On the other hand, most African Americans who were on the lowest social and economic levels experienced these advances to a lesser degree. However, over time, African Americans have experienced slow progress; and many of the old folkways are eroding. Over time, a large class of educated African Americans has emerged (Sowell, 1995). Atlanta, Georgia, with a large population of professional African Americans, is an example of a Southern city that has promoted these advances.

THE AFRICAN AMERICAN FAMILY

Colonial Family

In African societies, "survival of the tribe" was primary; and kinship bonds directed tribal life. The philosophy of Africentricity that fosters communality and cooperation, rather than Eurocentricity that upholds individuality and competition, has permeated the black family in both Africa and America (Asante, 1987; Hoskins, 1992). The following discussion will focus on the African American families of the Old Northwest to illustrate colonial family concepts.

Joan Cashin (1995) studied 100 black families in the Old Northwest (50 native Northwesterners, 50 Southerners) and noted that the average household size was five persons. Men, whose average age was 37, headed 88 of the households. Two-thirds of these men worked as farmers or laborers; and in an area where almost all whites were literate, only about 35% of the black men could read or write. Almost half of the southern households were extended, but most of the native northwestern households were nuclear in structure. Only 28% of the black households owned real estate, yet they were not affluent. The Southerners (mostly fugitives) were financially more successful than the northwestern natives. The Southerners' unique skills and qualities required to escape from slavery probably evolved into special abilities to succeed financially. At any rate, all blacks, regardless of origin, managed with limited resources and rare prospects for upper mobility.

Most black women of the Old Northwest resided in male-headed households and worked in low-paying jobs as domestic servants, laundresses, or seamstresses. Their central role, like that of their husbands, was duty to the family. In this 1850 sample, married women had an average of three children per household, well below the average of seven children for slave families. They probably practiced birth control to limit their families because children were vulnerable to kidnappers and/or the apprenticeship system. In naming their children, most parents in this sample selected not African names but rather Biblical names, most likely because of their devout Protestant faith.

Most often Northwestern black gender roles were determined less by the white middle class or free black philosophy than by the fugitive slaves' own experiences. Because the fugitive slave's family integrity was constantly threatened and daily life necessitated survival behaviors, men and women had to assume flexible gender roles. Men and women fugitives often cross-dressed in order to deceive slavehunters. Black women were seldom able to assume the traditional white role of the weak and dependent female; instead, they had to deviate more from traditional roles than did black men. Many assertive northwestern women including Maria Stewart, Sojourner Truth, Mary Shadd Cary, and Mary Bibb, became well-known public activists.

Contrary to proslavery propaganda, that depicted black men as uncaring husbands and fathers, most black men believed that caring for their family was basic to their masculinity. The deliberate disintegration of their families by slave owners was an outrage to their masculinity. Northwestern black men often had to bravely defend their families from kidnappings and other abuses. To "show yourself as a man" became an important concept specific to African American men of the Northwest; white men rarely, if ever, had to defend their families from such abuses (Cashin, 1995).

Many well-known northwestern African American men, including Frederick Douglass, Martin Delany, John Mercer Langston, and Henry Bibb, became active abolitionists in spite of dangerous, abusive treatment. African American men also fought bravely in the American wars. Unfortunately, however, the stereotype of the weak, cowardly, and submissive black male was perpetuated, for example, in the media's characterization of the submissive, contented Uncle Tom, the "humorous" Sambo, and later the blackface minstrels. Making the black man an object of laughter stripped him of his masculinity, dignity, and self-respect (Cashin, 1995; Dates & Barlow, 1990).

Modern Family

Steven Ruggles used new data sources to trace long-term national trends in African American family structure between 1880 and 1980. Two well-known features of the African American family are a high incidence of single parenthood and a tendency toward extended family structure. The black extended family has been a method of coping with single parenthood and other problems. Recent data analysis indicates that from 1880 to 1960, black children were two to three times more likely to reside with one parent than were white children. From 1960 to 1980, single parenthood rose sharply for both blacks and whites.

A simple socioeconomic interpretation of the black family's single-parent pattern may not be adequate. In 1980, it was noted that educated black mothers of young children were less likely to reside with a spouse than were illiterate mothers. Thus poor economic conditions were not necessarily related to single parenthood. Actually, a significant positive relationship was found between single parenthood and per capita wealth. Thus in 1880, poor and illiterate blacks were more likely to reside in a two-parent family, whereas educated blacks were more likely to reside in single-parent households, usually resulting from divorce. In contrast, in 1980, poverty among whites was associated with single parenthood.

However, today a growing number of African American children are being born into low-socioeconomic fatherless environments, currently increasing the association of single parenthood and poverty (Gaines, 1994). Apparently, in order to explain the family patterns of some African Americans, both socioeconomic and cultural explanatory factors may be inadequate. In view of their extremely different backgrounds, there have been consistent cultural differences between black and white norms related to residence of spouses (Ruggles, 1994). Empirical studies have suggested that European Americans and African Americans have differing value orientations (Fine, Schwebel, & James-Myers, 1987).

Staples (1991) believes that the high percentage of single African American parents is related to a number of factors that include the following considerations: Young black couples continue to have unprotected sex and are less likely to get married or to have an abortion if conception occurs. Fewer than one black teenager in ten (8.5%) gets married after premarital pregnancy, compared to half (50.8%) of whites. Also about 33.5% of premaritally pregnant white women have abortions, compared to only 5% of black women. Hudgins (1991–1992) believes that the significant tendency for African American women to keep children born out of wedlock reflects a tradition of caring and the willingness to assume multiple role responsibilities. The preponderance of young mothers with out-of-wedlock children may have diminished the stigma somewhat, but has failed to relieve the major resulting problems (Davis, 1993).

The Extended Family

The philosophy of the extended family is based on a sense of obligation. When family members are unable to survive alone, they depend on relatives (kin) for support. Martin and Martin (1978), who interviewed members of 30 extended families of small towns and urban areas of Southern communities, noted the following characteristics:

- The extended family is interdependent; members depend on each other for emotional, social, and material support. In contrast, the nuclear family reflects independence and individualism and most frequently is economically independent of relatives.

- The typical household consists of at least four generations. The nuclear family usually includes only two generations.

- A dominant family figure keeps the family together, and all members look to this person for leadership. That a female is the dominant figure does not necessarily indicate a matriarchal household, because several male relatives may be highly influential in the decision making. Uncles, cousins, brothers, boyfriends, and "big daddies" may serve as decision makers and father figures to children.

- Reaching across geographic boundaries, family members do not have to live in the base household to be active participants in family activities. The base household is the home of the dominant figure and is the most stable unit of the family network. This base is usually the site for family reunions, vacations, holiday celebrations, and other important family activities.

- The extended family has a built-in mutual aid system for providing aid and moral support to family members. For example, an elderly member who is no longer able to live alone will be taken in by another family member, and children will be cared for ("child keeping") when necessary by any other member, without the technicalities of legal adoption.

- The subextended family may resemble the nuclear family, since it is a separate household consisting of a husband, a wife, and children. However the subextended family is firmly rooted in the base household and is obligated to assist in any family crisis. A family with an absent father may be viewed by mainstream culture as a "broken home" or a dysfunctional family, but in reality this family may be an important link in the flexible extended family network with a strong support system (Martin & Martin, 1978).

- Adult children are expected to perform duties for their parents as reciprocal acts. The basic idea of reciprocity is "give and take" and "what goes around, comes around" (Hines & Boyd-Franklin, 1982).

Unlike many white families, which were patriarchies maintained by the economic dependence of women, many African American couples have been characteristically more egalitarian in their roles. This is partly because the system of slavery in the United States did not allow the black male to assume a superior role in the family, and the female was not economically dependent on him. Therefore, relationships between the sexes were based on social-psychological factors rather than on an economic compulsion to marry and remain married. This may be an important factor projected into the current philosophy of some African American male-female relationships (Staples, 1988).

Another consideration is that African American women are generally better educated than the men at all levels except the doctoral level. African

American women tend to have more positions in the expanding sectors of the economy, whereas African American men are overrepresented in the decreasing number of industrial jobs (Staples, 1988). Yet African American outmarriage is lowest of all ethnic groups; for example 40% of Japanese American and more than 50% of Native American women intermarry, whereas only 1% of African American women and 3% of African American men are interracially married (McDaniel, 1995).

Nevertheless, many African Americans are experiencing well-functioning marriages. Many have loving and dedicated relationships with their spouses and families. Unfortunately, little research exists on positive marital adjustment, happiness, and satisfaction among African Americans (Staples, 1988).

Strengths of African American Families

The major adaptive strengths of the African American family are strong kinship bonds of the extended family (renewed by regular reunions), role flexibility, egalitarian household structure, and religious orientation. Role flexibility is the unique ability of family members to perform both traditional and nontraditional gender-typed activities. For females (including those with preschool children), this flexibility often includes employment outside the home, household maintenance and repair, and family protection. Most African American couples are generally more egalitarian with respect to family roles of economic provider, homemaker, child caretaker, and decision maker than other couples in mainstream America (Hines & Boyd-Franklin, 1982; Hudgins, 1991–1992; Staples, 1988).

Elderly

Hill (1977) found that African American elderly were more likely than Caucasian elderly to describe themselves as "happy." Perhaps one reason may be that they often continue to play an important role in the extended family for advice and child care. Only 4% of African American families have dependent elders 65 years or older living with them. Instead, the elder (usually a grandmother) takes young children into her household. Because of this common practice, many African American families are headed by an elderly woman, caring for dependent children who are not her offspring (Hill, 1977; Staples, 1988). On the whole, African American elders reside with kin comparatively more frequently than whites (Ruggles, 1994).

Although statistics show that generally most whites live longer than blacks, African American elderly, male and female, who live to be 70–75 years old or older, have longer life expectancies than their white counterparts (Watson, 1990). This is known as the black/white mortality crossover: There is a lower white mortality rate at younger ages but lower black rates at older ages (Wing et al., 1985).

Children

Fertility rates of African Americans are related to socioeconomic status and regional characteristics. The birth rate of college-educated African American women is lower than that of their white counterparts (Staples, 1988). Although some African American women describe menstruation as being "sick," pregnancy is viewed as a state of wellness. Some African American men see their women as most beautiful during pregnancy and view pregnancy as a positive sign of their own virility and masculinity. Because pregnancy has been a symbol of fertility, an old Southern African American practice was to take the pregnant women to the fields and have them plant potatoes and onions. It was believed that this would insure a good crop for the farmer.

Naming the child confirms the child with an identity. Black Muslim fathers may name the baby, informing the mother of the name later, but most African American parents cooperate in the naming process. Names are frequently selected from the Bible, or babies are named after members of the extended family. Also, Black parents are selecting names of African origin, such as Faraja (leader of the way) and Turmani (our trust and hope) or names corresponding to days of the week; for example, Cudjoe for males and Juba for females, meaning Monday (Greathouse & Miller, 1981; Holloway & Vass, 1993).

African American mothers tend to start toilet training early and wean their babies from the bottle early. The toilet trained and weaned child will be easier for the working mother to place in a child-care facility. But in some instances the training and weaning from the bottle and pacifier (if used at all) represent a form of early discipline.

With respect to discipline, middle class families tend to be more liberal and less authoritarian with their children than lower-income families. Spankings are often a part of the discipline process, which is not considered to be child abuse. Although African American parents are more likely than their white counterparts to use physical, rather than verbal punishment, this form of discipline is often tempered by the love most African Americans express for their children (Staples, 1988).

Some studies have associated the African American child with low self-esteem. Yet other studies have found that African American children are not usually likely to suffer from low self-esteem because of many supportive influences such as religion, reference groups, group identification, and positive experiences in the extended family (Staples, 1988). Children build self-esteem based on the appraisal and reinforcement they receive from their significant others (Videbeck, 1960). More recent research findings noted that low self-esteem was rare in African American adolescents because these youngsters focused more on the perceived judgments of family members and other significant others than on the opinions of society (Verkuyten, 1988).

Socialization

African American families usually teach their children to develop pride in their race and culture and try to prepare them to cope with racism. The African American child is taught to function in two different societies, the black society and the white mainstream society, while maintaining his or her identity and self-esteem. Thus, African American parents' childrearing techniques are geared to prepare their children for a kind of existence that may be alien to middle-class white children (Staples, 1988).

Because of gender role flexibility in childrearing and household responsibilities within the family, the child may not internalize rigid distinctions between male and female roles. In comparisons of African American and white children, African American children were found to be more androgynous, that is, they had a less stereotypic concept of sex roles than did white children (Johnson, 1977; Kleinke & Nicholson, 1979).

SOCIOECONOMIC STATUS

One-third of African Americans live in poverty. Approximately one-half reside in central cities and in communities typified by poverty, poor schools, unemployment, periodic street violence, and generally high levels of stress (U.S. Department of Health and Human Services, 1990). Many African Americans experience conflicts and stresses related to discrimination.

Individuals vary in their perception and internalization of stressful racial situations. The perception and appraisal of a stressful event is determined by the person's socioeconomic status, intelligence, education, self-esteem, previous experiences, and coping styles. The higher the socioeconomic status, the greater the individual's ability to cope with a hostile society. Socioeconomic status also affects one's self-concept and determines one's sense of powerlessness. Thus, African Americans show vast differences in coping abilities (Dodson, 1981).

Comments by the Black Bourgeoisie

In his book *Race Matters*, Cornel West, then director of African American Studies at Princeton University, discusses the growing gulf between the African American underclass and the rest of black society. Ellis Cose discusses the problems of middle-and upper-income African Americans in his book *The Rage of the Privileged Class*. Many are disturbed that one segment of the African American community (the disadvantaged) has come to represent the whole.

Although, over the past 20 years, African Americans have made obvious professional and financial advances, many black leaders continue to present black communities as having universal needs such as social welfare programs, inner-city services, and job skills training. This perpetuates the myth of the stereotypic black underclass despite the growing number of upper-income black families. Several whites and, unfortunately, some blacks are surprised to confront a "proper-English-speaking" educated or professional African American.

Between 1970 and 1990, the number of black families with incomes under $15,000 rose from 34.6% to 37% of the black population. Whereas the number of black families with incomes of $35,000 to $50,000 increased from 9.9% to 14.5% of the black population (U.S. Bureau of the Census, 1990). Apparently there is a growing rate of above-poverty-level African Americans in the United States.

To be recognized as middle class often may be perceived by some as a threat to the political progress of black people. When the media presents the "official" opinion of all African Americans, the black bourgeoisie and intelligentsia generally remain silent because disagreement might assign one the label of traitor or "oreo." The label *oreo* refers to an African American who is black on the outside but white on the inside (considered an insult to be avoided). Leonce Gaiter, in his article "The Revolt of the Black Bourgeoisie," demands the right of any American to be recognized as an individual, to have his or her own opinions and talents, and not to be described within a universal complex of ethnic characteristics (Gaiter, 1994).

NUTRITION

"Soul food" is the expression used to describe native African American food. This type of food is preferred by many, but not all. During slavery and later, the black plantation worker in America was often allotted only the "undesirable" pieces of meat, such as the intestines and bony cuts. Later some ex-slaves purchased their own land and grew pigs and chickens. Consequently, African Americans learned to prepare skillfully spareribs (bony part of the pig), chitterlings or "chitlins" (hog intestines), and pigs' feet and ears. Pork is a popular meat product in the African American diet. Pork skins, fat, and ham hocks are often used to flavor other dishes. Black Muslims, however, do not eat pork. Other favorite foods that may be included in "soul food" diets are as follows:

- Vegetables: Collard greens, kale, poke salad, turnips, corn, sweet potatoes, yams, black-eyed peas, pinto beans, kidney beans, lima beans (butter beans).
- Cereals and breads: grits, oatmeal, hoecake (unleavened corn bread), flour dumplings.
- Dairy: clabber (similar to yogurt).

- Meats: fried chicken, fried pork chops (with gravy), smoked Virginia ham, chitlins, spareribs, scrapple (breakfast meat made from pork scraps), sage sausage, fried fish.
- Desserts: Rice and bread puddings, homemade biscuits (covered with blackstrap molasses), and various berries (Carrington, 1978).

Seventy-five percent of African Americans do not drink milk because their gastrointestinal tracts cannot tolerate lactose (Boyle & Andrews, 1989). Except for those individuals who do not eat pork or any meat products, African Americans generally enjoy foods that are high in fat content and highly seasoned, especially with salt. However, increasing public health information about the adverse effects of fats and salt in relation to heart disease and hypertension has motivated many African Americans to alter their eating habits (U.S. Department of Health and Human Services, 1990).

RELIGIOUS BELIEFS AND PRACTICES

Traditionally African Americans have had strong religious orientations. The church was the major institution in the lives of the slaves; its hymns and spirituals communicated ideas about salvation, freedom, judgment and punishment, and plans to escape.

Preachers have always been major speakers among African Americans, and many black politicians and leaders have also been powerful religious figures, such as Martin Luther King, Jr., Adam Clayton Powell, Malcolm X, and Jessie Jackson (Asante, 1987). The chief purpose of preaching is to stir up the emotions. The church continues to serve many functions in the lives of African Americans, playing an active role in the coping and adaptation processes of its members. The church sponsors activities for the entire family and also provides a network of people who are available as a support system in times of need (Hines & Boyd-Franklin, 1982). African American churches include the Baptist, Methodist, Jehovah's Witness, Church of God in Christ, Church of Christ, Seventh Day Adventist, Pentecostal, Nation of Islam, Presbyterian, Lutheran, Episcopal, and Roman Catholic (Hines & Boyd-Franklin, 1982).

The largest number of African Americans in the South are Baptists. The Baptist religion began in Switzerland and was brought to this country by the Pilgrims (Wood, 1978). By the middle of the twentieth Century, the Baptist religion became the largest Protestant denomination in the United States for both blacks and whites (Gaustad, 1987). Baptists stress an individual's personal relationship with God and seek to follow Jesus Christ as he is described in the Bible. Baptists emphasize the individual and attempt to apply their faith to daily life. They believe that the New Testament associates baptism with one's faith in Jesus. Thus since babies are not old enough to establish beliefs, baptism is withheld until individuals can make their own decisions and commitments. According to the New Testament, baptism is synonymous with death and resurrection, cleansing individuals of one way of life so that they can begin a new quality of life as Christians. Most Baptist churches have a baptistery in the floor. This is a pool of water about waist deep where believers are baptized by immersion (Wood, 1978).

Many African Americans are Methodists. The Methodist church began as a group within the Church of England. Methodists are Protestants. The name Methodist arose from the description of a follower as a person who lives according to the method laid down in the Bible (Baker, 1987). The early Methodists practiced a methodical daily schedule of duties, visiting the sick and imprisoned, conducting schools for the poor, and praying silently every hour and aloud three times a day (Sockman & Washburn, 1975). The Salvation Army was founded by a Methodist minister, William Booth (Bates, 1977). Methodists teach how to live a Christian life and communicate directly with God. They believe in infant baptism by sprinkling water on the infant's forehead. Methodists view the infant as a member of the church from birth and believe that the child can later decide whether to continue in the faith by making a committed response in confirmation (Bates, 1977; Wood, 1978).

Jehovah's Witnesses comprise a Bible-based Christian faith founded in 1872 by Charles Taze Russell. Witnesses proclaim that there will be an imminent end to Satan's rule and an ultimate reign of Christ on earth. Jehovah's Witnesses maintain a moral and neutral stance, refraining from saluting images or symbols, seasonal gift exchanging, or celebrating major American holidays. They operate active recruitment, missionary, and publication programs. Their most popular publication is the *Watchtower* magazine (Eliade & Couliano, 1991). Jehovah's Witnesses generally oppose the teachings of other religious groups. They often reject modern scientific advances, including medicines, and they refuse transfusions of another person's blood. Jehovah's Witnesses oppose abortion, artificial insemination, sterilization, euthanasia, organ donations, and faith healing (Spector, 1991).

Seventh Day Adventist members regard Saturday as their Sabbath. They accept the Bible and believe that evidence of salvation will be through keeping the commandments. Many groups refrain from alcohol, coffee, tea, narcotics, and stimulants. Most accept therapeutic abortions, autopsy, organ donations, medications, blood transfusions, and surgical procedures. Euthanasia is not practiced. Most Seventh Day Adventists believe in divine healing and prefer a vegetarian diet (Spector, 1979).

The Nation of Islam represents members of the Islamic faith (Muslims/ Moslems), of which there are diverse groups throughout the country. Islam is a way of life based on the concept of brotherhood. For the orthodox, all life is dependent on the will of God (Allah), which one understands by reading the holy book, the Quran (or Koran), and the teachings of the prophet Mohammed. This religion directs all activities of life. A strong emphasis is placed on self-discipline, as exemplified by prayer and fasting rituals. Muslims pray five times a day and fast during the entire month of Ramadan, when nourishment may be taken only after sunset. Young children, the elderly, pregnant women, and ill persons are exempt from the Ramadan fast. Family roles are traditional, the husband is the major provider and the spiritual leader. In traditional Muslim centers the women are isolated. They usually wear veils and a long outer garment called the abba or chador. Muslims do not eat pork or pork products and beans. They do not consume alcoholic beverages or substances that interfere with the ability to think clearly. Thus, alcoholism and drug abuse problems are virtually nonexistent in the Muslim community (Ramsey, 1986).

CULTURALLY BASED HEALTH BELIEFS AND PRACTICES

African American beliefs about health and related practices vary depending on the degree of adherence to traditional ideas, geographical location, education, scientific orientation, and socioeconomic status of the individual. Nevertheless, the Africentric heritage has caused most African Americans to retain a holistic philosophy of health, perceiving mind and body as inseparable and the total person in interaction with the environment. Consequently, many believe that life events affect all aspects of one's life, including one's job, one's family, and one's health (L. F. Snow, 1983). Thus illness results from disharmony or conflicts in some area of a person's life (Cherry & Newman-Giger, 1991).

According to J. Snow (1985), low-income African Americans use a large variety of home remedies, traditional healing practices, and over-the-counter drugs. The use of herbs is a common practice, noted more in rural than urban areas. Herbs and home remedies are frequently used in conjunction with mainstream professional prescriptions.

Home remedies include sugar and turpentine for worms and to cause an abortion; poultices applied to various parts of the body to treat infection and pain; herb teas to treat pain, fever, and gastrointestinal problems; soda to treat chest pain; vinegar and garlic for high blood pressure; and hot tea with lemon and honey and a dash of brandy and/or Vicks Vaporub swallowed to treat a cold.

Health maintenance practices by some African Americans may include the following:

- Proper nutrition, which means eating three meals a day, including a hot breakfast.
- Laxatives used periodically to keep the system open (castor oil commonly used).
- Cod liver oil taken, especially during the winter months to help prevent colds.
- Copper and silver bracelets worn by some young girls through adulthood to

protect against ill health. Pending illness will cause the skin around the bracelet to turn black, alerting the wearer of a need to change her health habits by improving her diet and/or increasing her rest and prayer periods.

For many African Americans, prayer is a common method used for the treatment of illness. Frequently the next move would be the "lay referral system," which involves seeking advice from relatives or significant others. As a final resort, if illness persists, the professional health care system would be consulted (Snow, 1985).

AFRICAN AMERICAN HEALTH STATUS

There are real disparities between the health status of African Americans and that of White Americans. Poor health is attributed to decreased access to health care services, discrimination in the health care system, economics, and inadequate utilization of available health care facilities (Byrd, 1990; Russell & Hewell, 1992). Statistics indicate that generally African Americans do not receive enough early, routine, and preventive health care (DHHS PHS, 1990). Although poverty may appear to be an underlying element in the disparity of African Americans' utilization of the professional health services, results of research found that even when socioeconomic factors were controlled, health status indicators remained consistently poorer for African Americans than for white Americans (National Center for Health Statistics, 1990).

Hypertension

Hypertension morbidity and mortality rates are at least three to five times higher in African Americans than in Caucasians (Saunders, 1991). African Americans of lower socioeconomic experience higher rates of hypertension as compared to their advantaged peers (Sorel et al., 1992).

Diabetes

Diabetes is 33% more prevalent in African Americans than in Caucasians in the United States. African American women, especially those who are overweight experience the highest rates (U.S. Department of Health and Human Services, 1990).

Coronary Heart Disease

African Americans experience a high rate of coronary heart disease. The higher prevalence of hypertension, diabetes, cigarette smoking, and obesity contribute to the higher level of coronary heart disease in African Americans (Curry, 1991). However, when heart disease rates were compared within income levels, African American levels were lower than those for whites (U.S. Department of Health and Human Services, 1990)

Cancer

Although cancer also remains a major health problem for African Americans, improvement has been noted. Since 1984, the cancer mortality rate for African Americans has declined by 2%. Black women are having Pap smears more frequently than women of any other ethnic group. The use of tobacco has decreased much more among African American adolescents than among their white counterparts. There is evidence also that high cancer rates in African Americans may be related to poverty, limited access to health care, and lack of education (Boring, Squires & Health, 1992).

AIDS

The rate of AIDS among African Americans is more than triple that of whites. The number of AIDS cases associated with intravenous drug abusers is greater for African Americans than for other AIDS victims. Also, there are higher rates of heterosexual transmission of the HIV virus and thus of transmission from mother to newborn (U.S. Department of Health and Human Services, 1990; Selik, Castro & Papaionnou, 1988).

Sickle Cell Anemia

Sickle cell anemia is a genetic abnormality found predominantly in persons of African origin. The disease is discussed in Chapter 1, on Africans.

BELIEFS ABOUT DEATH AND DYING

These beliefs vary; they are generally determined by religious affiliation, family conditioning, and/or country of origin. Many African American funerals are elaborate and attended by the extended family from within and outside the country. These funerals are often preceded by a wake.

CONCLUSION

African Americans are a diverse group of people who are a composite of European, Caribbean, Native American, and North American cultures and are not necessarily identified by skin color. Having survived periods of preslavery, slavery, segregation, and desegregation/integration, in addition to persistent negative portrayals by the media, many African Americans believe that their strengths will help them to overcome current problems.

Most African Americans would like to eliminate classifications based on past stereotypes and prefer to be recognized for their individuality and diversity.

REFERENCES

Asante, M. K. (1987). *The Africentric Idea*. Philadelphia: Temple University Press.

Bailey, J. (1973). *The God-Kings and the Titians*. New York: St. Martin's Press.

Baker, F. (1987). Methodists. In Mircea Eliade (Ed.), *Encyclopedia of religion* (vol. 2) (pp. 493–95). New York: Macmillan.

Bates, J. (1977). *The Methodist church*. New York: Religious Education Press, a division of Pergamon Press.

Boring, C., Squires, T. S., & Health, C., Jr. (1992). Cancer statistics for African Americans. *CA: Cancer Journal for Clinicians*, 42(2), 1251.

Boyle, J. S., & Andrews, M. M. (1989). *Transcultural concepts in nursing care*. Glenview, Ill.: Foreman/Little, Brown.

Branch, M., & Paxton, P. (1976). *Providing safe nursing care for ethnic people of color*. New York: Appleton-Century-Crofts.

Byrd, W. (1990). Race, biology, and health care: Reassessing a relationship. *Journal of Health Care for the Poor and Underserved*, 1(3), 278–96.

Carrington, B. W. (1978). The Afro-American. In A. L. Clark (Ed.), *Culture and childbearing* (pp. 34–52). Philadelphia: F. A. Davis.

Cashin, J. E. (1995). Black families in the Old Northwest. *Journal of the Early Republic*, 15(3), 449–77.

Cherry, B., & Newman-Giger, J. (1991). Black Americans. In J. Newman-Giger & R. E. Davidhizer (Eds.), *Transcultural nursing: Assessment and intervention* (pp. 147–82). St Louis, Boston, Chicago: Mosby Year Book.

Curry, C. (1991). Coronary artery disease in African Americans. *Circulation*, 83(4), 1474–75.

Dates, J. L., & Barlow, W. (1990). Introduction: War of images. In J. L. Dates & W. Barlow (Eds.), *Split image: African Americans in the mass media* (pp. 1–21). Washington, D.C.: Howard University Press.

Davis, R. A. (1993). *The black family in a changing black community*. New York: Garland Publishing.

De Quatrefages, A. (1905). *The human species*. New York: Appleton and Co.

Dodson, J. (1981). Conceptualizations of black families. In H. P. McAdoo (Ed.), *Black families* (pp. 23–36). Beverly Hills, Calif.: Sage.

Douglass, F. (1845). *Narrative of the life of Frederick Douglass, an American slave: Written by himself*. Boston: Anti-Slavery Office.

Drinkard-Hawkshawe, D. (1974). *David Augustus Straker: Black lawyer and reconstruction politician (1848–1908)*. Ann Arbor, Mich.: University Microfilm Publishers.

Du Bois, W. E. B. (1903, first reprint 1968). *The souls of black folk: Essays and sketches*. Chicago: McClurg. Reprint, New York: Johnson Reprint.

Eliade, M. & Couliano, J. P. (1991). *The Eliade Guide to World Religions*. San Francisco: Harper.

Fine, M., Schwebel, A. I., & James-Meyers, L. (1987). Family stability in black families: Values underlying three different perspectives. *Journal of Comparative Studies*, 18(1), 1–23.

Franklin, J. H. (1974). *From slavery to freedom: A history of Negro Americans* (4th ed.). New York: Knopf.

Gaines, S. O., Jr. (1994). Generic, stereotypic, and collectivistic models of interpersonal resource exchange among African American couples. *Journal of Black Psychology*, 20(3), 294–304.

Gaiter, L. (1994, June 26). The revolt of the black bourgeoisie. *New York Times Magazine*, p. 42, col. 1.

Gaustad, E. (1987). Baptists. In M. Eliade (Ed.), *The encyclopedia of religion* (vol. 2) (pp. 63–66). New York: Macmillan.

Greathouse, B., & Miller, V. G. (1981). The Black American. In A. L. Clark (Ed.), *Culture and childrearing* (pp. 68–95). Philadelphia: F. A. Davis.

Heyerdahl, T. (1971). Isolationist or diffusionist? In G. Ashe (Ed.), *The quest for America*. New York: Praeger.

Hill, R. B. (1977). *Informal adoption among black families*. Washington, D.C.: National Urban League Research Department.

Hines, P. M., & Boyd-Franklin, N. (1982). Black families. In M. McGoldrick, J. K. Pearce, & J. Giordano (Eds.), *Ethnicity and family therapy* (pp. 84–107). New York: Guilford Press.

Holloway, J. E., & Vass, W. K. (1993). *The African Heritage of American English*. Bloomington: Indiana University Press.

Hoskins, L. A. (1992). Eurocentrism vs. Afrocentrism: A geopolitical linkage analysis. *Journal of Black Studies*, 23(2), 247–57.

Houk, J. (1993). The terminology shift from "Afro-American" to "African-American": Is the field of African-American anthropology being redefined? *Human Organization*, 52(3), 325–28.

Hudgins, J. L. (1991–1992 Winter). The strengths of black families revisited. *Urban League Review*, 15(2), 9–20.

Johnson, J. (1977). Androgyny and the maternal principle. *School Review*, 86 (1), 50–69.

Katz, W. L. (1986). *Black Indians*. New York: Atheneum.

Kleinke, C. L., & Nicholson, T. (1979). Black and white children's awareness of de facto race and sex difference. *Developmental Psychology* 15(2), 84–86.

Lassiter, S. M. (1994). Black is a color, not a culture: Implications for health care. *ABNF Journal* (Association of Black Nursing Faculty), 5(1), 4–9.

Martin, E. P., & Martin, J. M. (1978). *The black extended family*. Chicago: University of Chicago Press.

McDaniel, A. (1995, Winter). The dynamic racial composition of the United States. *Daedalus*, 124(1), 179–99.

National Center for Health Statistics. (1990). *Health, United States, 1989, and Prevention Profile*. Hyattsville, Md.: U.S. Department of Health and Human Services.

Osborne, O. H. (1978). Aging and the black diaspora: The African, Caribbean, and Afro-American experience. In M. Leininger (Ed.), *Transcultural nursing: Concepts, theories and practices* (pp. 317–33). New York: John Wiley & Sons.

Piersen, W. D. (1988). *Black Yankees: The development of an Afro-American subculture in eighteenth century New England*. New York: Amherst.

Ramsey, D. E. (1986). The lifestyles of Afro-American Sunni Moslems in New York City. *Journal of the New York State Nurses Association*, 17(1), 21–30.

Ruggles, S. (1994). The origins of African American family structure. *American Sociological Review*, 59(1), 136–51.

Russell, K., & Jewell, N. (1992). Cultural impact of health care access: challenges for improving the health of African Americans. *Journal of Community Health Nursing*, 9(3), 161–69.

Saunders, E. (1991). Hypertension in African Americans. *Circulation*, 84(3), 1465–67.

Selik, R. M., Castro, K. G., & Papaionnou, M. (1988). Racial/ethnic differences in the risk of AIDS in the United States. *American Journal of Public Health*, 78(12), 1539–44.

Sertima, I. V. (1976). *They came before Columbus*. New York: Random House.

Snow, J. (1985). *Common health care beliefs and practices of Puerto Ricans, Haitians and low-income blacks in the New York/New Jersey area*. Contract #120–83–0011, Region II. Prepared by the National Health Service Corps, Dept. of Health and Human Services. John Snow Public Health Group, Inc.

Snow, L. F. (1983). Traditional health beliefs and practices among lower class black Americans. *Western Journal of Medicine*, 139(6), 820–28.

Sockman, R. W., & Washburn, P. A. (1975). What is a Methodist? In L. Rosten (Ed.), *Religions of America: Ferment and faith in an age of crisis* (pp. 170–85). New York: Simon and Schuster.

Sorel, J., Raglan, D. R., Syme, S. L., & Davis, W. B. (1992). Educational status and blood pressure: The Second National Health and Nutrition Examination Survey. *American Journal of Epidemiology*, 135(12), 139–48.

Sowell, T. (1995). Cultural baggage. *Forbes*, 156(13), 150.

Spector, R. E. (1979, 1991). *Cultural diversity in health and illness* (2nd and 3rd eds.). New York: Appleton-Century-Crofts.

Staples, R. (1988). The black American family. In C. H. Mindel, R. W. Haberstein, & W. Roosevelt Wright, Jr. (Eds.), *Ethnic families in America: Patterns and variations* (pp. 303–24). New York: Elsevier.

Staples, R. (1991). Changes in black family structure: The conflict between family ideology and structural conditions. In R. Staples (Ed.), *The black family: Essays and studies* (pp. 28–36). Belmont, Calif.: Wadsworth.

U.S. Bureau of the Census. (1990). *Statistical abstracts of the United States*. Washington, D.C.: U.S. Government Printing Office.

U.S. Department of Health and Human Services (DHHS), Public Health Service. (1990). *Healthy people 2000: National health promotion and disease prevention objectives*. DHHS Publication PHS 91–50212. Washington, D.C.: U.S. Government Printing Office.

Verkuyten, M. (1988). General self-esteem of adolescents from ethnic minorities in the Netherlands and the reflected appraisal process. *Adolescence*, 23(92), 863–71.

Videbeck, R. (1960). Self-conception and the reactions of others. *Sociometry*, 23, 351–59.

Watson, W. (1990). Family care, economics and health. In Z. Harel, E. A. McKinney, & M. Williams (Eds.), *Black aged: Understanding diversity and service needs* (pp. 50–68). Newbury Park, Calif.: Sage.

Wing, S., Manton, K. G., Stallard, E., Hames, C. G., & Tryoler, H. A. (1985). The black/white mortality crossover: Investigation in a community-based study. *Journal of Gerontology*, 40(1), 78–84.

Wood, J. (1978). *The Baptists*. New York: Religious Education Press, a division of Pergamon Press.

3

Alaskan Americans

The name Alaska is derived from the Aleut language, meaning "great land," a fitting description for the largest state. Alaska enjoys magnificent expanses of natural undisturbed areas and a coastline longer than that of the contiguous 48 states. The state is more than twice the size of Texas, has the tallest mountain in North America (Mount McKinley) and a glacier larger than the area of Rhode Island, and has experienced North America's largest oil spill. Alaska has been called "Russian America," "The Last Frontier," and "The Land of the Midnight Sun."

THE STATE

Located at the northwest tip of the North American continent, Alaska expands over 570,374 square miles and is actually a large peninsula, surrounded by water on three sides. The state is bounded on the south by the Gulf of Alaska and the Pacific Ocean and on the northwest by the Arctic Ocean. A narrow channel 56 miles wide, the Bering Strait, separates Alaska's western shores from the Soviet Union. The Canadian provinces of British Columbia and the Yukon Territory form Alaska's eastern border. Alaska and Hawaii are the two states that do not border on any other state.

Alaska has more than 18,000 islands, the largest located off the south coast. The Aleutian islands form a chain to the southwest between the Bering Sea and the Pacific Ocean. Alaska has about 100,000 glaciers, mostly along the southern coast. Malaspino Glacier, extending over 850 square miles, is the largest of these ice masses in North America. With more than three million lakes and about 3,000 rivers, Alaska has more waterways than any other state; the Yukon River, flowing from Canada to the Bering Sea, is the longest river. Alaska has the world's largest chain of active, or potentially active, volcanoes, whose peaks are part of the Pacific Ocean's "Ring of Fire." Redoubt Volcano was active much of 1990, and Pavlof Volcano has erupted 41 times since 1760.

Although forests cover about one-third of the land, Alaska has fewer native trees than any other state. Much of Alaska's land north of the Arctic Circle is a permanently frozen barren area called "tundra." Bears (black, brown, grizzly, and polar) are natural to Alaska. Kodiak brown bears that inhabit Kodiak Island are the largest carnivorous mammals in the world. Other animals found naturally in Alaska include caribou, moose, reindeer, wolves, beavers, foxes, and raccoons. Strict state and federal conservation laws protect marine mammals such as walruses, sea otters, seals, sea lions, and whales. Natives who traditionally hunt these animals for subsistence are exempted from the laws. Salmon, herring, cod, and halibut are important commercial fish (Heinrichs, 1991; Hunter, 1996–1997; Vick, 1983).

Climate

The Arctic refers to the area around the North Pole lying north of the Arctic Circle and north of the 50 degree Fahrenheit isotherm. An isotherm (equal temperature) is a line on a climate map between regions with the same mean temperature. The 50 degree isotherm marks the southern limits of the area where the average monthly temperature never goes above 50 degrees Fahrenheit, and the coldest month averages below 32 degrees Fahrenheit. The 50 degree isotherm follows roughly the Arctic Circle. The area north of the Arctic Circle is commonly called "The Land of the Midnight Sun." The region below the Arctic Circle is the subarctic (Damas, 1984; Encyclopedia Americana, 1994).

Winters in the subarctic last over eight months with high winds, snow (up to 20 feet), and temperatures as low as minus 80 degrees Fahrenheit. A December day may have less than six hours of daylight. The short summers are hot, with temperatures reaching 90 degrees Fahrenheit, and days in June and July lasting 20 hours. The gound is permanently frozen below a depth of about 15–18 inches. Because no plant life can grow, the inhabitants depend on hunting and fishing for survival.

In southern regions of Alaska, temperatures are moderated by warm winds blowing in from Japan's Pacific Ocean currents, making the weather milder than the rest of the state. The average January temperature is about 28 degrees Fahrenheit, and the July average is about 55 degrees Fahrenheit. Alaska's interior, without the benefit of ocean breezes, is colder in the winter but warmer in the summer than the coastal areas. Inland January temperatures may drop to 9 degrees Fahrenheit, while summers may average about 59 degrees Fahrenheit. In Barrow, the city nearest the North Pole,

January temperatures may dip to minus 30 degrees Fahrenheit, while Anchorage, further south, might register 20 degrees Fahrenheit (Hunter,
1996–1997; Vick, 1983).

"The Land of the Midnight Sun"

Alaska has been called "The Land of the Midnight Sun" because the sun
actually shines at night. Astronomers explain that the closer the North Pole
leans toward the sun, the more daylight hours there are in a summer day.
On June 20 or 21, the summer solstice, the North Pole is closest to the
sun, causing a peak period of daylight hours. In the Arctic Circle latitude,
the summer solstice extends over 24 hours, during which time the sun does
not set. The farther north one travels, the longer the "longest day." Since
more than one-quarter of Alaska lies north of the Arctic Circle, daylight
hours are extended in this area. For example, Barrow experiences the most
diverse daylight changes. After sunrise on May 10, sunset does not occur
until August 2, causing 84 days of continuous daylight. During the winter,
after the sun sets on November 18, Barrow does not experience daylight
for 67 days, with the sun finally rising again on January 24 (Heinrichs,
1991; Lefever & Davidhizar, 1991).

Population

About 550,000 Alaskans, of ethnic, racial, and philosophical diversity,
reside in a few large cities and several small towns. Anchorage is the largest
city; the capital is Juneau. Because connecting roads are limited, transportation is often by fishing boats, small planes, snow machines, or sleds. The
1990 census reported 53% of Alaska's population as male, 68% urban,
and 69% aged eighteen and older. It was noted that only 36% of the
residents were natives; the rest were foreign-born. The population represents 33 different cultures, including (in decreasing numerical order)
German, English, Irish, French, Norwegian, American, Swedish, Scottish,
Dutch, Polish, French, Canadian, and Russian. The census indicated that
3% of Alaskans were African American and about 2% were Hispanic.
Alaska's strong antidiscrimination laws, primarily designed to protect Alaskan natives, have benefited all ethnic groups (Hunter, 1996–1997; U.S.
Bureau of the Census, 1990).

Outsiders have referred to Alaskan natives as Eskimos. The Oxford English and Webster's New World dictionaries have maintained that the name
"Eskimo" was derived from a proto-Algonquian root translating as "eaters
of raw flesh." This translation has been perpetuated by the world's desire
to visualize the Eskimo as the ultimate natural man. However, in fact the
name originated from a Montagnais form meaning "snowshoe-netter" (Damas, 1984, p. 6). Because of the varying definitions, some Eskimos, espe-

cially those residing in Canada and parts of Greenland, have preferred to be called "Inuit," meaning "people." Many Eskimos of western Alaska have called themselves "Yup'ik," meaning "genuine people" (Fienup-Riordan, 1990a). Generally, Alaskan Natives are classified into three major groups: Aleuts, Yup'ik Eskimos, and Inuit Eskimos.

The original Eskimos, who were extremely adaptable, built their homes from whatever materials were available. For example, during the summers most lived in tents made of skin-covered poles. In winter, families in the eastern Arctic built houses of stone, while many in the west used driftwood and sod for housing. The familiar domed igloo (a word that means any type of house to many Eskimos) was found most commonly in northern Canada, seldom in Alaska. Although the snow igloo appeared cold, it was actually warm and cozy inside. Construction of the igloo used the principle that hot air rises. The entrance was usually a long passage below ground level so that the warm indoor air could not escape via the door. In addition the inside was insulated with furs (Josephy, 1991). If caught in a blizzard, an Eskimo could survive by cutting a circle in the icy snow crust covering the ground, digging a hole, and crawling in. The individual would then replace the lid and remain there until the storm ended. Eskimos wore clothing well adapted to the harsh climate. Traditional men and women wore fur trousers and shirts, usually made of caribou, polar bear, or other furs. Hooded parkas were added in winter. Stockings, boots, and mittens (attached to the jackets) were also made from furs (Fienup-Riordan, 1990a; Lefever & Davidhizar, 1991).

Language

Eskimo and Aleut comprise the two related branches of the Eskimo-Aleut linguistic family. The Eskimo branch has two distinct subgroups, Yup'ik and Inuit-Inupiaq. Yup'ik, consisting of five languages, was spoken originally in Siberia and some sections of Alaska, while Inuit-Inupiaq was spoken in Arctic Alaska and Canada. Aleut, the other major branch, was spoken on the Aleutian Islands. Contact with Europeans affected the intensity of the languages spoken in native communities, especially between 1910 and 1970, mainly because of their suppression in the schools by foreigners. The only native language with large numbers of speakers today is Central Yup'ik, for the culture of Yup'ik is believed to be the most traditional (Sprott, 1994; Woodbury, 1984).

The Russian Orthodox Mission to Alaska established formal bilingual education in 1784. Bilingual education evolved from the native and Orthodox philosophies that enhanced the success of the Orthodox mission with minimal social disorientation. During the Russian era, that lasted until about 1912, books were published in the four native languages that became most familiar to the Russians: Aleut, Central Yup'ik, Alutiiq, and Tlingit.

Many bilingual natives went on to higher education in Russia. However, during the early American period, native languages were forbidden in the schools; only English was permitted. Consequently, most Alaskan native languages are almost extinct today, which has caused lowered self-esteem in many native families and communities, resulting in significant social upheavals. Although bilingual/bicultural education is legally permitted and encouraged in the schools today, the value of bilingual education remains a topic of heated discussion among American educators (Dauenhauer, 1990).

BRIEF HISTORY

Archaeologists believe that the ancestors of today's native Alaskans crossed the Bering Land Bridge or Beringia from Siberia perhaps about 15,000 years ago. When the land bridge became covered with water (Bering Strait), crossings continued by boat. These early Alaskans formed three distinct groups: Eskimos (more than half), Aleuts, and Indians. The Eskimos generally resided in Canada, along the Arctic Ocean and Bering Sea, along the Yukon and Kuskokwin River valley, and on Kodiak island. There were two major groups of Eskimos: the Inupiaq of the northwest and the Yup'ik of the west. The Eskimos became efficient hunters of caribou and musk-oxen for meat and hides. They also hunted walruses, seals, and polar bears, using small skin-covered boats called *kayaks*.

The Indians were divided into two groups, Interior and Maritime. Athabascan Indians (relatives of the Apache and Navajo of the southwestern United States) occupied Alaska's interior regions, where they developed snowshoes for walking on the snow in order to hunt. The three groups of maritime Indians—Tlingits, Haidas, and Tsimshians—resided in the forests and islands of the southwest, where they thrived on the plentiful fish, game, and edible plants available in this mild climate.

The Aleuts, the smallest group, occupied southwest Alaska, or what is now the Aleutian Islands. They also hunted and used skin-covered canoes called *baidarkes*. Eskimos and Aleuts have shown several biological and linguistic similarities, along with some diversities.

European Contact

On his second voyage to the Arctic, in 1742, Vitus Bering and his crew, under the auspices of Peter the Great of Russia, became the first Europeans known to set foot on Alaskan soil. Siberian fur traders established the first permanent Russian settlement in America on the Aleutian Islands. By 1743, the Russian presence in Alaska was motivated by a desire for furs ("soft gold") that brought high prices from the Chinese traders of the Canton market. The Russians were fascinated by the Alaskans' skill at hunting and soon exploited the native labor to hunt for the fur traders. The area was claimed as a Russian colony and became known as Russian America.

The first Russian Orthodox missionaries arrived on Kodiak Island in 1794 and at the Bering Sea region in 1829. Between 1838 and 1839, a smallpox epidemic eliminated about two-thirds of the native population. Because the Russians had been vaccinated they were unaffected, causing the Eskimos to assume that the disease was deliberately introduced to destroy them. To seek revenge, many Eskimos attacked trading stations and killed the Russian employees. Consequently fur trade with the Russians diminished, but Alaskan imports from Russia continued including bracelets, beads, knives, needles, soap and tobacco. Tobacco became the first drug available to the Alaskan natives. Also, the Russian-American company introduced intoxicants such as rum and alcohol to the natives. Alcohol abuse became a problem with some natives (Fisher, 1990; Josephy, 1991; Heinrichs, 1991; Lidfors & Peterson, 1990; Oswalt, 1990).

In the meantime, as word of the new land spread, British, Spanish, and French ships set out for Alaska, some in search of trade and others to establish colonies. In 1773, Juan Perez and, in 1775, Juan Francisco de la Bodega y Quadra arrived on the southern coast of Alaska. Alaskan towns such as Valdez and Cordova trace their names to the era of these Spanish expeditions. In 1778, British Captain James Cook sailed to the Bering Strait; fourteen years later one of his lieutenants, Captain George Vancouver, explored, surveyed, and made geographical charts of Alaska's Pacific coast. Vancouver gave British names to Prince William Sound, Cape Prince of Wales, and Bristol Bay. In 1786, French Captain Jean Francois Galaup sailed to northeastern Alaska, where he studied and traded with the Tlingit Indians (Fisher, 1990; Heinrichs, 1991).

American Presence

By 1861, Russia, preoccupied with European wars and losing interest in the Russian-American Fur Trading Company, became aware of America's desire to purchase Alaska. After the Civil War, Secretary of State William Seward, with the strong support of Senator Charles Sumner, began negotiations to purchase Alaska. Many Americans felt that this was an unwise idea because Alaska was believed to be just a frozen wasteland; the venture became known as "Seward's Folly." Nevertheless, on April 9, 1867, America signed the treaty with Russia and purchased Alaska (about a half million square miles) for 7.2 million dollars, a price amounting to less than two cents per acre (Shannon, 1990).

Ever since gold had been discovered in California, prospectors had continued to search the west coast, until rumors traveled that Alaskan women were wearing necklaces of gold and Alaska became a new destination. Prospectors arrived and set up "tent cities" in Juneau, Douglas, and Treadwell.

Juneau, with gold mines that were active for decades, became the capital of Alaska. Although gold was found in many other areas of Alaska, the biggest gold strike of all was in the Klondike region of Canada's Yukon territory in 1896. The gold rush caused Alaska's population to almost double between 1890 and 1900. Although the Bureau of Indian Affairs (BIA) had planned designated areas for the relocation of northwest Alaskan Eskimos to protect them from the influence of the foreigners, most Eskimos ignored the relocation plan and continued to live in their traditional manner. Because their lands were not alluring to the Westerners who had forced the relocation of natives in other places, many natives were able to retain their relative independence while interacting with the foreigners (Ducker, 1996).

During World War I (1914–1918), when many residents entered the military, Alaska's population decreased; but increased again during the Great Depression of the 1930s, when the federal government resettled farm families in Alaska to help them start a new life. After the Japanese bombing of Pearl Harbor, Hawaii, in 1941, when the United States entered World War II, Alaska's population escalated with the arrival of military personnel and civilian workers. In order to provide a land route for military equipment, the federal government built the Alaska Highway in 1942. Alaska's geographical location was dangerously close to Japan and later, during the Cold War, proved to be strategically near the Soviet Union. After the war, many military returned to set up residence in Alaska, which soon demanded statehood. Therefore, on January 3, 1959, President Eisenhower officially recognized Alaska as the forty-ninth state of the Union. Statehood stimulated a new consciousness in and about the Alaskan native population (Chance, 1984).

By 1971, large oil reserves were found in Alaska, and pipelines were run by major oil companies. Residents of Cordon complained and filed a lawsuit to prevent pipeline terminals in Valdez because the economy depended on fishing, and a possible oil spill could destroy their livelihood. However, after several safety measures were ensured, the pipeline was approved. But in 1989, the oil tanker *Exxon Valdez*, after leaving the port of Valdez, struck a reef in Prince William Sound and spilled 11 million gallons of crude oil into the Sound. The Exxon Valdez oil spill, that destroyed countless birds, fish, sea otters, and seals, was the largest in United States history. An accurate estimate of the long range effects on Alaska's environment and economy will take many years to determine (Heinrichs, 1991).

Modern Alaska

Not having the hazards of warfare or issues of land ownership that characterized the colonization of America's West, outsiders readily moved into Alaska to set up permanent residences. Fur traders, whalers, gold prospectors, and oil miners were followed by missionaries, school teachers, nurses, doctors, and military personnel. Encounters with outsiders, especially after World War II, greatly affected Alaska's traditional lifestyles. Today, interest in traditional activities such as hunting and fishing, games and dances, skin sewing, and skilled crafts has lessened, and it is apparent that modern Eskimo people have tended to identify with Western cultural patterns. However, many Eskimos continue to live in village communities far removed from areas of rapid economic growth (Chance, 1984; Condon, Collings & Wenzel, 1995).

Many traditional practices persist in Alaska's recreational activities, including sled-dog racing and winter games such as ice skating and skiing. Dog mushing or sled-dog racing is Alaska's official state sport. Today, dogsleds, once a major form of daily transportation, have been replaced by mechanical snow machines. Alaska's world-famous Iditarod Trail Sled Dog Race was shortened in 1967 to cover a trail across Alaska from Anchorage to Nome using traditional dogsleds. The race begins every year on the first Saturday of March and lasts from ten days to three weeks. The first twenty mushers to complete the race are awarded prizes up to $50,000.

Festivals and celebrations are frequent in Alaska. The "rondy" (short for rendezvous) is a unique occasion, when Alaskans gather for fun. Several towns may have an annual rondy featuring races, games, sporting events, and crafts exhibits. Held in February, the Anchorage Fur Rondy, called the Mardi Gras of the North, is one of the major winter events of the nation and attracts visitors from all over the world. A favorite festival game is called "blanket tosses," modeled after the traditional habit of using walrus skins to toss a hunter into the air as high as 20 feet so that he could spot distant game. In addition, Alaska today is a major tourist attraction; cruises are particularly popular.

ALASKAN FAMILY

Traditional

The extended family, numbering up to 30 persons, was the basic social unit of the Aboriginal family. Usually consisting of from two to four generations, the family included parents, offspring, grandparents, married siblings, and their children. Extended families, consisting of a network of consanguineal and affinal ties, often formed a single community. In larger villages, most marriages occurred within the group. Although in some areas small family groups moved out to spring sealing camps along the coasts and summer fishing camps along rivers, the extended family reunited in their permanent villages during the winter.

Early Yup'ik Eskimos formed communities of up to 300 persons, who occupied residences divided by the sexes. A large communal men's house, or *qasgiq*, was located at the center of the village and surrounded by smaller sod houses, or *enet*, where the women and children lived. The *enet* appeared to have a reproductive function; its interior was likened to the womb from which children were born and, concurrently, from which spirits of the dead were reborn into human form. Children were usually given the name of a deceased relative, in the belief that the soul of the departed would pass on to the baby at birth (Fienup-Riordan, 1990a).

At the age of five, boys moved to the men's house to reside with their fathers and other male relatives. Thus the males of the community lived in a separate residence where they worked, ate, slept, bathed, conversed, and entertained visitors. This living arrangement did not foster conjugal bonds, because the husband was an outsider to the house where his wife lived. However, a husband could stay overnight in the women's house whenever he wished or when he was ill. Only shamans lived permanently in houses occupied by their wives. During the winter, the mens' house, the heart of the village, was the focus of community activities and elaborate ceremonies (Fienup-Riordan, 1990a).

In the *qasgiq*, early morning routine was ritualistic, beginning with morning teachings about proper behavior, such as keeping conversations subdued, avoiding horseplay and quarreling, and showing respect toward the adult males. After the teachings, the shaman arrived to perform morning religious rituals, that were followed by daily activities including eating meals, hunting, fishing, repairing equipment, and bathing.

The day in the women's household began with the preparation of the morning meal. The wives watched for the shaman to return from the men's house, indicating that the men were awaiting their morning meal, which the women then delivered to their husbands. Women visited the men's house to bring meals or attend ceremonies but never stayed overnight. Sometimes a man would eat the morning meal at his wife's house and then return to the *qasgiq*. Women were responsible for harnessing dogs to the sleds for their husbands' hunting trips and, on their return, unharnessing the dogs and processing the catch. In addition, women made all the family's clothing using sinew for thread. They processed skins and shaped and sewed them into waterproof boots and heavy parkas. They also stitched canoe coverings, wove mats and baskets of grass, and made clay cooking vessels and lamps.

In order to utilize local resources efficiently, most families lived at three different places each year: their village, tundra camp, and fish camp. During the winter, families did very limited hunting, depending on the quantity of fish and game stored before the freeze. Since most supplies were depleted by spring, most families anxiously awaited the longer spring days, ending their winter isolation. They would pack up much of their household and set out on dogsleds to their tundra camps. In the spring women gathered berries and fished in the streams that had thawed. Men trapped beavers, land otters, and muskrats or canoed out to hunt for marine animals. After a couple of months the families returned to their village. In late fall, some families revisited their spring camps to obtain additional food for the winter. As the days shortened, they again returned to their home village to settle in for the winter.

Although most traditional Eskimos did not live in nuclear family units, marriage was preferred for economic reasons because a male or female had difficulty functioning independently in this culture. A husband depended on his wife to prepare his meals, process and preserve his catch, make and repair his clothing, and care for him when he was ill. A wife relied on her husband to provide food and skins for herself and her children (Oswalt, 1990).

Childrearing

Traditionally, the first pregnancy was an important event for a couple, especially if the child was a boy. To symbolize the importance of the birth, the couple relinquished their personal names and became known as the parents of their firstborn, a convention called *teknonymy*. Children gradually became integrated into the community through daily activities and special ceremonies. Special ceremonies were held to honor a boy's development of hunting skills; at a girl's puberty, a special ceremony (Putting Away the Doll) indicated the advent of adulthood. Shortly after the girl's puberty ceremony, her relatives arranged her marriage. Traditional marriage, with no special ceremony, consisted of an elaborate feast with the presentation of new garments to the couple. The bride continued to live in her mother's home, and the groom returned to the men's house, maintaining a matrilocal marital residence pattern (Fienup-Riordan, 1990a; Oswalt, 1990).

Modern Family

Assimilation, enhanced by intermarriage with outsiders, has contributed to a loss of Alaskan natives' distinctive culture. Today, individuals of mixed heritage outnumber full-bloods. Many Alaskan people of culturally mixed backgrounds tend not to perpetuate a separate identity as a group. However some individuals, living predominantly in native villages, especially the elders, have tended to maintain a native identification and engage in several traditional practices (Sprott, 1994).

As the federal government improved living conditions by building new log houses with spun glass insulation, aluminum roofs, and two or three rooms, these physical changes altered the look of villages, and a new lifestyle was introduced, abandoning the women's and men's houses. By the early 1900s, Moravian missionaries had determined that couples living in a Yup'ik village should marry in a church service and live together in their own dwelling. Legal marriages restricted the flexibility of former male-female relationships, destroying the male bonds nurtured by *qasgiq* life as well as the closeness of related females in their traditional matrifocal household. A missionary would arrive at a village early in the morning and marry all couples that he found sleeping in bed together. By 1950, some natives felt that forced legal matrimony may have produced more permanent but, undoubtedly, many unhappy marriages (Oswalt, 1990).

Changes in attitudes indicated that Alaskan natives were absorbing many ways of the outsiders, including Western-style dress, enjoyment of television, radio, and popular music, as well as the use of alcohol and other drugs. Although, today many Alaskans still recognize the elders as advisors, baby-sitters, and providers of material and emotional support, the deference once shown to older people no longer exists among some younger people. Some elders complain that children are no longer respectful and shy in the presence of adults.

Today, generally, the extended family remains the most important social group, and ties are strong as in the past, regardless of where relatives live. Many villages remain insular, with residents tending to distrust strangers without local connections. Some natives also tend to disapprove of outsiders who marry into a village and particularly those who do not successfully participate in the subsistence activities that are a major aspect of village life. However, many modern Alaskans live in the large cities and have adapted to the Western lifestyle. The federal government is the major employer in Alaska; but for some whose work is seasonal, hunting and fishing as subsistence is an option (Chance, 1984; Oswalt, 1990; Sprott, 1994).

Socialization

Alaskan natives tend to be considerate and sharing with each other as well as outsiders. They seldom disagree publicly with others and are usually polite and noncritical. Eskimos often use nonverbal communication and are able to evaluate others by observing and interpreting body language. Some Eskimos may prefer an intimate communication distance, especially with family and friends, because traditional Alaskan natives lived in close quarters with family members, sharing crowded space, in contrast to the Western concept of territoriality. Apparently, hunting and fishing trips provided the traditional Eskimo with any needed privacy. Further, unlike the Western intolerance of silence, some Eskimos can tolerate long periods of silence even in the presence of others and do not believe in filling quiet time with idle chatter. The more acculturated the individual, the less prominent these behaviors will be (Lefever & Davidhizar, 1991; Oswalt, 1990).

NUTRITION

Traditional Alaskans have consumed a high protein diet of various fish and game. Fish could be boiled, pickled, fried, iced, shredded, or dried. Wild berries have been popular, especially blueberries and salmonberries, often mixed with congealed fat into *akutaq*, or Eskimo ice cream, a favorite dessert for special occasions.

The diets of modern Alaskans may include preparations of vension stew, caribou swiss steaks, and breast of ptarmigan (large bird), braised bear chops, pot-roast beaver, grilled Alaska spot prawns or other large shrimp, smoked halibut, stewed clams, and seafood fettuccini. Garnishes include salmonberry-rhubarb jelly and sweet kelp relish. Alaska is the home of sourdough, which is used to make sourdough pancakes, biscuits, and French toast.

Radishes, carrots, onions, potatoes, peas, broccoli, cauliflower, and particularly rhubarb thrive well in Alaska's short summer. Favorite salads include Alaskan coatal salad (containing a variety of local seafood with curried mayonnaise, brown rice salad, and grilled chicken salad). Favorite soups are halibut bisque, bean supreme (three beans—dried black turtle beans, red Mexican beans, and navy beans), and curried cream of carrot soup. Among the most popular desserts are espresso-chocolate cheesecake, strawberry-rhubarb pie, and ice cream made from snow (evaporated milk, sugar, vanilla, and enough fresh-fallen snow to produce a consistency of ice cream) (Brown, 1970; DeCherney et al., 1991).

RELIGION

Some traditional Alaskan Americans have practiced a shamanistic religion. Because their livelihood had been based on fishing and hunting, they often held ceremonies of atonement for the spirits of killed game. Traditionally, Yup'ik Eskimos have viewed the relationship between human and animals as collaborative reciprocity, game submitted to the hunter in response to the hunter's respectful treatment of animals as persons. Since humans and nonhumans shared the basic characteristics of personhood, both required mutual respect.

Traditional belief holds that all living things participated in a cycle of birth and rebirth, dependent on proper thoughts and actions. The soul was the principle that sustained life for both humans and animals, and some believed that inanimate objects also had souls. For humans and animals, the soul was the aspect of the person that after death was reborn into the next generation (Fienup-Riordan, 1990a, p. 167).

Shamanism, having its center in Asia, is not actually a religion, but rather a system of contacting the parallel but invisible universe of spirits to obtain their support in dealing with human affairs. This practice existed among most Aboriginal Arctic peoples. Male or female shamans were believed to have special relationships with the spirits, enabling them to heal the sick and foresee the future (Eliade & Couliano, 1991).

During the 125 years of Russia's occupation of Alaska and for 120 years after her departure, Christianity in the form of Russian Orthodoxy remains the largest single religious denomination among Alaskan American natives. The Russian Orthodox mission began in Alaska about 1794 as an instrument of pacification. The mission emphasized lay leadership, literacy, advocacy on the behalf of the natives, and tolerance of native culture and language. By maintaining old churches, chapels, and practices, more than eighty native communities, especially Aleuts and Yup'ik Eskimos, have kept the faith alive and thereby preserved Russian America's unique contribution to North American culture (Smith, 1990).

Selaviq, a Christmas celebration, is the largest celebration of the year in many Russian Orthodox communities throughout Alaska. The celebration combines ritual activities and religious practices. A practice known as "starring" highlights the Christmas festival. Starring involves the use of a decorated five-point star (two and a half feet in diameter) with an icon of the Nativity at the center. The star is carried aloft throughout the village the week of Orthodox Christmas, beginning January 7. Today, preparation for starring begins in the summer, with families spending thousands of dollars to prepare for the feasting and gift giving. In some areas, Selaviq is preceded by a Holy Supper on Christmas Eve, January 6. The supper is a meatless meal that ends the pre-Christmas fasting. *Kolyadi* (folk carols) are sung in the home before the family leaves for church. Selaviq officially begins with a two-and-a-half-hour church service on the morning of January 7. During the service, Christ, the saints, and the people of the community celebrate the glory of Christ's birth, after which the star, carried by four young men, is presented to the congregation and then carried from house to house in the village. Some believe that the star entering their home symbolizes Christ's rebirth in their souls. Today multiple cultures interact in Kasigluk, a Yup'ik Eskimo village that has celebrated Selaviq since the late 1800s. Russian Orthodox, Ukranian, and indigenous beliefs and practices all contribute to the event of Selaviq, which has been modified to accommodate the increasing cultural diversity and growing population (Fienup-Riordan, 1990a).

HEALTH BELIEFS AND PRACTICES

The traditional health concept of most Alaskan Americans has been holistic. In contrast to the narrow concept held by Westerners, traditional Alaskans have viewed health as a synthesis of the individual state of being, which is a combination of the body and soul, and the social well-being of the community maintained through hunting, food sharing, and observance of taboos. The role of the spiritual leader, the shaman, was to maintain the health of the community by interceding between humans and the spiritual world (Borré, 1994).

Tradition held that a specific set of taboos (or superstitions) guided healthy behaviors. These taboos were enforced by each person's spiritual healer. It was believed that illness was caused either by the breaking of one's taboos and thus offending one's spiritual healer or by becoming possessed by harmful spirits. An example of a traditional taboo was that a pregnant woman must pass through doorways rapidly so that her delivery (the passing out of her baby) will be quick. Many taboos were associated with the salmon harvest and other events. For example, during the salmon harvest, the first fish caught for the season received special treatment, including using every part of it; when salmon were plentiful, noise near the river was prohibited; and fresh salmon was never fed to dogs. These taboos were intended to show respect to the fish and thereby insure plentiful catches in the future. Generally, health was maintained by reliance on the shaman's rituals, observance of the taboos, and the use of various seal products believed to be preventive and therapeutic. When illness persisted, it was believed to be one's fate, never the shaman's fault (Borré, 1994).

Health and Diet

The Aboriginal Arctic Eskimos were more heavily dependent on meat than any other peoples of the world. Their diet was characteristically high in protein and fat, and low in carbohydrate. Diabetes mellitus and cardiovascular disease were rare in early Eskimos. Recent study findings have indicated that marine fat may have a preventive effect on cardiovascular disease, thrombosis, and arteriosclerosis. The low incidence of coronary heart disease among Arctic individuals has been related to the intake of a high fish diet (Mulvad et al., 1996). Findings of earlier studies have suggested that the low incidence of cardiovascular disease in traditional Alaskan Americans may have been due to their adaptation to a high fat, high protein diet that in temperate zones would have caused elevated triglycerides and cholesterol. Eskimos differ from American whites in their unique ability (due to genetic and environmental factors) to absorb dietary cholesterol but inhibit cholesterol synthesis.

Triglyceride lowering is the most consistent effect of fish oils, without altering cholesterol levels (Harris, 1996). Eskimos who are consuming traditional diets have significantly lower triglycerides and other fats in the blood than Eskimos consuming Western diets (Szathmary, 1984).

Lactose Intolerance

Lactose intolerance, common among individuals with limited milk supplies, occurs in Eskimos. About 80% of Alaskan Americans and 70% of their children are lactose intolerant. Signs of lactose intolerance include various degrees of gastric discomfort such as flatulence and bloating and/or diarrhea that occur after ingesting milk or milk products. Also because of the limited milk in traditional diets, causing calcium and iron deficiencies, some traditional children developed nutritional rickets and /or anemia. The possibility that aboriginal Eskimos had a genetic ability to metabolize calcium and thus prevent more damaging bone disorders and osteoporosis in adult women has been considered for further research (Lefever & Davidhizar, 1991; Szathmary, 1984).

Cancer

More than one-third of all cancers in the United States are believed to be attributed to various nutritional factors. Epidemiological studies indicate that a consistent pattern of lower risk for cancers of the colon and lung exists for individuals who eat large amounts of fruits and vegetables and that a higher risk exists for cancers of the colon and prostate for those who eat larger amounts of fat. Although the cancer rates among Alaskan American natives are currently lower than that for nonnative Americans, the natives' rates appear to be increasing. Today, most foods of Alaskan American natives are similar to the current American diet, high in fats and low in fruits and vegetables (Byers, 1996).

A higher risk of colon and rectal cancer was found among Alaskan Inuits as compared to a lower risk in Canadian and Greenland Inuits. Alaskans also indicated high rates of liver and gallbladder cancers. Both groups had a high incidence of esophageal cancer. Rates of nasal cavity cancer were high for Inuit men, and rates for lung cancer for both men and women were among the highest in the world. Their heavy smoking and alcohol consumption patterns correlated to environment and diet were believed to be significant causal factors (Miller & Gaudette, 1996; Storm & Nielsen, 1996).

Obesity

Recent findings have indicated that the prevalence of obesity among Alaskan Americans is essentially similar to that of the general North American population. Apparently, Alaskan obesity does not usually affect glucose and insulin levels, resulting in a low incidence of obesity-related diabetes (Young, 1996).

Alcoholism

The prevalence of alcoholism and fetal alcohol syndrome is high among some Alaskan American natives. Causative factors such as loss of identity, unemployment, changing lifestyles and values, and other social problems have been identified (Burd & Moffatt, 1994).

Death and Dying

Traditional Alaskan Americans have believed that a person is composed of a body, a soul, and the name of a deceased relative (to provide the soul). Great respect was shown for the dead. Traditional Eskimo hunters carefully disposed of the remains of the animals that they had killed, and warriors attended to the bodies of their victims. Some traditional Eskimo women would remove a tassel from their favorite parkas after the death of a relative or close friend and later sew the tassel back after the birth of a child considered to be the deceased's replacement (Fienup-Riordan, 1990a).

Traditionally, in the event of human death, the body was pulled through the smoke hole located at the center of the *qasgiq*. In this manner the deceased, passing from the realm of the living to that of the dead, would exchange the mortal sight that was lost at death for the supernatural clairvoyance of the spirit world (Nelson, 1899, p. 425). The numbers four and five were significant in Central Yup'ik rituals, primarily representing the number of steps leading to the underworld land of the dead. The symbol of a circle with a dot in the center (an eye and a hole) represented physical movement between two worlds (Fienup-Riordan, 1990a).

The coastal Yup'ik held an annual Bladder Festival to honor the souls of seals killed during the year. The seal's bladders, believed to contain their souls, were inflated and hung on the men's house during four days of celebration. On the fifth day the families would take the bladders and push them through a hole in the ice so that the seals might be reborn (Fienup-Riordan, 1990a).

CONCLUSION

Today, many traditional Alaskan American practices have been abandoned, especially among the younger generations. Generally, scientific medical technology has replaced shaman healing rituals. Religious practice and beliefs about death and dying are now related to the various currently practiced religions, with some individuals combining Christian and spirit world beliefs. Theory has it that intermarriage and loss of a mother tongue indicate the demise of a distinct Alaskan American culture and strongly suggests assimilation into the Western lifestyle. A study of Alaskans in Anchorage (Sprott, 1994) noted that although there were no well-demarcated ethnic enclaves and scant available information on specific native traditions or customs, aspects of symbolic culture and social affiliations were observed that reflect the tenacity, rather than the demise, of ethnic groups in Alaska.

REFERENCES

Arctic. (1994). *The Encyclopedia Americana: International Edition: Vol. 2* (pp. 412–14). Danbury, Conn.: Grolier.

Borré, K. (1994). The healing power of the seal: The meaning of Inuit health practice and belief. *Arctic Anthropology*, 31(1), 1–15.

Brown, D. (1970). *American cooking: The northwest.* New York: Time Life Books.

Burd, L., & Moffatt, E. K. (1994). Epidemiology of fetal alcohol syndrome in American Indians, Alaska Natives, and Canadian Aboriginal peoples. *Public Health Reports*, 109(5), 688–693.

Byers, T. (1996). Nutrition and cancer among American Indians and Alaska Natives. *Cancer*, 78(7, Suppl.), 1612–16.

Chance, N. A. (1984). Alaska Eskimo modernization. In W. C. Sturtevant (Ed.), *Handbook of North American Indians* (vol. 5) (pp. 646–56). Washington, D.C.: Smithsonian Institution.

Condon, R. G., Collings, P., & Wenzel, G. (1995). The best part of life: Subsistence hunting, ethnicity, and economic adaptations among young adult Inuit males. *Arctic (Canada)*, 48(1), 31–46.

Damas, D. (1984). Introduction. In D. Damas (Ed.), *Handbook of North American Indians* (vol. 5) (pp. 1–7). Washington, D.C.: Smithsonian Institution.

Dauenhauer, R. L. (1990). Education in Russian America. In B. S. Smith & R. J. Barnett (Eds.), *Russian America: The forgotten frontier* (pp. 155–64). Tacoma: Washington State Historical Society.

DeCherney, N., DeCherney, J., Marshall, D., & Brook, S. (1991). *Recipes from Alaska's most celebrated restaurant and bakery.* New York: St. Martin's Press.

Ducker, J. H. (1996). Out of harm's way: Relocating northwest Alaska Eskimos, 1907–1919. *American Indian Culture and Research Journal*, 20(1), 43–71.

Eliade, M., & Couliano, I. P. (1991). *The Eliade guide to world religions.* San Francisco: Harper.

Fienup-Riordan, A. (1990a). *Eskimo essays: Yup'ik lives and how we see them.* New Brunswick, N.J.: Rutgers University Press.

Fienup-Riordan, A. (1990b). Following the star: From the Ukraine to the Yukon. In B. S. Smith & R. J. Barnett (Eds.), *Russian America: The forgotten frontier* (pp. 227–35). Tacoma: Washington State Historical Society.

Fisher, R. H. (1990). Finding America. In B. S. Smith & R. J. Barnett (Eds.), *Russian America: The forgotten frontier* (pp. 17–31). Tacoma: Washington State Historical Society.

Harris, W. S. (1996). Dietary fish oils and blood lipids. *Current Opinion in Lipidology*, 7(1), 3–7.

Heinrichs, A. (1991). *America the beautiful: Alaska.* Chicago: Children's Press.

Hunter, B. (1996–1997). *The Statesman's Year-Book: A statistical, political and economic account of the states of the world for the year 1996–1997* (133rd ed.). New York: Chelsea House.

Josephy, A. M., Jr. (1991). *The Indian heritage of America.* Boston: Houghton Mifflin.

Lefever, D., & Davidhizar, R. E. (1991). American Eskimos. In J. N. Giger & R. E.

Davidhizar (Eds.), *Transcultural nursing: Assessment and intervention* (pp. 261–90). St Louis: Mosby Year Book.

Miller, A. B., & Gaudette, L. A. (1996). Cancer of the respiratory system in Circumpolar Inuit. *Acta Oncologica, 35*(5), 571–76.

Mulvad, G., Pedersen, H. S., Hansen, J. C., Dewailly, E., Jul, E., Pedersen, M., Deguchi, Y., Newman, W. P., Malcom, G. T., Tracy, R. E., Middaugh, J. P., & Bjerregaard, P. (1996). The Inuit diet: Fatty acids and antioxidants, their role in ischemic heart disease, and exposure to organochlorines and heavy metals: An international study. *Arctic Medical Research, 55*(suppl. 1), 20–24.

Nelson, E. W. (1899). *The Eskimo about Bering Strait.* Bureau of American Ethnology Annual Report for 1896–1897, vol. 18(1). Washington, D.C.: Smithsonian Institution (reprinted 1983).

Oswalt, W. H. (1990). *Bashful no longer: An Alaskan Eskimo ethnohistory, 1778–1988.* Norman and London: University of Oklahoma Press.

Shannon, M. (1990). Charles Sumner and the Alaska Purchase. In B. S. Smith and R. J. Barnett (Eds.), *Russian America: The forgotten frontier* (pp. 109–20). Tacoma: Washington State Historical Society.

Smith, B. S. (1990). Russia's cultural legacy in America: The Orthodox Mission. In B. S. Smith & R. J. Barnett (Eds.), *Russian America: The forgotten frontier* (pp. 245–51). Tacoma: Washington State Historical Society.

Sprott, J. E. (1994). "Symbolic ethnicity" and Alaska Natives of mixed ancestry living in Anchorage: Enduring group or a sign of impending assimilation? *Human Organization, 53*(4), 311–22.

Storm, H. H., & Nielsen, N. H. (1996). Cancer of the digestive system in Circumpolar Inuit. *Acta Oncologica, 35*(5), 553–70.

Szathmary, E. J. E. (1984). Human biology of the Arctic. In W. C. Sturtevant (Ed.), *Handbook of North American Indians* (vol. 5) (pp. 64–71). Washington, D.C.: Smithsonian Institution.

U.S. Bureau of the Census (1990). *Statistical abstracts of the United States.* Washington, D.C.: U.S. Government Printing Office.

Vick, A. (1983). *The Cama-i book: Kayaks, dogsleds, bear hunting, bush pilots, smoked fish, mukluks, and other traditions of Southwestern Alaska.* Garden City, N.Y.: Anchor Press/Doubleday.

Woodbury, A. C. (1984). Eskimo and Aleut languages. In W. C. Sturtevant (Ed.), *Handbook of North American Indians* (vol. 5) (pp. 49–63). Washington, D.C.: Smithsonian Institution.

Young, K. (1996). Obesity, central fat patterning, and their metabolic correlates among Inuit of the central Canadian Arctic. *Human Biology, 68*(2), 245–263.

4

Asian Americans

Asian and Pacific Islander Americans number 7,273,662 and represent 2.9% of the American population. From 1970 to 1980, the Asian population grew at a rate of 165%; and from 1980 to 1990, the rate of increase was 107%. Of the Asian and Pacific Islander Americans, Chinese have the highest population, followed by the Filipinos, and then by the Japanese. Asian Indians represent the fourth largest Asian American group, followed by Koreans, Vietnamese, Hawaiians, Guamanians, and finally, Samoans (U.S. Bureau of the Census, 1990).

GENERAL CHARACTERISTICS

Immigration

Asian immigration began in the mid-nineteenth century, when large numbers of Chinese migrated to California to work in mining and railroad construction. However, during the late nineteenth and early twentieth centuries, the United States government enacted restrictions on the immigration of Asians into the country. Consequently the Asian population increased slowly until about 1968, when the Immigration Act of 1965 became fully effective. This new immigration law abolished Asian exclusion and permitted Asians admission based on the following three criteria: (1) possession of occupational skills needed in the United States labor market; (2) family unification; or (3) status as victims of political or religious persecution. The 1965 Immigration Act abolished discrimination based on national origin, thereby facilitating immigration from Asia, South America, and the Caribbean. A major consequence of the new act was to shift the major source of immigrants from European countries to non-European countries. Most recently, the Immigration Act of 1990 revised the 1965 law, expecting to attract skilled Europeans as occupational immigrants (Arnold, Minocha, & Fawcett, 1987).

Most post-1965 Asian immigrants came to the United States for economic reasons. In 1987, the U.S. standard of living (per capita income) was ten times higher than that of the Philippines, three times higher than that of South Korea, and twelve times higher than that of India. Because Japan was the only Asian country to achieve a standard of living comparable to that of the United States, only a small number of Japanese have migrated to the United States in the past twenty years. In addition to economic motivations, some Asians migrated because of political, cultural, and military connections between the United States and their countries. The U.S. military presence in the Philippines, South Korea, and Vietnam fostered immigration of kin. Thus, Asians migrated as wives and/or families of U.S. servicemen stationed in those areas (Gordon, 1987; Min, 1995a). During the 1950s, 86% of the Japanese immigrants to the United States were women, three-quarters of whom were admitted as wives of U.S. servicemen. Asian children fathered by U.S. servicemen are referred to as "Amerasians" (Nishi, 1995; Rutledge, 1992).

Settlement Patterns

Currently, nearly 40% of all Asian and Pacific Islander Americans have settled in California, although in previous years the major settlement area was Hawaii. New York and Hawaii are the second and third largest settlement areas. The largest number of Chinese Americans are located in (in descending order) California, New York, and Texas. Since 1980, New York City's Chinatown has become the largest Chinatown in the Western world, surpassing that of San Francisco (U.S. Immigration and Naturalization Service, 1979–1992).

The largest number of Filipino, Korean, and Indian Asian Americans have settled in California, New York, and New Jersey. After the Chinese, East Indians are the second largest group of Asian Americans in New York City, forming the largest Indian center in the United States. Vietnamese Americans have settled heavily in California and lightly in Texas and in Washington state. Thus the major areas (in descending order) that have the largest Asian and Pacific Islander American populations are California (Los Angeles, San Diego, Orange Counties), New York (New York City), and Hawaii (Honolulu) (U.S. Immigration and Naturalization Service, 1979–1992).

Earlier Chinese immigrants to New York, California, and other cities established segregated communities or Chinatowns. Chinatowns were created in response to racial oppression and violence against the immigrants at the end of the nineteenth century (Wong 1995). Because Chinatowns offered convenient employment in ethnic businesses, ethnic food, and language, a large number of recent immigrants and Chinese businessmen prefer to reside in Chinatowns. Also, new immigrants who are not yet assimilated prefer to live closer to their own ethnic group. Koreatown, established in Los Angeles, is the only officially recognized Korean enclave in the United States (Min, 1995b). In a study of Asian groups, whites, and blacks in California, Jiobu (1988) found that Vietnamese Americans were the most ethnically segregated Asian group.

By contrast, recent Asian Indian and Filipino immigrants have not established ethnic enclaves in major cities but rather have spread throughout suburban areas, probably because they consist of subgroups that are not culturally homogeneous. Asian Indians and Filipinos have migrated from various regional areas that differ in language, customs, and ethnicity. Also, their assimilation into areas of American culture may be facilitated because Filipino and Indian immigrants are generally characterized by higher educational and occupational levels and are more fluent in English than other Asian immigrants. Japanese also fall into a similar category with respect to education and occupation. Indian, Filipino, and Japanese Americans, often of higher socioeconomic status, apparently have less need for ethnic community unity than other Asians. The highest percentage of Asian Americans living in central cities' ethnic enclaves are the Chinese (54%) and the Vietnamese (52%). Fewer Japanese (41%), Filipinos (45%), and Indians (40%) reside in central cities (U.S. Bureau of the Census, 1990; Min, 1995a).

Diversity

Asian Americans manifest genetic and cultural diversity. Asian groups speak different languages, practice different religions, and experience various levels of segregation and socioeconomic status in the United States. By contrast, Hispanics, who are also diverse, generally share apparent similarities such as the Spanish language and the Catholic religion. However despite significant differences, many Asian Americans tend to share certain values that differ from mainstream American values. Many Asian Americans are group-oriented, in contrast to the American individual-oriented value system. Other Asian values include filial piety, emphasis on educational achievement, restraint in emotional expression, shame as a behavioral control, high regard for the elderly, importance of family loyalty, and respect for authority. Some Asians may demonstrate respect by avoiding eye contact while conversing with a respected person (Chung, 1991; Lassiter, 1995; Min, 1995a; Ross-Sheriff, 1991).

Cultural and Religious Diversity

Korean, Chinese, and Japanese Americans are culturally and physically similar. Culturally, China has influenced the other two nations through the Chinese written characters and the philosophy of Confucianism. Confucianism, a code of ethics (rather than a religion) began in China in the second century and spread to Korea and then Japan. Perhaps because of their similarities, intermarriage among Koreans, Chinese, and Japanese Americans is common in Hawaii and California (Kitano et al., 1984). Some Vietnamese also are strongly influenced by Confucian moral philosophy. The major religion of Vietnam, Cambodia, and Thailand is Buddhism, although a significant number of Vietnamese in America are Catholic. Most Korean immigrants are Christians, compared to a smaller proportion of Chinese and Japanese.

Asian Indians and Filipinos were not influenced by Confucianism, making them different from some other Asian groups. In India and Pakistan, Hinduism or other religions (Islam, Sikhism, and Jainism) regulate family, social, and religious life (Williams, 1988). The Philippines, with a long history of Western colonization, is probably the most westernized Asian country. Influenced by the early Spanish colonists, most Filipinos are Roman Catholic (Min, 1995a).

Language Diversity

Generally, Asians speak several languages and many dialects. Mandarin is the official Chinese language, but many Chinese Americans speak only Cantonese. Problems caused by the variety of Chinese dialects are overcome by use of the written Chinese language, which is constant (Rawl, 1992). Ilocano is the language most commonly spoken by Filipinos in Hawaii and on the United States mainland. Tagalog, renamed Pilipino (pronounced Filipino) in 1946, was then proclaimed the national language (Melendy, 1980). Hindi is the East Indian national language. There are many other languages and dialects spoken in India, but individuals of higher socioeconomic status usually speak Hindi and English (Kamar, 1994). Many Vietnamese, Korean, and Japanese Americans speak some English in addition to their national languages.

Socioeconomic Diversity

Generally, a large proportion of recent Asian immigrants have high educational and pre-immigration occupational levels, yet some are at the poverty level. The educational success factor associated with many Asian Americans is related to their respect for education and commitment to hard work in achieving an education, rather than to genetic factors or special abilities (Rutledge, 1992). Some older immigrants have achieved financial success in the United States through hard physical work. The highest median family income was reported (in descending order) for the Japanese, Indian, and Filipino Asian Americans (U.S. Bureau of the Census, 1990).

Occupations are also diverse. A large proportion of Filipino and Indian Asians are professionals, especially in the medical field. Some Korean and Chinese Americans are self-employed in small businesses; others are professionals in science and education. Several Korean Americans own and operate small family businesses such as grocery/fruits and vegetables businesses, dry cleaning services, sale of Korean imports (wigs, jewelry, etc.), and American fast-food services. On the other hand, a large number of Chinese businesses are concentrated in the garment industry, Chinese restaurants, and gift shops (Min, 1995).

The following sections briefly discuss specific Asian American groups with respect to family, socialization, religion, nutritional patterns, health beliefs and practices, common diseases, and concepts of life and death. The largest Asian American groups—Chinese, Filipinos, Japanese, East Indians, Koreans, and Vietnamese—are included for discussion. Chapter 6 discusses Hawaiians.

CHINESE AMERICANS

Chinese Americans are the largest Asian group in the United States and the first Asian group to migrate in significant numbers to this country. In 1990, numbering about 1.7 million individuals, they represented 0.7% of the American population, an increase from 0.4% in 1980. Although Chinese Americans reside in every state, their largest populations are on the West Coast and in the Northeast (U.S. Bureau of the Census, 1990).

Family

Traditional Family

Familism is a significant Chinese value. Traditionally, the family has been the major unit of socialization for the Chinese. In the typical traditional Chinese extended family:

- The father, undisputed head of the family, is responsible for the economic support and the discipline of family members.
- The mother is responsible for care of the children and the home. She is subordinate to her husband and insignificant until she gives birth to a son (Lee, 1982).
- Sons are blessings because they carry on the name for the family and ancestors. Boys are so important that, in the distant past, girl babies were often killed or given away. Girls were thought to be a bother to feed and care for since they would only leave and marry into another family some day (Char, 1981).
- Filial piety is an important value of the traditional Chinese family system. Sons,

especially the oldest, have specific obligations to the family. Sons are controlled by their father, whom they call "yeh" (dignity and sternness), in a patrilocal residence arrangement. Thus, married sons with their families would live in their father's house where the "yeh", the oldest male, would remain the head of the household. After the father's death, the oldest son would assume responsibility for the household (Char, 1981) and divide the property among the sons (Kleinman & Lin, 1981).

Ancestor worship is an integral aspect of the familism concept. The traditional belief has held that the living and the dead are enmeshed by kinship and descent and that many problems encountered by the living could be avoided if one maintains a balance in relationships with the souls of the dead. Generally, the traditional belief has been that spirits of dead ancestors are constantly present to protect family members; so one must respect these ancestors. Thus, familism has demanded respect for both the living and the dead (Char, 1981; Kleinman and Lin, 1981).

Modern Family

A common family type in today's Chinatowns is the non-residential extended family, which consists of a group of related nuclear families living in separate homes but in close proximity, often on the same street. This grouping may be called a clan. Although these units are independent, they often share a common family business, such as a restaurant or grocery store. In Chinese communities, stores serve as socialization centers for families, friends, and new immigrants (Wong, 1985).

Many of the first-generation Chinese who arrived in America prior to the 1965 Immigration Act, referred to as the "old immigrants," have retained traditional values (father-son dyad and emphasis on filial piety). The new immigrant families who arrived in the United States after 1965 are less traditional, tend to prefer the nuclear family model and to prefer that their children affiliate with both cultures, the American and the Chinese. In China today many families, especially those of higher socioeconomic status and those who are more westernized, prefer the nuclear family model. The new immigrants appear to be more affluent and better educated and enter this country possessing more Western values than the old immigrants (Wong, 1985).

Elderly

Traditionally, Chinese have demonstrated great respect for their elderly, based not only on recognition of the elder's experience, technical knowledge, and property ownership (in upper socioeconomic levels) but mainly on the Confucian philosophy of reverence for age. Also elders were respected because they were close to becoming ancestors (Morrisey, 1983). However, acculturation may have altered these values, and some modern

Chinese youngsters may not necessarily show this respect for elders (Chang, 1991; Lassiter, 1995).

Socialization Patterns

The Chinese have had a traditional philosophy regarding suicide. In pre-modern China, suicide was not regarded as deviant behavior. Suicide for reasons related to duty or loyalty was socially acceptable, as opposed to suicide committed merely because of unhappiness. For example, a woman who committed suicide after the death of her husband to avoid being forced to remarry and transfer her loyalty was acting in an admirable manner (Kleinman & Lin, 1981).

Bourne (1973) noted that the suicide rate among early Chinese immigrants was three times the U.S. national average. Interpersonal conflicts or a reprimand could provoke a suicide attempt, and this attempt would frequently motivate the family to seek guidance, counseling, and/or psychotherapy (Lee, 1982). Chinese suicide statistics indicate a high female suicide rate as compared to other countries. This rate increases with age. Most common methods of suicide are jumping from a height or hanging. These methods differ greatly from suicide methods used by other cultures (Hau, 1993). The suicide rate of Chinese Americans appears to be lower in states where there is a large Chinese population (Lester, 1992).

In summary, major Chinese personality traits include familism, collective responsibility between kinship members, group solidarity, conformity, respect for authority, and suppression of individuality. Some Chinese have been noted to be strongly past-oriented and may experience rigidity of role and status (father-son dyad and filial piety). Chinese culture emphasizes adherence to tradition, loyalty to family, and the relative unimportance of individual feelings. In contrast, American culture emphasizes independence, freedom, and individualism (Rawl, 1992).

Other characteristics observed among Chinese Americans are a desire for harmony and balance, an ability to suppress emotions, stoicism, passivity, frugality, and fatalism. Behavior patterns are often based on a moral code of ethics (Kleinman & Lin, 1981; Lee, 1982; Wong, 1985). Traditionally Chinese families and schools have stressed moral rules (based on Confucianism) to maintain proper behavior, which children are expected to internalize. Kleinman and Lin (1981) noted that the Chinese use moral values as guides to behavior to a greater extent than many other cultures.

Religious Beliefs and Practices

Traditionally, there have been three major religions and one basic philosophy in Chinese culture. The religions are Buddhism, Taoism, and Ancestor Worship. Although some Westerners have questioned whether or not

Confucianism is a religion (Taylor, 1990), Chinese Americans view Confucianism as a philosophy, not a religion (Huang, 1996). Confucius, born in 551 B.C., developed the first Chinese code of ethics. His teachings stress moral virtue, goodness, reciprocity, empathy, and the use of shame to develop one's own moral conscience.

Buddhism was developed from the teachings of Gautama Buddha, who lived in India from 563 to 483 B.C. An early form in China was Chan, meaning "meditative." Today, this form of Buddhism in both China and Japan is known as Zen. Buddhism has been called a negative religion because it emphasizes the inevitable suffering of humans and the impermanence of life (Dumoulin, 1976). Buddhism teaches the individual to think more intensely about the meaning of human existence in order to experience intuitive understanding and ultimately to relieve suffering. The underlying principle of Buddhism is that enlightenment is attained through intuitive understanding, which is experienced by complete absence of thought and by nonattachment. An individual may accomplish this by assuming a meditative state in order to reach the original pure nature of one's inner self (Summerfield, 1991). Buddhism also emphasizes passivity, stoicism, benevolence, self-respect, self-control, preservation of family honor, and reincarnation (Eliade & Couliano, 1991; Lee, 1986; Miller, 1988; Seward, 1972).

Taoism is based on the philosophy of Lao Tzu (or Laotse), who was born about 604 B.C. Taoism emphasizes the mystical aspects of human nature. It professes that immortality is the reward of true faith. Taoism is often associated with health (well-being) practices. Whereas Confucianism is mainly concerned with the proper way of conducting one's social life (a moral code), Taoism focuses on achieving the optimal state of well-being by maintaining harmony with cosmological and natural spheres (Kleinman & Lin, 1981). Taoism teaches that life is a cycle consisting of birth, death, and reincarnation (Lee, 1986).

Traditionally, the foundation of Ancestor Worship has been the belief that the natural and the supernatural are interrelated. This religious practice assumes that there is an afterlife and that the living are able to communicate with the dead (Summerfield, 1991). A shaman (*tang-ki*), or medium, is able to enter into a trance state, where he becomes possessed by supernatural powers and is able to contact spirits of the dead. Often the shaman is used to seek advice from dead spirits in order to help a believer deal with a problem. By worshiping ancestors, the traditional Chinese family expects to be rewarded by good fortune. Ancestor worship has been practiced in various ceremonies, of which the most important is Ching Ming or First Feast of the Dead at Spring Festival time. (Kleinman & Lin, 1981; Lassiter, 1995).

Today, religions practiced in the Peoples' Republic of China also include Christian religions (Roman Catholic and Protestant denominations) and

Islam, in the Muslim communities. Many Chinese Americans are affiliated with Christian religions in the United States (Lassiter, 1995).

Health Beliefs and Practices

Health Beliefs

In contrast to the Western health system, that emphasizes crisis intervention, Chinese philosophy emphasizes prevention and health maintenance. Many Chinese believe that because the body is a gift from one's parents and/or ancestors, it should be well cared for and properly maintained, and it is best to die with the body intact (Spector, 1991). The Chinese have a holistic concept of health. Psychosocial, physical, religious, and cultural factors are an integral part of the human system. A dominant theme of the traditional Chinese belief pattern is the importance of maintaining harmonious relationships ("psychosocial homeostasis") with family and community. Psychological problems are often related to interpersonal stress among family members (Kleinman and Lin, 1981).

The basic concept of Chinese health practices is the balance and harmony of energy fields. Since changes are unavoidable in the universe, balance is dynamic rather than static. Yin and yang are polar terms that describe the contrasting aspects of the universe. Although yin and yang are contradictory, they are also complementary. The interaction of yin and yang is the essence of all change in the universe. Thus a yin-yang imbalance within the human body results in dysfunction or disease.

Yin represents the female, negative energy—the passive, unassertive, inhibited, unclear, internal, dark, and cold, plus material and concrete human factors. Yin stores the vital strength of life. Winter and spring diseases are yin. Yang signifies male, positive energy—the active, excited, aggressive, external, bright, and hot, as well as abstract and functional human aspects. Yang protects the body from outside forces. Summer and fall diseases are yang.

Body parts correspond to the dualistic concept of yin and yang. The surface of the body is yang; the inside of the body is yin. The front of the body is yin; the back is yang. Liver, heart, spleen, lungs, and kidneys are yin. The gallbladder, stomach, large and small intestines, bladder, and lymph are yang (Kleinman & Lin, 1981; Spector, 1991; Wollnofer & von Rottauscher, 1972).

Yin-Yang dichotomy is also manifested in the polar relationship of hot and cold. Yin conditions are classified as cold, and yang conditions are hot. Diseases may be classified as hot or cold, and remedies similarly classed are used as treatment. Foods are also classified as hot or cold.

Yin conditions such as cancer, pregnancy, and postpartum problems are treated with yang (hot) foods. Examples of yang foods are chicken, beef, eggs, and spicy foods. On the other hand, yang conditions such as infections, hypertension, and venereal diseases are treated with yin (cold) foods. Yin foods include pork, fish, fresh fruits and vegetables, soybean curd, and bland foods (Chang, 1991; Chow, 1976).

Major concepts related to care of the body include balancing, replacement, and moderation. The goal of balancing is to achieve harmony by an awareness of the hot-cold status of the body as well as the status of substances taken into the body. This awareness promotes measures to prevent imbalance, such as eating a balanced diet. Replacement maintains balance. Replacement is the process by which any bodily deficiency can be altered by the use of supplemental foods and herbs. And finally, the practice of moderation instead of extremes avoids disrupting the system and throwing the body out of balance (Kleinman & Lee, 1981; Louie, 1976).

Apparently for some Chinese Americans somatization is a common method of expressing emotional distress (Lee, 1982). As a coping method or manipulating strategy, emotions such as depression and anxiety are frequently articulated as somatic rather than psychological distress. For example, instead of regarding depression as a psychological disturbance, the resulting lack of energy and loss of appetite may be viewed as a disturbance in the *chi* (vital energy). Generally, emotions are not considered harmful or disruptive to the body, except when they become excessive (Kleinman & Lee, 1981).

Healing Practices

Meditation is a form of deep concentration, usually in a trance-like state, during which the mind becomes attuned to unique internal energy forces. Meditation is used to alleviate stress in order to prevent stress-related disease.

Acupuncture is a popular demonstration of the energy fields theory. Fine hairlike needles are inserted into specific predetermined points in the skin, located on meridians, or pathways of energy, *chi*. These points lead to various organs of the body. Acumassage, acupressure, and martial arts (such as kung fu) use acupressure points in the body and the meridians through which energy flows. Western measures, such as the electrocardiogram and electroencephalogram, Kirlian photography, and biofeedback are similar uses of energy systems (Chow, 1976).

Cupping is a traditional healing practice in which a heated bamboo cup is placed on selected skin sites. As the cup cools, the skin and energy are drawn into the cup. Pinching, an alternative form of cupping, applies friction to special areas by pinching the skin. These procedures are believed to reduce stress and relieve congestion, headache, and cold symptoms (Chow, 1976).

Herbology is the use of natural elements from plants and/or animals that help counteract deficiencies and stimulate the body's *chi*. One of the most popular herbs is ginseng, sold as teas, candies, powders, and tablets in most health food stores. Ginseng is frequently used as a rejuvenator. Other uses for ginseng are as a sedative, to stimulate digestion, for faintness after childbirth (Spector, 1991), and to treat hypertension (Chang, 1991) and diabetes (Lu, 1986).

The physician has been the primary healer in traditional Chinese medicine. A problem was encountered when male physicians had to treat women, because men were not permitted to touch women directly. In order to demonstrate areas of discomfort or pain on her body, the female patient used a figurine. Traditionally, women healers were usually midwives or shamans. Female shamans were believed to possess gifts of prophecy (Spector, 1991).

Nutritional Patterns

The Chinese American focus on health maintenance and disease prevention is reflected in their dietary practices. Food mixtures are prepared with a specific balance in mind. Traditionally, a balance between the foods classed as hot and cold (unrelated to temperature) has been essential to the maintenance of good health. Hot foods (e.g., chicken and beef) are balanced by cold (e.g., fresh fruits and vegetables) (Rose, 1978).

Chinese cuisine is high in vegetables, low in fat and sweets, and high in salt. Vegetables are cooked for short periods to retain the vitamins. Roasts and large portions of meat are not generally eaten. Rather, meat is served in small pieces that can be handled easily with chopsticks. Typical foods include rice, pork, chicken, eggs, various soy preparations, and a variety of vegetables. Hot and warm beverages are preferred to cold beverages. Hot tea is a favorite. Milk is not a part of the typical Chinese diet because there appears to be an almost universal Asian (94%) intolerance to lactose (Boyle & Andrews, 1989; Char, 1981).

World-renowned Chinese cuisine is enjoyed by many cultures. Notable styles of Chinese cookery are the Cantonese, Shanghai, and Sichuan. Cantonese style consists of foods steamed in water rather than fried. Vegetables, prepared to retain their crispness, are combined with a variety of other foods such as eggs, chopped liver, smoke-cured ham, or prawn slices wrapped in rice flour. Few spices are used, and dishes tend to taste sweet. Shanghai-style foods are somewhat heavier and take longer to prepare than Cantonese cuisine. The longer cooking causes the vegetables to be softer and to absorb more of the sauces. Shanghai style offers more fried foods with more spices. Sichuan style is the most spicy with a liberal amount of spices, hot peppers, and pimientos (Summerfield, 1991).

Common Diseases

Neurasthenia is probably the most frequent diagnosis made by Chinese psychiatrists. Symptoms of neurasthenia include a wide range of complaints: headache, various kinds of pain, pressure and heaviness in the head, noises in the ears, lack of concentration, insomnia, exhaustion, and poor appetite (Kleinman, 1982; Lin, 1983). Kleinman noted that patients diagnosed with neurasthenia most often attributed the symptoms to nonorganic causes such as work problems, political concerns, family and marital problems, and school crises.

Chinese Americans manifest a high incidence of the genetic diseases thalassemia and glucose-6-phosphate dehydrogenase deficiency. Thalassemia is a hemoglobin abnormality characterized by a high rate of red blood cell destruction, requiring the client to have frequent blood transfusions. G-6-PD, also a blood cell disorder, causes the production of fragile red blood cells (Molnar, 1983; Overfield, 1985). Another genetic condition found in many Chinese causes marked facial flushing and vasomotor reaction when alcohol is ingested. This may explain the low rate of alcoholism among Chinese (Overfield, 1985).

Other observations about Chinese American health include the following:

- Chinese Americans tend to have fewer dental caries than other Americans (Bullough & Bullough, 1982).
- Chinese Americans have a lower mortality from heart disease (32%) than white Americans (39%), but a higher mortality from cancer (27%) than white Americans (21%).
- Suicide ranks seventh as a cause of death for Chinese Americans as compared to a ranking of tenth for white Americans (Hau, 1993; Yu, 1986).

Beliefs about Death and Dying

For the most part, Chinese Americans tend to be stoic and fatalistic when faced with terminal illness and/or death of self or family members. Some Chinese Americans believe in an afterlife, in reincarnation, and that the living may be influenced by spirits of the dead, the basis of ancestor worship (Kleinman & Lin, 1981; Lassiter, 1995).

Buddhists believe that when a person dies, the individual goes to "the pure land" and is welcomed by Buddha. The deceased then becomes an ancestor with whom the living may maintain contact (Eliade & Couliano, 1991). Consequently, Buddhists tend to have less difficulty than some other individuals in accepting the loss of a loved one due to this expectation of continued contact (Grippin, 1979).

FILIPINO AMERICANS

Filipino Americans are the second largest Asian group in the United States. In 1990, numbering 1.5 million, they represent 0.6% of the American population, an increase from 0.3% in 1980. Most Filipino Americans reside in the West, the South, and Hawaii (U.S. Bureau of the Census, 1990).

Family

Traditional

Four major relationships characterize the traditional Filipino American family concept. These may be categorized as blood kinship, marriage kinship, compadrazgo, and reciprocity relationships (Affonso, 1978; Vance, 1991). The most common relationship is the blood bond of a bilateral kinship system, which means that the individual's descent is acknowledged with respect to the families of both parents. The mother's maiden name may be used as a child's middle name, while the surname remains that of the father's family. Each parent is considered of equal importance, and together both families provide a bilateral inheritance system (Aquino, 1981).

The second type of relationship is affinial, resulting from marriage. At the wedding, the relatives of the bride are accepted by the groom; in like manner, his relatives become the bride's family. Thus, the bilateral kinship practice is initiated by marriage.

A third type of relationship is known as *compadrazgo* kinship. Originally a Roman Catholic ritual, godparents (*compadres*) are selected at the time of the child's baptism. These godparents serve as co-parents and assume responsibility for the child's welfare thereafter. Generally the *compadres* are selected on the basis of socioeconomic status and access to power. Ideally the *padrino* (godfather) is someone to whom the godchild can go when in need of financial or political favors. Although this role may have altered somewhat among modern Filipinos in the United States, godparents are still viewed as surrogate parents as well as active participants in the socialization and education of their godchildren. Today it is still customary to expect the godparents to assume some of the financial expenses for baptism and to give gifts at Christmas, birthdays, weddings, family funerals, thus becoming involved in family rites of passage. Godparent obligations may also include helping to finance their godchild's education and later assisting the child to find employment, build a home, and/or purchase a car (Affonso, 1978; Almirol, 1982). The *compadrazgo* system also embodies reciprocal obligations. If the godparents have no children of their own, their godchildren are expected to provide care during the godparents' illness and old age. Thus the *compadrazgo* system extends the kinship ties of loyalty, obligations, reciprocity and interdependence. When Filipinos migrate and are not among blood kin, often the *compadrazgo* and/or the *utang* system can increase their allies and provide support while adjusting to the new environment (Affonso, 1978; Agbayani-Siewert & Revilla, 1995).

The fourth type of relationship, *utang na loob*, is a system of reciprocal obligations; a person must be ready to repay another's kindness by goods or services, often on demand. Kin members borrow money and exchange food and other necessities among themselves. An individual who refuses to help a relative may be regarded as *walang hiya* (shameless). *Hiya* means shame or losing face, and this label must be avoided at all cost. To be *walang hiya* means to be publicly condemned (Almirol, 1982).

Some traditional Filipino Americans believe that they are judged primarily by their loyalties to the extended family. Social status could be associated with one's capacity to improve the family socioeconomic level, maintain family harmony and cohesion, and protect the honor of women kin. The kin group relationship is based on a complex system of reciprocal rights and obligations in a setting of interdependence. Loyalty and unity, which are essential to family relationships, serve to promote strong ties between kin that can be advantageous. On the other hand, these strong ties tend to isolate socially some Filipino Americans from other Americans (Almirol, 1982; Lassiter, 1995).

Modern Family

Filipino Americans differ from most other Asian groups in that many Filipino surnames are Hispanic rather than Asian. Also, the structure of many Filipino American families is somewhat different from that of other Asian groups with respect to distribution of authority and power. This difference may be due to the influence of indigenous Filipino customs prior to Spanish colonialism. Unlike several other Asian groups, family authority is not usually patriarchal, but more often egalitarian, where husband and wife share in financial and family decisions (Andres & Illada-Andres, 1987; Yu & Liu, 1980). A Filipino legend has it that in the beginning, man and woman emerged simultaneously from a large bamboo tube, unlike the Judeo-Chistian concept of Eve being created from the rib of Adam (Andres & Illada-Andres, 1987). Thus Filipino descendants are traced bilaterally through both parents (Agbayani-Siewert & Revilla, 1995).

In the Philippines, families may be either nuclear or extended, but more often are extended. Nuclear Filipino families are more common in the United States. Although the nuclear Filipino American family is the basic socioeconomic unit, this family is actually a subunit of the extended kin group. It is an acceptable practice for adult unmarried employed children to live with parents in the nuclear family and contribute to family support

(Almirol, 1982). Although the Filipino heritage is a blend of various cultures, there is a strong Chinese influence of Filipino family solidarity (Lassiter, 1995; Vance, 1991).

Elderly

Filipino American elders are highly respected and viewed as wise, but do not maintain an ascribed authority over younger family members, as is characteristic of many other Asian groups. Whenever possible the elders provide financial assistance for the education of their grandchildren and help with household chores and child care. Many Filipino children feel responsible for the care of their elderly parents (Peterson, 1978).

Children are taught to respect their elders. The expression *po* (similar to the English expressions *madam* and *sir*) is often used when addressing an elder (Vance, 1991). Another important Filipino practice is that of kissing the hand of the elder as a sign of respect and reverence. In greeting the elder, the right hand is kissed, with the words, *"mano po."* The elder may then reply with "God bless you" (Affonso, 1978).

Socialization Patterns

Many Filipino Americans value smooth interpersonal relationships (SIR). Many encourage passive nonconfrontation and discourage aggressive outward displays of behavior that might cause conflict (Bulato, 1981; Tagaki & Ishisaka, 1982). SIR are primarily maintained by four methods: reciprocal obligations (*utang na loob*), shame (*hiya*), protection of self-esteem (*amor proprio*), and going along with (*Pakikisama*) (Lynch, 1981).

Utang ng loob is a from of social control that assures the individual help and protection, but the recipient must be prepared to return favors or suffer *hiya*. *Hiya* serves to emphasize the importance of the group over the individual.

Amor proprio is related to *hiya*. Although some Filipinos are very sensitive to criticism that could cause humiliation, affront one's self-esteem, and thereby provoke aggression, the value of *hiya* helps to repress behavior that might shame others. Thus some Filipino Americans are careful not to criticize or provoke others (Agbayani-Siewert & Revilla, 1995).

Pakikisama, the final Filipino value, means maintaining good feelings in all personal interactions and being able to get along with others at all costs. The individual is expected to forfeit personal interests and desires (and those outside the kin unit) for the good of the family; cooperation among family members is more important than individualism (Agbayani-Siewert & Revilla, 1995; Lynch, 1981).

In summary, many Filipino Americans generally have mild, passive temperaments and tend to place great importance on balance and harmony in social interactions. Many seldom express disagreement, especially with those in authority. They are usually quiet, polite, respectful of authority, and able to outwardly suppress hostility. Anger may be dealt with in a passive aggressive manner using behavior manifestations such as procrastination, stubbornness, desire for acceptance, and various attention-seeking tactics (Aquino, 1981; DeGracia, 1979; Lassiter, 1995; Vance, 1991).

Religious Beliefs and Practices

During the Spanish colonial period (1521 to 1898), the Roman Catholic church was an important political, educational, and economic power in the Philippines. Consequently, the Philippines became the only Christian nation in the Far East, and so most Filipinos are Roman Catholic (Aquino, 1981; Lassiter, 1995; Melendy, 1980; Vance, 1991).

Health Beliefs and Practices

Traditional belief has held that illness results when the internal and external elements of the body are disturbed. Factors that may disturb the normal equilibrium of these elements are changes in seasons, improper diet, witchcraft, accidents, and inappropriate behaviors. Some Filipino Americans say special prayers of protection, perform rituals, use holy water, and/or wear such articles as charms, medals, or crucifixes for protection against external disease agents (Aquino, 1981).

Traditional Filipino American health beliefs and practices may be based on three concepts:

1. Flushing, the perception of the body as a container that is able to collect and hold impurities. A common home remedy used to cause flushing is vinegar, believed to be able to flush out the system in the treatment of a cold or fever.
2. Heating practices, based on the belief that hot and cold must be kept in balance within the body. Extremes of hot and cold can cause illness.
3. Protection, to keep the body's external boundaries safe from disease and other evil forces (McKenzie & Chrisman, 1977; Vance, 1991).

Because the culture of the Philippines has been influenced by different ethnic groups, including the Chinese, East Indian, Arab, Spanish, and American, a variety of folk practices exist (Vance, 1991). Some folk beliefs associated with illness and health include:

- Combing the hair at night will cause diseases of the eyes.
- Sleeping with wet hair will result in blindness.
- Bathing during menstruation will cause insanity.
- Bathing on Fridays is unhealthy.
- Large ears are an indication of longevity.

• Crucifixes, charms, or medals should be attached to the clothing of babies to protect them from evil spirits and effects of the evil eye (Aquino, 1981, p. 182).

Nutritional Patterns

Filipino Americans who believe in the hot-cold dichotomy may prepare meals by including "hot" and "cold" (unrelated to temperature) foods. For example, beans, considered "hot," are served with vegetables, considered "cold" (Orque, Bloch, & Monrroy, 1983). Favorite Filipino American foods are fish, vegetables, and rice. Typical dishes might include *adobo*, a highly seasoned, spicy dish made of pork and chicken cooked in vinegar and lard; *lumpia*, prepared with selected vegetables and similar to Chinese egg roll; and *pancit*, consisting of rice or noodles cooked with ham, chicken, or shrimp in soy and garlic sauce (Ignacio, 1976; Lassiter, 1995; Vance, 1991).

Common Diseases

Thalassemia (Cooley's anemia) is prevalent among Filipinos (Vance, 1991). Filipinos of Chinese descent may also exhibit lactose intolerance (Gerber, 1983).

Except for Filipino Americans, the prevalence of controlled and uncontrolled hypertension in the United States is generally lower for persons of Asian ethnicity (Stavig, Igra, & Leonard, 1988). Filipino American men and women have the highest rate of hypertension among the Asian population in the United States (Klatsky & Armstrong, 1991). Although they show a high prevalence rate for hypertension, they record low rates of hypertension mortality. This low mortality rate may be related to appropriate control practices, knowledge of risk factors, and behavior modification. Filipino Americans demonstrate a lower risk for cigarette smoking and alcohol abuse than Caucasians (Stavig, Igra, & Leonard, 1988).

In Hawaii, where Filipinos constitute 20% of the population, Filipino American women were found to have the lowest incidence of breast cancer, as compared to Japanese, Chinese, ethnic Hawaiians, and Caucasians. However late-stage diagnosis is common among the Filipino Americans, and thus their death rate from the disease is greater than that for the other cultures (Goodman, 1991; Lassiter, 1995).

Beliefs about Death and Dying

Filipino American beliefs about death and dying are generally related to the Catholic religion.

JAPANESE AMERICANS

Japanese Americans comprise the third largest Asian group in the United States. In 1990, numbering about 850,000 individuals, they represented 0.3% of the United States population, with no percentage change from the 1980 census. In contrast to the increase in other Asian populations, the number of Japanese Americans has grown very slowly, constituting a decreasing proportion of the Asian population. Currently, with little incentive to migrate from modern Japan, two-thirds of Japanese Americans are native born, as compared to the 40% of other Asian ethnic groups born in their native countries (Nishi, 1995). The states with the largest proportion of Japanese ancestry are Hawaii and California (U.S. Bureau of the Census, 1990).

Family

Japanese Americans are the only ethnic group that has named its generational levels. The first generation (first immigrants to settle in America) is called *Issei*, the second (their offspring) is *Nisei*, and the third generation is known as *Sansei*. The fourth and fifth generations are called the *Yansei* and the *Goset*, respectively (Kitano, 1988; Okamoto, 1978).

Traditional Family

The *Issei* were not eligible for citizenship until after the 1952 McCarran-Walter Act (one provision of which removed the racial bias of eligibility for citizenship). Prior to the act, during World War II, the *Issei* (considered "aliens") and their children, constituting about 90% of the Japanese in the continental United States, were removed to internment camps. From 1942 to 1945, these camps, located in isolated areas of the West, enclosed by barbed wire, and staffed with armed guards, restricted the lives of their Japanese residents (Kitano, 1988; Nishi, 1995; Okamoto, 1978; Sodetani-Shibata, 1981). Consequently, the *Issei* established strong ethnic communities that they maintained even after resettlement. Japanese have been considered a uniquely homogeneous people (Fugita & O'Brien, 1991). Today, most *Issei* are no longer alive (Nishi, 1995).

Characteristics of the traditional Japanese American family (*Issei*) are:

- Patriarchal, hierarchical structure.
- Emphasis on obedience to elders, filial piety, and rank.
- Interdependence of family members.
- Women subordinate to men.
- Purpose of marriage is to continue the family. Marriage for love is considered

immoral because it places personal feelings before the family. Traditional marriages are often arranged by parents (Kitano, 1988; Nishi 1995).

Modern Family

Presently most *Nisei* are 50 years of age or older. Many experienced internment with their *Issei* parents and are influenced by traditional Japanese family values as well as those of mainstream America. *Nisei* families demonstrate some of these characteristics:

- Marriage partners tend to be freely chosen on the basis of romantic love.
- The bond between husband and wife (conjugal bond) takes priority over the bond between parent and child (filial bond).
- The marital relationship is more egalitarian, with greater flexibility of sex roles.
- The emphasis is on upward socioeconomic mobility (Yanagisako, 1985).

The modern *Sansei*, typically born in the United States, comprise the majority of the present young adult Japanese American population. *Sansei* retain some traditional Japanese family values but are more likely to follow American mainstream family practices. The following exemplify some Sansei family values and practices:

- Some *Sansei* select non–Japanese Americans as spouses.
- Attitudes about marriage are closely related to those of most Americans.
- Love is viewed as the most important aspect of marriage.
- The conjugal bond takes precedence over filial bonds and kinship relationships.
- Although some male dominance persists within the family, many *Sansei* couples have adopted an egalitarian model of family relationships.
- Separation and divorce are becoming more common.
- Some families maintain strong identification with the extended family network; hierarchies may persist (Sodetani-Shibata, 1981).

Some *Nisei* and *Sansei* have demonstrated a high degree of assimilation into American culture by indices such as use of the English language, out-of-group marriages (60–65%), residing outside of concentrated Japanese areas, high educational levels, and a wide range of professional occupations (Kitano, 1988; Lock, 1983).

Elderly

Some Japanese Americans have retained a strong sense of duty, respect, and dedication to the elderly, based on filial piety and the fundamental concept of ancestor worship (Chee & Kane, 1983). Palmore (1975) noted that because the Japanese are relatively homogeneous racially and ethnically, this facilitates the integration of elderly persons. However, the elderly are more integrated into their families in Japan than in the United States. According to Yanagishita and Guralnik (1988), Japanese elders have the longest life expectancy of any other ethnic group in the world.

Socialization Patterns

In contrast to the Western emphasis on individualism, Japanese Americans value collectivism. Many place more importance on the smooth functioning and preservation of the whole group than on any individual, and consensus is more important than personal autonomy. Some Japanese Americans define a successful person as one who avoids conflict, displays an appropriate amount of modesty, observes formal ranking, and identifies with the group (Fugita & O'Brien, 1991).

An important characteristic of Japanese American socialization is the concept of *iemoto*, which encourages the development of superior-subordinate relationships not only within the family but also within larger social groupings. Traditional beliefs of the *Issei* have held that a person must have associational ties outside the immediate family and kin. The modern version of *iemoto* is the Japanese corporation (Fugita & O'Brien, 1991).

Another socialization theme is *enryo*, which encompasses the norms of restraint, reserve, and lack of assertion in social interactions. A dominant personality aspect of some Japanese Americans is the tendency to suppress negative feelings towards others, including family, intimates, and those in authority (Kitano, 1988; Lassiter, 1995; Lock, 1983; Sodetani-Shibata, 1981). Many Japanese Americans believe that one must "fit in," not cause conflict, adapt, and maintain harmony. The ability of many Japanese Americans to adapt harmoniously may have facilitated their high level of assimilation into American society (Fugita & O'Brien, 1991).

Religious Beliefs and Practices

The predominant religions of Japan are Shinto and Buddhism. Less than 1% of Japan's population practices Christianity (Ensminger et al., 1983). Confucianism, a Chinese philosophy has greatly influenced Japanese thinking, although it never became strongly organized in Japan (Katagawa, 1988; Miller, 1988).

Shinto, the native religion of Japan, is a complex of beliefs, customs, and practices distinguished from the religions of India and China (Buddhism and Confucianism, respectively) (Eliade & Couliano, 1991). Shintoists worship gods and goddesses (*kami*) who are forces of nature residing in trees, rivers, rocks, mountains, the wind, some animals, and particularly the sun and moon (Eliade & Couliano, 1991; Miller, 1988; Seward, 1972). Japanese ancestor worship is basically a Shinto institution, often altered by Confucian and Buddhist rituals.

Buddhism, from the teachings of Gautama Buddha of India, was brought to Japan from China during the sixth century. Buddhism amalgamated with the existing Shinto religion, and its followers practiced Shinto-Buddhism (Katagawa, 1988; Seward, 1972). Buddhism is discussed in this chapter in the section on Chinese Americans.

Zen is a form of Buddhism. The term Zen means silent meditation. Zen Buddhism was brought from China and established in Japan by two monks, Eisai and Dogen, during the thirteenth century. Zen emphasizes meditation and enlightenment through intuitive thought, self-discipline, and direct and unhesitating style of life. Because of Zen's focus on direct unhesitating behavior, this form of Buddhism became popular among the Japanese military (Dumoulin, 1988; Lassiter, 1995; Seward, 1972).

Health Beliefs and Practices

Many Japanese Americans believe in the holistic concept of health: All parts of the body are interrelated; the mind and the body are inseparable; and social, psychological, and physiological factors contribute to health and illness. Consequently, many believe that treatment of illness should involve the entire body rather than only the area of complaint and should also address the social and environmental implications of the condition (Lock, 1980; Lock, 1983).

Some Japanese Americans believe that illness is related to yin or yang states and that a dietary balance between yin and yang is required to maintain health as well as to treat disease conditions (Chow, 1976; Lock, 1980). Yin-yang theory was discussed earlier in this chapter, under Chinese Americans. Herbs, classified by traditional practitioners according to the yin-yang theory, form important medications. Some Japanese American families ingest herbal liquid mixtures (two to four times a day) to prevent illness (Lassiter, 1995; Lock, 1980).

Ginseng or ginseng root (often called the "root of life") is a popular herb used by Japanese Americans. Classed as a yang substance, it is often ingested as a rejuvenator by pregnant women, athletes, older persons, or anyone in a "weakened" condition (Andrews, 1989). Adverse reactions associated with the long-term use of ginseng include nervousness, insomnia, edema, or irregularities in blood glucose levels (Ginseng, 1980; Lassiter, 1995).

Nutritional Patterns

Rice is the staple food of the Japanese diet and is served with almost every meal. Fish and soybean products are major sources of dietary protein.

Soybean curd (tofu) is used extensively. Japanese Americans usually eat less meat and more vegetables than other Americans. Fresh vegetables are slightly cooked (often stir fried) to preserve crispness and nutrients. Edible seaweed is popular in Japanese cuisine.

Japanese Americans prefer their food chopped in small pieces that are easy to manage with chopsticks. Favorite desserts are fruits, especially melons, berries, and tangerines (Burtis, Davis, & Martin, 1989; Tien-Hyatt, 1987). Tea is the favorite beverage. Sake, a rice wine, is a popular alcoholic drink (Ensminger et al., 1983).

Strict Buddhists are vegetarians. They avoid eating the flesh of any animal (except fish), as well as milk and eggs. They also abstain from alcoholic beverages (Burtis, Davis, & Martin, 1989).

Common Diseases

Japanese Americans (both sexes) demonstrate the longest life expectancies of any large population subgroup in the United States (Curb et al., 1990). Between 1972 and 1982, Japan reached and surpassed Sweden's record as the country with the longest life expectancy (Yanagishita & Guralnik, 1988).

Lactose enzyme deficiency is found in about 90% of Japanese American adults. Individuals with this condition are unable to digest the lactose in milk and other dairy products. Symptoms of lactose intolerance include gastrointestinal upset, cramping, and diarrhea (Burtis, Davis, & Martin, 1989).

Because feelings are not readily expressed, Japanese Americans often convert their emotions into somatic conditions. They are vulnerable to stress-related illnesses (Grippin, 1979; Lock, 1983).

Japanese American women were found to have a lower rate of breast cancer than Caucasian women, but a 3.5 times higher rate of breast cancer than their peers in Japan. These findings indicate that environmental factors play a larger role than genetic factors in determining breast cancer risk (Nomura et al., 1984; Shimizu et al., 1991).

Coronary heart disease rates are much lower in Japanese Americans than in Caucasians, but hemorrhagic stroke rates are higher in Japanese Americans than in Caucasians. Plasma fibrinogen levels and coagulation factors were found to be significantly higher in Caucasians than in Japanese Americans. This may partly explain the difference in mortality from cardiovascular disease between these two populations. These differences may be related to diet and genetics (Iso et al., 1989).

There is a significant positive relationship between coffee consumption and serum cholesterol. This relationship is not present with other sources of caffeine such as tea and cola. Thus tea drinkers tend to have lower serum cholesterol levels than coffee drinkers. Tea is usually the preferred beverage among Japanese Americans (Curb et al., 1986).

Cancer of the digestive organs appears to be more prevalent in Japanese Americans than in Caucasians. However, in general Japanese Americans have a lower incidence of other cancers.

Japanese Americans tend to have a slightly higher incidence of diabetes and pneumonia than Caucasians. Their most common health problems are peptic ulcer, hypertension, arthritis, diabetes, and gout.

Older age groups (ages 75–81) have a higher incidence of heart disease and stroke (Curb et al., 1990; Gerber, 1983; Park, Yokoyama, & Toku-yama, 1991; Peterson, Rose, & McGee, 1985). Among Japanese Americans, arteriosclerotic disease ranks highest as a cause of death, followed by COPD, infection, and diabetes (Park, Yokoyama, & Tokuyama, 1991).

Coronary occlusion is the major cause of sudden death among Japanese Americans. Although the incidence of stroke is high, it is not the major cause of sudden death (Yano, McCarthy, Reed, & Kagan, 1987; Lassiter, 1995).

Beliefs about Death and Dying

Some Japanese Americans may avoid discussions related to impending death because they believe that nonverbal methods are the most effective means of communicating feelings (Lock, 1983). Some may express grief by developing somatic ailments (Lawson, 1990). According to Buddhist philosophy, an individual's mind should be calm, hopeful, and clear at the time of death in order to reincarnate into a better person. Thus a dying Buddhist might refuse any pain medication that could alter consciousness (Tien-Hyatt, 1987).

ASIAN INDIAN AMERICANS

Asian Indian Americans, who also refer to themselves as East Indians, Indo-Americans, or Indians, are the fourth largest Asian American group in the United States. Although a few thousand Indians, mostly farmers, came to the United States in the early 1920s, most Indian migrants arrived after the reformed 1965 Immigration Act took effect. Recent Asian Indian immigrants consist of college-educated, urban, middle-class professionals and students. Of all the Asian countries, more immigrants from India and China have entered the United States as students (often graduate students) and then adjusted their status to that of permanent residents (Kamar, 1994; Sheth, 1995).

Asian Indians number approximately 815,000 individuals, representing 0.3% of the American population. Although large numbers live in California, the largest proportion, 35%, of Asian Indians reside in the Northeast, mostly in New York and New Jersey, as well as Washington, D.C. (U.S. Bureau of the Census, 1990).

Family

Family practices are influenced by India's caste system, a traditional religious cultural method of structuring life. The system establishes and maintains highly defined social levels that permeate all religious, linguistic, and ethnic associations. This traditional system is practiced in some Indian villages; however, many of these practices have changed with population shifts to the cities of India and migration to the United States.

Traditional beliefs held that purity was essential to one's interaction with the gods. Brahman priests, the highest rank, were the purest. In contrast, the untouchables, the lowest order, performed the most polluting duties (those that placed them in contact with pollutants such as human excrement, human hair and nails, water, garbage, and dead bodies) (Nyrop, 1986). Intermediate castes were, second to the Brahman, the Kshatriya (warriors); the Vaisya (farmers and merchants); and finally, just above the untouchables, the Sudras (poor farmers) and artisans. Mahatma Gandhi (of the vaisya class) named the untouchables Harijans, (people of God) (Fishlock, 1983). Traditionally, many believed that the only emancipation from a particular caste or level in society was to be reborn into a higher caste (Miller & Supersad, 1991).

Traditional Family

The traditional caste structure has been intrinsically related to kinship, with all of a person's kin belonging to the same caste. As caste affiliation is patrilineal, children are members of their father's caste. Traditionally, marriage was arranged by kin and partners were selected from among caste mates, assuring the perpetuation of the caste system (Aris, 1990; Nyrop, 1986). Traditionally, the family structure of India has been patriarchal and patrilineal, and the residential norm is patrilocal. The preferred joint household consisted of a senior couple, their unmarried children, their married sons' families, and perhaps the parents of the senior couple (particularly the husband's mother) and any other relatives (Nyrop, 1986). A major function of the family was to insure its continuity through the production of male heirs. All family property was divided evenly among the males, regardless of age. The female portion consisted only of the amount that would be given to her husband as a dowry when she married (Nyrop, 1986). An important traditional family value was concern for the welfare of the family as a whole. Individual members were expected to make sacrifices and/or pool their resources for the benefit of the total family unit (Chekki, 1988; Heitzman & Worden, 1996; Kamar, 1994).

Traditionally, marriage was the normal and most respectable state for

Indians. Unmarried daughters past the age of 25 were a poor reflection on the family. Marriage was extremely important, not only for the marriage partners but also to maintain the respectable status of the family and caste, as well as to unite two families (Nyrop, 1986). In traditional India, divorce was not common. Although divorce today in modern India poses no problem for an Indian man, in some areas divorce could lower the social status of a woman, unless she is wealthy and/or well educated (Patibandla, 1994).

Marriage arrangements vary somewhat in different regions of India. In southern regions, some castes prefer consanguineous (kin) marriages, for example, between a man and the daughter of his eldest sister (that is, a mature uncle and his young niece). The marriage between a woman and her mother's brother (again, young niece and older uncle) is also an acceptable union. Typically, the next preference would be marriage between first cousins. The age gradient is always important. The bride's age usually ranges from 16 to 21 (frequently about 18), and the groom is in his late 20s or older. Today, with the greater number of Indian women attaining higher education, their typical age at marriage is older. Depending on the caste community, the frequency of kin marriages still exists in several regions of South India, but they tend to occur between less close kin (Driver & Driver, 1988; Patibandla, 1994).

Although the traditional mother is close to her daughter, there may be a stronger bond with her son, who will take care of her in her old age while her daughters live with their in-laws. Mothers may compromise the interests of their daughters for those of their sons. The close bond between mother and son can cause problems when the son's wife enters the home and the mother has to share her son with another woman. Therefore, fear of mistreatment by the mother-in-law has always been a major concern of young brides. A few reports exist of disastrous mishaps befalling young brides who could not get along with their mothers-in-law (Dhruvarajan, 1988; Heitzman & Worden, 1996; Nyrop, 1985; Patibandla, 1994).

Modern Family

Most post-1965 Indian immigrants had married in India and brought their spouses with them to the United States. Some students either sent for their spouses or returned to India to be married and then brought their new spouses back to the United States. Of the six major Asian groups, Asian Indians and Chinese have the lowest rate of marriage outside of their ethnic group. Asian Indians in India as well as the United States tend to marry within their ethnic group. Some modern Asian Americans still observe the traditional practice of having parents select their mates (to be approved by the involved individuals) (Patibandla, 1994). Indian Asians show the lowest divorce rate among all Asian groups. The high stability of Asian Indian American families may be explained by traditional Indian attitudes and values that place strong emphasis on marriage and the family with a stigma on divorce and also by the high socioeconomic backgrounds of many Indian Americans (Patibandla, 1994; Sheth, 1995).

Elderly

Traditionally the Indian mother-in-law or grandmother and eldest son are frequently the most important family decision makers. The mother-in-law is often the main decision maker in family health care practices (Kakar et al., 1989).

Socialization Patterns

Some Asian Indian American family systems may encourage timidity, laissez-faire, dependency, humility, and deference in their members. Women tend to be stoic and self-sacrificing (Miller & Supersad, 1991). The Asian Indian American way of life, especially that of tolerance, accommodation and docility, may have facilitated their assimilation into American society. In addition, most adhere to the middle class value system in America (Chandras, 1977).

Many Asian Indian American women wear the traditional long, gracefully draped *sari*. Others may wear the soft pants (*salwar*) with a long top (*kameez*) and scarf (*dupatta*) (Ratnaraj, 1994). A fashionable married woman may wear a dot on her forehead, colored to coordinate with different outfits. Earrings in the ears and/or an earring in the side of the nose are also decorative and fashionable. Asian Indian men generally wear Western attire. However, attire is generally determined by the area of India where the person resides. Sikh men usually wear turbans in public (Kamar, 1994; Rajamani, 1994).

Religious Beliefs and Practices

Hinduism, probably the oldest religion in the world, is practiced by 80% of the people of India. The Hindu religion has its origin in the concepts of the early Aryans, who came to India more than 4,000 years ago. Three modern Hindu sages, Gandhi ("Mahatma," often used before his name, means "great souled" or "saint"), Maharshi, and Bhaktivedanta have greatly influenced Hindu philosophy in the twentieth century (Herman, 1991). Gandhi sought to solve the problem of suffering in others through civil disobedience to unjust laws, carried out in an attitude of nonviolence and love. Gandhi's philosophy, called *satyagraha*, has inspired many people throughout the world, such as Dr. Martin Luther King, Jr. By contrast, Maharshi was not concerned with the suffering of others but rather emphasized liberation from personal suffering through recognition of God dwelling within the self of every individual. Bhaktivedanta sought to solve the problem of personal suffering, but only by experiencing the presence of the legendary god *Krsna* as the self. These three apparently opposing philosophies are basic to the modern Hindu way of life (Herman, 1991).

Hinduism teaches the immortality of the human soul and the ultimate union of the individual with the all-pervasive spirit. The "self" is eternal, changeless, and ancient and is never destroyed even when the body is destroyed. Hinduism's theological rationale is based on a body of sacred literature known as the Vedas, that was composed between 1200 and 600 B.C. (Heitzman & Worden, 1996; Nyrop, 1986).

To the Hindu, religion is a spiritual expression of the reality of the universe. The knowledge of reality is the ultimate goal. Only specially gifted individuals can achieve a state of high spiritualism enabling them to know the truth. They are then said to experience *Moksha* (or *mukti*), which means "release from the false illusions of the external world." This heightened state of spiritualism may be reached through exercise of the intellect, devotion to deities, expansion of the senses, heightened control of the body, and disciplined meditation.

It is believed that the divine spirit permeates the universe and that people perceive the divine in accordance with their spiritual level. All life forms (including animals and gods) exist as a hierarchy, depending on spiritual advancement or purity. Many life forms pass through a chain of incarnations, thus assuming various positions in a hierarchy during their different lives. All souls are considered equal; thus, the rationale for the principle of *ahimsa* (noninjury to living things) is manifested in the practice of vegetarianism (Nyrop, 1986).

The law of Karma determines life cycles through birth and rebirth. Karma is the spiritual merit or demerit that an individual acquires during his or her lives. Thus, all lives are ordered in a hierarchy dependent on one's moral behavior in a previous life. Perfection of karma leads to emancipation from the burdens of birth and rebirth (*moksha*). (In Buddhism, this release is known as *nirvana*). (Heitzman & Worden, 1996).

Reincarnation is the central belief of Hinduism. The Hindu's goal in life is to acquire the highest spiritual merit or karma, which will determine his or her future lives. Each Hindu strives for a final release from the burden of birth and rebirth, which can be achieved only through a knowledge of truth and the experience of reality. Reality will be understood when there is a spiritual union of the individual soul and the universal soul. This ultimately desirable state may be attained by only a few of the purest and most highly spiritual, who are thereby released from the burden of reincarnation (Boyle & Andrews, 1989; Herman, 1991; Nyrop, 1986). Hinduism respects other religions and does not seek converts (Government Publication of India, 1993).

Among the other religions practiced by Asian Indians are Buddhism, Jainism, Islam, Sikhism, Zoroastrianism, Christianity, and Judaism (Government Publication of India, 1993; Nyrop, 1986). The majority of Asian

Indian Americans are Hindus. Although Sikhs represent only 2% of the population in India, Sikhs represent about 30–40% of the Asian Indian population in California. Muslims, Jains, and Zoroastrians make up small groups both in the homeland and in America (Jensen, 1980; Heitzman & Worden, 1996; Kamar, 1994; Lassiter, 1995).

Health Beliefs and Practices

Traditionally, many Asian Indians have believed that health is based on the body's intrinsic ability to heal itself. Illness may be caused by internal or external forces. Some have held the belief that an individual unable to control such internal forces as anger, fright, and jealousy becomes susceptible to disease (Henderson & Primeaux, 1981). Ilnesses caused by external forces are explained as the gods' way of punishing a person for his or her present sins or those committed in a previous life. Other external forces capable of causing illness may be spirits of dead ancestors, powers of jealous living relatives, and various demons and spirits empowered by evildoers. Charms, medals, and trinkets may be worn to help ward off evil (Boyle & Andrews, 1989; Miller & Supersad, 1991).

In addition to acceptance of modern or Western medicine, East Indian Americans tend to believe in several highly developed health and illness systems based on complex folk beliefs and practices. These belief systems include the Ayurvedic, the Unani, and the Homeopathic health theories (Heitzman & Worden, 1996).

The Ayurvedic system is based on the belief that disease is caused by the imbalance of essential body elements. Some East Indians acknowledge three fundamental elements of the human body—*dasa*, *dhatu*, and *mala*—that must be in a state of balance to maintain equilibrium or optimal health. *Dasa* directs the physiological functions of the body, *dhatu* is the basic structure of the human cell, and *mala* constitutes products of metabolism (Kakar, 1977). Within the Ayurvedic system, diseases are believed to be of psychosomatic origin and are treated accordingly (Dash, 1974). Most Ayurvedic medications, extracted from plants, are herbal remedies. To maintain or reestablish balance, diet is an important consideration in the therapeutic regime (Miller & Supersad, 1991).

The Unani health belief system was introduced by the Muslims. Its local practitioners are called *hakims*. Unani, which uses herbal remedies from every known plant, is similar to the Ayurvedic system.

The Homeopathic health belief system has no religious affiliation. It was introduced by a German doctor Samuel Christian Friedrich Hahnemann in 1796. Homeopathic medicine is based on the law of similars "like cures like." The theory states that large doses of drugs that produce symptoms of a disease in healthy people will cure the same symptoms when given in small amounts. Vaccination and inoculation to produce immunity are frequently offered in support of the homeopathy theory (Heitzman & Worden, 1996).

Nutritional Patterns

The preparation of an Indian meal is time consuming. Onions must be ground to a paste, often done by hand. Most Indian dishes have a base of an onion spice mixture browned in oil. Meat, vegetables, and water are added to this browned mixture and cooked until tender. Curry, a popular seasoning, is a mixture of typical Indian spices added to gravy that turns the food a yellowish-green. Other spices commonly used in Indian cookery are tumeric, ginger, tamarind, garlic, and coriander (Patibandla, 1994).

Most Hindus are vegetarians. Those who do eat meat do not eat beef. Muslims do not eat pork. Meat curry dishes are frequently made from goat meat or chicken.

Most Asian Indian Americans eat rice daily, often with dal, a bowl of lentil soup. Individuals of southern India like the hot and spicy sambar, a dal eaten with thin rice-flour pancakes.

A popular bread is called *roti*, which is a flat pancake-like bread, prepared on a black iron griddle. One type of roti is prepared by dropping balls of dough into boiling oil, where they become puffy. These puffed-up roti are enjoyed on festive occasions with halwa (a sweet cereal).

Chapatis are a form of roti made of whole wheat flour, salt, butter or margarine, and water, usually baked on a heavy iron convex griddle or an earthen stove (a *chulha*). When chapatis are stuffed with grated vegetables and fried in oil, the dish is called *parata* and is often served with yoghurt, a favorite milk dish. Another favorite dish is *panir*, a homemade cheese, which may be cut up into small pieces, deep fried, and then curried with peas and potatoes. Alcohol is forbidden to Muslims but not to Hindus; nevertheless, the latter rarely serve alcoholic beverages (Sarin, 1985).

Some Asian Indians, especially in rural areas, prefer to eat their food with their hands while sitting cross-legged on the floor. They wrap a piece of roti around meat or vegetable, dip it in dal, gravy, or sauce, and thus convey it to the mouth (Sarin, 1985). The right hand is used for feeding oneself; the left hand is reserved for toileting procedures (Nyrop, 1986).

Common Diseases

Some Asian Indian Americans have a genetic predisposition to thalassemia (Cooley's anemia) and lactose intolerance (Miller & Supersad, 1991). A study performed in the United Kingdom revealed that South Asians (Indians, Pakistanis, and Bangladeshis) averaged a lower alcohol consumption rate than the native British population. However, in spite of the lower consumption, alcohol morbidity rates for some South Asian communities were higher than for the general population. Alcohol consumption rates were found to be higher in Sikhs than in Hindus or Muslims (McKeigue & Karmi, 1993).

Another British study of adult Asian patients revealed a notable proportion of metabolic bone disease. Osteomalacia, most prevalent in Hindu women, was associated with strict vegetarian diet and the covering of skin from the sun when outdoors (Finch et al., 1992). Chapatis, a staple bread in some East Indian communities, are known to have a high concentration of phytate, which may decrease calcium absorption in the small intestine. Vitamin D levels appear lower in individuals who consume chapatis (Freimer, Echenberg, & Kretchmer, 1983).

Beliefs about Death and Dying

Many Hindus perceive death as a passing from one existence to another through reincarnation. Each person strives through rebirths to attain perfection of karma. Thus, the ultimate goal is to reach the highest spiritual level and become released from the burden of birth and rebirth. Because many Hindus believe that the self is greater and different from the body, cremation of the body is preferred (Nyrop, 1986).

KOREAN AMERICANS

Korean Americans comprise the fifth largest Asian group in the United States. Numbering about 800,000 individuals, they represent approximately 0.3% of the American population. The Korean American population has increased by about 125.3% between 1980 and 1990 (U.S. Bureau of the Census, 1990). Although Korean Americans have had a century-long immigration history, their entry into the United States peaked significantly after the Korean War in 1950. War brides of American servicemen constituted about 40% of all Korean legal immigrants between 1950 and 1964. In addition, Korean war orphan immigrants accounted for 60% of all alien children adopted by American citizens. (U.S. Immigration and Naturalization Service, 1950–1964). Today, the Korean community is largely composed of post–1965 Immigration Act immigrants. The significant improvement in living conditions in South Korea and publicity about Korean immigrants' adjustment difficulties in the United States has slowed Korean immigration in the past seven years. Because many comfortable middle-class individuals have remained in South Korea, a large number of recent immigrants have been from lower socioeconomic levels, migrating to improve their economic status. Some have migrated to join family members and/or to study at universities (Min, 1995).

With the exception of "Koreatown" in Los Angeles, Korean immigrants generally have not settled in tightly segregated ethnic communities. Instead, they have settled in and around the urban areas of America, where many are self-employed in small businesses (Hurh & Chung, 1984; Kim, 1980; Min, 1995b; Yu, 1983). The largest number reside in the West (44%), followed by the Northeast (22%), the South (20%), and the lowest number in the Midwest (14%) (U.S. Bureau of the Census, 1990). Cities with the largest Korean-ancestry population (in descending order) are Los Angeles, New York, Chicago, and Honolulu (Allen & Turner, 1988).

Family

Traditional Family

Confucianism, the traditional philosophy of Korean thought and behavior, has influenced the relationships among some members of Korean families (Korean Overseas Information Service, 1979). Confucian teachings emphasize patriarchy, filial piety, and educational achievement (Min, 1988). The traditional Korean family has the following characteristics:

- *Patriarchy.* The father is the head of the household, the authority, primary breadwinner, and decision maker in the family.

- *Extended structure.* In addition to the parents and their children, the family might include other relatives such as in-laws, uncles, aunts, cousins, grandparents, and grandchildren living together or in close proximity.

- *Continuity.* In a patrilineal rule of descent, the oldest son is the father's heir. The family's name and lineage are passed down through the male members (Kim, 1989).

- *Inclusiveness.* A strong kinship organization is based on a patrilocal rule of residence and genealogical records (Kim, 1989).

- *Authority.* The father has unchallengeable authority over his wife and the children, the elders control the younger members, and the males dominate the females (Kim, 1989).

- *Asexuality.* The father-son relationship is more important than the husband-wife relationship. Arranged marriage is a basic manifestation of asexuality in Korean kinship. Ideally, traditional Korean couples remain aloof from each other, symbolic of asexuality. Sexual pleasure between husband and wife is less important than bearing a male heir. They seldom display affection in public, especially in the presence of their respected parents and elders. Marriages were often arranged by the elders (Kim, 1989; Min, 1988).

- *Filial piety (hyo'song).* This special obligation requires that the eldest son remain with his parents after his marriage in order to assure them care and financial support. Filial piety is extended even after death through ancestor worship (Min, 1988).

- *Confucian philosophy* directed the role of women, who must conform to a "Rule of Three Following." A woman must follow her father as a child, her husband as an adult, and her son when she is old (Kim, 1989; Lassiter, 1995; Shon & Ja, 1982).

Modern Family

Most second-generation Korean Americans are between 35 and 45 years of age and tend to be strongly influenced by American mainstream family practices. Generally, modern Korean marriages are no longer arranged by families, and relationships between husband and wife are more egalitarian, although Korean immigrant couples tend to be less egalitarian than the average American couple with respect to authority and decision making (Min, 1988).

Many second-generation Korean-American families maintain a successful small business, in which both husband and wife work together. A wife's help in the store (usually as the cashier) is essential to the success of the business, affording her an economic role equal to her husband in the family. However, her level of education is the most important factor in determining her authority and decision-making power in the family relative to her husband (Min, 1988). A low divorce rate, a low percentage of female-headed households, and a high percentage of couple families foster a high degree of family stability among Korean immigrants (Min, 1988; Lassiter, 1995; Tienda & Angel, 1982).

Elderly

Because Confucian ideology places emphasis on age, the elderly are usually highly respected and viewed as authorities by the family. In the event of illness, the elder's son and his wife assume responsibility for the parent's health care (Min, 1988).

Socialization Patterns

Confucianism (previously discussed) directs the behavior of some Korean Americans. Many attempt to maintain harmony, avoid conflict in social interactions, and show respect for elders and those in authority.

Korean Americans maintain a higher level of ethnic attachment than other Asian immigrant groups. Several reasons might explain this tendency. First, Korean immigrants are culturally homogeneous, speaking one native language and having no subgroup differences, unlike some other Asians who speak several native languages from various subgroups. Second, most Korean Americans are affiliated with Korean churches that provide ethnic socialization. And finally, more than 75% of Korean Americans work in a segregated Korean subeconomy, either as business owners or employed by co-ethnic–owned businesses. Although this cultural homogeneity and economic segregation has helped to maintain strong ethnic solidarity, it has hindered Korean assimilation into American society (Min, 1995b).

Religious Beliefs and Practices

The three religious and philosophical cultural traditions that have significantly shaped Korean American attitudes about life, death, and social interactions are Confucianism, Buddhism, and Taoism (all previously discussed). Prior to immigration, about 55% of Koreans attended Christian churches. In the United States, 75% of Korean immigrants are affiliated with Korean ethnic churches, most of them of Protestant denomination (Hurh & Kim, 1984; Min, 1995).

Health Beliefs and Practices

Many Korean Americans believe in a holistic concept of health and view health and illness as an integration of biological, social, psychological, and emotional aspects of the human. This holistic concept also emphasizes the inseparable nature of mind and body. Also, some Korean Americans believe in concepts of balance between humans and the universe, yin and yang, and/or hot and cold (Do, 1988; Lassiter, 1995; Tien-Hyatt, 1987).

Health Practices

Korean American folk health practices tend to vary from the use of *mudang* or shamans (mediums), herbalists, and acupuncturists to American mainstream medical methods (Kraut, 1990). Some traditional Korean American clients who practice ancestor worship may seek advice or assistance from spirits through a shaman. Often this practice does not replace or influence the medical therapeutic regime (Moon, 1974; Lassiter, 1995).

The practice of acupuncture is based on the concept of vital energy forces within the body and the universe. Acupuncture is superior to general anesthesia for some surgical procedures because the client remains awake and alert, and there are no post-anesthesia blood pressure and respiratory complications (Beare & Myers, 1990; Miller & Keane, 1987).

Ginseng or ginseng root (often called the "root of life") may be used by some Korean Americans as a rejuvenator for pregnant women, athletes, older persons, or anyone in a weakened condition. Ginseng is also believed to be an aphrodisiac (Andrews, 1989; "Ginseng," 1980).

Middle-class Korean Americans tend to share health-related values and practices with the American mainstream culture. However, those who follow Western health methods often retain some traditional remedies for selected illnesses and practice them concurrently or consecutively with Western health care (Chang, 1981; Do, 1988; Kraut, 1990).

Nutritional Patterns

Rice is the staple food of the Korean diet. In order to add nutrients, white rice is often boiled with barley, millet, and red beans. Rice cakes are favorites. Fish (raw, steamed, salted, or dried) and soybean products (soy sauce, bean curd or tofu, soy milk) are major sources of dietary protein. Soups containing fish, beef, or seaweed are served frequently.

Korean American diets include several fresh fruits and vegetables. Vegetables are lightly cooked to preserve crispness and nutrients and are highly seasoned with red and black pepper, garlic, and soy sauce. Food is preferred chopped in small pieces that are easy to manage with chopsticks. Barley water, a favorite beverage, usually accompanies every meal, served cold in the summer and warm in the winter (Burtis, Davis, & Martin, 1989; Handbook of Korea, 1979). A popular dish is *kimchi*, prepared with chopped vegetables that are highly seasoned, salted, and fermented for one to three months. Some variety of kimchi is usually served at each meal. Because kimchi is not readily available in the United States, a Mexican salsa may be an acceptable substitute. Beef, heavily marinated with sugar to produce a crisp coating, is also a favorite (Burtis, Davis, & Martin, 1989).

Korean Americans generally consume a diet high in fruits and vegetables and low in meat (protein). They also tend to use seasonings that are high in sodium (Burtis, Davis, & Martin, 1989). Strict Buddhists are vegetarians who avoid eating the flesh of any animal except fish. Many Buddhists also refrain from eggs, milk, and intoxicating beverages (Ensminger et al., 1983; Freimer, Echenberg, & Kretchmer, 1983; Lassiter, 1995).

Common Diseases

Lactose enzyme deficiency is found in about 90% of Korean American adults (Chang, 1981).

One potentially life-threatening illness that soldiers faced during the Korean War and that still exists today is Korean hemorrhagic fever (Gill, 1991). Hemorrhagic fever with renal syndrome (HFRS) is characterized by fever, headache, fatigue, abdominal pain, renal dysfunction, and various hemorrhagic manifestations. A lethal form of the disease occurs in Korea, and a milder nonlethal form is found in Europe. The disease is caused by hantaviruses spread by rodents and transmitted to humans via aerosol from rodent urine, saliva, and feces (Niklasson, 1992).

Beliefs about Death and Dying

Christian Korean Americans tend to believe that illness and death are determined by fate, which God has destined, and that one must go peacefully to the final destination. Some Korean American Protestants believe that group prayers and hymns foster a peaceful death or transition to another life (Tien-Hyatt, 1987).

VIETNAMESE AMERICANS

Vietnam, Cambodia, and Laos are often referred to as Indochina or Southeast Asia. A major exodus from Southeast Asia began after the U.S. military withdrawal and the fall of Saigon in 1975. The 130,000 (mostly Vietnamese) refugees who entered the United States during 1975 to escape persecution by the North Vietnamese communists were sent to government reception areas in California, Pennsylvania, Arkansas, and Florida, where they were matched with voluntary sponsors throughout the country.

Unlike the Chinese and Japanese, the Vietnamese (the newest Asian Americans) have not experienced a long history in America. Unlike the Filipinos, neither have they experienced colonization by the United States. Also, unlike the recent Indian Asians who migrated as highly educated professionals, with the exception of the early first wave, Vietnamese refugees have generally consisted of a larger proportion of rural individuals with less education than the other Asian groups (Rumbaut, 1995). Differing from Filipinos, Chinese, Japanese, Koreans, and Indians, most Vietnamese entered as "refugees" rather than "immigrants." There is a significant difference between refugee and immigrant status: Immigrants voluntarily migrate from one location to a planned destination, whereas refugees are forced to leave their countries hastily under traumatic circumstances in order to avoid persecution. The United States places limitations on the number of immigrants but not on refugees and in addition facilitates refugees' access to a number of public assistance programs that are not available to immigrants (Rumbaut, 1995; Rutledge, 1992).

Vietnamese Americans number 615,000, representing 0.2% of the U.S. population. Fifty-four percent of Vietnamese Americans reside in the western United States, and 20% reside in the South (U.S. Bureau of the Census, 1990). The largest numbers of this population are found in California, Virginia, Texas, and Florida (Lan, 1988). California is the Vietnamese capitol in the United States. California Vietnamese Americans control the Vietnamese market in America, publish Vietnamese books, and produce Vietnamese videos, movies, and food for their population in America and throughout the world (Tran, 1988). Over 90% of Vietnamese Americans were born in Vietnam and generally tend to be a young population when compared to other immigrant groups in the United States (U.S. Bureau of the Census, 1990).

Family

Traditional Family

Traditional Vietnamese Americans believe that the family, not the individual, is the basis of society. A person's name is written with the family name first, followed by the middle name and then the given name, in order to emphasize the importance of one's heritage. The traditional family is patriarchal, patrilineal, and patrilocal. Before 1959, polygamy was legal in Vietnam (Rutledge, 1992).

The immediate (*nha*) family consists of the nuclear family in addition to the husband's parents and the sons' spouses and offspring. The extended family (*ho*) includes the immediate family plus relatives of the same name and kin residing in close proximity. Family members have a specific kinship term used to refer to each other, such as "son," "brother," or "sister" (Rutledge, 1992). Traditionally, the oldest male (*Truong Toc*) is the head of the family. The *Truong Toc* is responsible for maintaining the family land and ancestral graves and perpetuating ancestor worship. The father is usually the head, to be succeeded by his son. The head of the family completely controls his family and even assumes responsibility for the behavior of individual members. He is legally accountable for failing to prevent any member of his family from committing a crime (Rutledge, 1992; Tran, 1988).

Family loyalty focuses on filial piety, which emphasizes that children should honor and obey their parents. This obligation extends even after the parents' death, when children commemorate their parents and care for their graves. Family behavior is based on Confucian philosophy of "only do to others what you would have them do to you" (Rutledge, 1992; Tran, 1988).

Traditional Vietnamese women have had no power and few privileges. A woman is expected to honor and obey her father, then her husband, and finally her eldest son with whom she will live when she is a widow. However, the traditional Vietnamese woman gains status when she becomes a mother because she then ranks second in the family after the father (Lassiter, 1995; Rutledge, 1992; Tran, 1988).

Modern Family

Many traditional values are still held by some Vietnamese Americans. However, the American economic system has necessitated some changes. Vietnamese American children tend to become more economically independent. Because many children quickly become more knowledgeable about American society than their parents, they demand more freedom than tradition allowed. Many young Vietnamese, having moved away from their families to pursue educational and professional opportunities, were unable to maintain the traditional practice of living with their parents until marriage. The modern Vietnamese American father has lost some of his absolute power over the family. His children often react differently because they are becoming acculturated to a different culture. The father finds that methods of punishment used in Vietnam may be inappropriate in America (Tran, 1988).

Due to economic necessity the Vietnamese American woman may obtain a job outside the home. Working and contributing to the family support gives her increased status and power in the family, although the husband usually remains the dominant authority figure. Vietnamese Americans were found to be the only Asian group with a relatively high percentage (14.2%) of households headed by women (Gardner, Robey, & Smith, 1985; Lassiter, 1995; Rutledge, 1992).

Elderly

Traditionally Vietnamese elderly were powerful and highly respected for their wisdom. However, as the traditional wisdom that could be passed down is less useful in American society, Vietnamese American elderly have lost a great deal of their power. Since many do not speak English and cannot drive, they are often highly dependent on and yet often isolated from their families. Their grandchildren often prefer to speak English and watch American television. In many Vietnamese American communities, the elderly experience loneliness and homesickness for the homeland. Often their only social outlet is the church (Rutledge, 1992; Tran, 1988).

Socialization Patterns

Societal concepts held by many Vietnamese Americans include living in harmony, extending peace to all life, and showing respect and tolerance for cultural preferences. They value the family and collective advancement. Achievement and strong motivation to excel are general characteristics. Their self-descriptive expression *tran can cu* means the combination of hard work, patience, and tenacity into a strong drive to survive or be successful. Vietnamese Americans have been described as adaptable, resourceful, passive, indirect, and resilient (Rutledge, 1992).

Religious Beliefs and Practices

Although most Vietnamese acknowledge Buddhism, several also ascribe to Taoism, Confucianism, and Roman Catholicism in America. Traditional Vietnamese cultural and religious beliefs reflect a blending of Buddhist theories of reincarnation and the law of moral retribution, the Taoist concept of harmony, and Confucian ethical and social principles. Some combine these principles with those of Roman Catholicism. It is estimated that about 40% of Vietnamese Americans claim to be Roman Catholic (Rutledge, 1992).

Health Beliefs and Practices

Traditionally, Vietnamese Americans have a holistic concept of health, a belief that a person's health is dependent on family, religion, food, morality, and metaphysical forces. Some traditional Vietnamese Americans perceive three basic causes of illness: physical, supernatural, and metaphysical. Physical causes are simple and apparent, such as a broken limb, a cut, or a burn after an injury. However, supernatural causes are more complex and less apparent, resulting from the actions of demons, deities, or angry spirits. Supernaturally caused illness serves to punish an individual for inappropriate behavior. The most commonly acknowledged supernatural phenomenon is *phong*, or bad wind, which once in the body can lead to anything from asthma to a heart attack. Some believe that *phong* can only be cured by traditional rituals (Rutledge, 1992).

The metaphysical cause of illness is based on the Taoist concepts of balance. Good health stems from harmonious interactions; poor health is a result of disharmony. The metaphysical theory is based on a balance of hot and cold or yin and yang, previously discussed (Muecke, 1983; Rutledge, 1992; Stauffer, 1991).

Dermabrasive procedures represent a group of self-care practices noted among some Vietnamese Americans. These procedures are used to alleviate a wide variety of symptoms such as headache, nausea, myalgia, cough, and backache. The procedures abrade the skin with minor scrapes that are rarely harmful but help the person experience a sense of control over the problem. A cutaneous hematoma is sometimes created over an affected area of the face, neck, chest, or back to release excessive "air" believed to cause certain conditions. There are various methods used to induce hematomas: by pinching the skin (*bat gio*); by rubbing an oiled skin with the edge of a coin (*cao gio*) or spoon (*tzowsa*); or by placing a cup from which oxygen has been extracted through heating over the affected area for 15–30 minutes (*giac* cup suction). American health professionals should be cautious not to confuse these indications of home treatment with evidences of abuse (Golden & Duster, 1977; Muecke, 1983; Rutledge, 1992; Stauffer, 1991; Yeatman & Dang, 1980).

Nutritional Patterns

Vietnamese American food reflects Chinese and French influences. The common staple of the Vietnamese diet is rice. A salty fish paste or sauce is added to many dishes for flavor (Tran, 1990). Rice and other dishes are seasoned with this sauce (*nuoc nam*), made by marinating small fish in salt for a month or more. Meat cut into small pieces may be eaten with rice and vegetables. Bean curd is another favorite, although dry bean dishes are not common (Stauffer, 1991). Lemon beef salad and shrimp crepes are favorites (Tran, 1990).

The traditional Vietnamese diet is low in fat and sugar, moderate in fiber, and high in complex carbohydrates (Burtis, Davis, & Martin, 1988). Although tea is considered the favorite drink, many Vietnamese Americans enjoy water and soft drinks. Before migration, Vietnamese were not great fluid drinkers, a practice that has been related to bladder stones in males. Also, since many Vietnamese Americans have lactose intolerance, milk was seldom included in their diet (Hoang & Erickson, 1982).

Strict Buddhists are vegetarians. Many avoid eating the flesh of any animal and may not eat eggs or drink milk. They will eat fish because fish are merely removed from the water, not slaughtered. Many strict Buddhists abstain from intoxicating beverages (Ensminger et al., 1983; Lassiter, 1995).

Common Diseases

Reizian and Meleis (1987) studied and compared symptoms reported by Arab Americans, Vietnamese Americans, native-born Americans, and other cultural groups at the University of Oregon Medical School Hospital. Arab Americans and Vietnamese Americans reported the highest number of symptoms pertaining to the digestive system, and both groups demonstrated similarly high psychological symptom patterns for feelings of inadequacy. Feelings of tension were noted as the second most common psychological symptom for Vietnamese Americans. Generally, the Vietnamese Americans reported slightly more psychological symptoms than the Arab Americans. Also, Vietnamese Americans reported more symptoms related to the respiratory and nervous systems than the Arab Americans.

A significant number of Vietnamese Americans have been diagnosed as having psychiatric or psychosomatic problems. A high prevalence of depression exists among the second-wave refugee groups as determined by the Vietnamese Depression Rating Scale, which was developed for testing this group (Sutherland et al., 1983). Although the origins of some emotional responses and illnesses of Vietnamese migrants may be unrelated to traumatic events, refugee trauma increases the likelihood of certain emotional responses such as anxiety, depression, delayed grief, and post-traumatic stress disorder (Muecke, 1983).

Results of a study by Chung and Kagawa-Singer (1993) indicated that Vietnamese women were more likely to experience distress than were their husbands. They also found that, regardless of the number of years in the United States, premigration trauma events and refugee camp experiences served as significant predictors of psychological distress for up to five years after migration. Results of another study (Buchwald et al., 1993) also noted the prevalence of depressive symptoms among Vietnamese Americans. Although physical symptoms that created anxiety about health status existed, psychological and emotional symptoms were much more prevalent. However, Ganesan, Fine, and Lin (1989) observed that Vietnamese Americans tend to refuse mental health services until symptoms are severe (Lassiter, 1995).

Beliefs about Death and Dying

Generally, major beliefs are related to religious affiliation. Some Vietnamese Americans believe in the constant presence of ancestors' spirits. Buddhists uphold the theory of reincarnation (Fabrega & Nguyen, 1992). Because white (not black) symbolizes death, mourning families may wear white clothing or headbands. Vietnamese generally bury their dead, whereas Cambodians and Laotians tend to prefer cremation. Some Vietnamese Americans may express grief as somatic complaints (Lassiter, 1995; Lawson, 1990; Rutledge, 1992).

CONCLUSION

According to Huang (1996), although cultural deviations exist among Asians, as a group they exhibit overall similarities in beliefs and values relating to family, social behavior, education, and ancestor worship (today, more accurately termed, "ancestor respect"). The preceding discussions are intended to motivate further investigation of Asian Americans. Noting the number of references involved, these pages can only serve as a brief outline. It is hoped that the reader has acquired a beginning understanding of some Asian cultures, has become aware of the great diversity among and within Asian Americans, and will utilize some of the references for further study.

REFERENCES

Affonso, D. D. (1978). The Filipino American. In A. L. Clark (Ed.), *Culture, child-bearing, health professionals* (pp. 128–53). Philadelphia: F. A. Davis.

Agbayani-Siewert, P., & Revilla, L. (1995). Filipino Americans. In P. G. Min (Ed.), *Asian Americans: Contemporary trends and issues* (pp. 134–68). Thousand Oaks, Calif.: Sage.

Allen, J. P., & Turner, E. J. (1988). *We the people: Atlas of American ethnic diversity.* New York: Macmillan.

Almirol, E. B. (1982). Rights and obligations in Filipino American families. *Journal of Comparative Family Studies,* 13(3), 291–306.

Andres, T., & Illada-Andres, P. (1987). *Understanding the Filipino.* Quezon City, Philippines: New Day.

Andrews, M. M. (1989). Culture and Nutrition. In J. S. Boyle & M. M. Andrews (Eds.), *Transcultural concepts in nursing care* (pp. 333–35). Glenview, Ill.: Scott, Foresman/Little, Brown College Division.

Aquino, C. J. (1981). The Filipino in America. In A. L. Clark (Ed.), *Culture and childrearing* (pp. 166–90). Philadelphia: F. A. Davis.

Aris, H. (1990, April 11). View from the East. *Nursing Times,* 86(15), 44–45.

Arnold, F., Minocha, U., & Fawcett, J. T. (1987). The changing face of Asian immigrants to the United States. In J. Fawcett & B. Carino (Eds.), *Pacific bridges: The new immigration from Asia and the Pacific Islands* (pp. 105–52). New York: Center for Migration Studies.

Beare, P. G., & Myers, J. L. (1990). *Principles and practice of adult health nursing.* St. Louis: C. V. Mosby.

Bourne, P. P. (1973). Suicide among Chinese in San Francisco. *American Journal of Public Health,* 63(8), 744–50.

Boyle, J. S., & Andrews, M. M. (1989). *Transcultural concepts in nursing care.* Boston: Scott, Foresman/Little, Brown College Division.

Buchwald, D., Manson, S. M., Dinges, N. G., Keane, E. M., & Kinzie, J. D. (1993). Prevalence of depressive symptoms among established Vietnamese refugees in the United States: Detection in a primary care setting. *Journal of General Internal Medicine,* 8(2), 76–81.

Bulato, J. (1981). The Manileno mainsprings. In F. Lynch & A. de Guzman, III (Eds.), *Four readings in Filipino values* (pp. 70–118). Quezon City, Philippines: Ateneo de Manila University Press.

Bullough, V. L., & Bullough, B. (1982). *Health care for the other Americans.* New York: Appleton-Century-Crofts.

Burtis, G., Davis, J., & Martin, S. (1989). *Applied nutrition and diet therapy.* Philadelphia: W. B. Saunders.

Chandras, K. (1977). *Arab, Armenian, Syrian, Lebanese, East Indian, Pakistani and Bangladeshi Americans: A study guide and source book.* San Francisco, Calif.: R&E Research Associates.

Chang, B. (1981). Asian-American patient care. In G. Henderson & M. Primeaux (Eds.), *Transcultural health care* (pp. 255–78). Menlo Park, Calif.: Addison-Wesley.

Chang, K. (1991). Chinese Americans. In J. N. Giger & R. E. Davidhizar (Eds.), *Transcultural nursing: Assessment and intervention* (pp. 359–77). St. Louis: C. V. Mosby.

Char, E. L. (1981). The Chinese American. In A. L. Clark (Ed.), *Culture and Childrearing* (pp. 140–64). Philadelphia: F. A. Davis.

Chee, P., & Kane, R. (1983). Cultural factors affecting nursing home care for minorities: A study of black American and Japanese-American groups. *Journal of the American Geriatrics Society,* 31(2), 109–12.

Chekki, D. (1988). Family in India and North America: Change and continuity among Lingayat families. *Journal of Comparative Family Studies,* 19(2), 329–43.

Chow, E. (1976). Cultural health traditions: Asian perspectives. In M. F. Branch and P. P. Paxton (Eds.), *Providing safe nursing care for ethnic people of color* (pp. 99–114). New York: Appleton-Century-Crofts.

Chung, D. (1991). Asian cultural commonalities: A comparison with mainstream American culture. In S. Furuto, R. Biswas, D. Chung, & F. Ross-Sheriff (Eds.), *Social work practice with Asian Americans* (pp. 27–44). Newbury Park, Calif.: Sage.

Chung, R. C., & Kagawa-Singer, M. (1993). Predictors of psychological distress among southeast Asian refugees. *Social Science and Medicine,* 36(5), 631–39.

Curb, J. D., Reed, D. M., Kautz, J. A., & Yano, K. (1986). Coffee, caffeine, and serum cholesterol in Japanese men in Hawaii. *American Journal of Epidemiology*, 123(4), 648–55.

Curb, J. D., Reed, D. M., Miller, F. D., & Yano, K. (1990). Health style in elderly Japanese men with a long life expectancy. *Journal of Gerontology*, 45(5), 5206–11.

Dash, V. B. (1974). *Ayurvedic treatment for common disease*. Delhi, India: Delhi Diary.

DeGracia, R. T. (1979, August). Cultural influences on Filipino patients. *American Journal of Nursing*, 79(8), 1412–14.

Dhruvarajan, V. (1988). Religious ideology and interpersonal relationships within the family. *Journal of Comparative Family Studies*, 19(2), 273–85.

Do, H. K. (1988). *Health and illness beliefs and practices of Korean Americans.* Doctoral dissertation, Boston University.

Driver, E. D., & Driver, A. E. (1988). Social and demographic correlates of consanguineous marriages in South India. *Journal of Comparative Family Studies*, 19(2), 229–43.

Dumoulin, H. (1976). *Buddhism in the modern world*. New York: Macmillan.

Dumoulin, H. (1988). Zen. In M. Eliade (Ed.), *Encyclopedia of religion* (vol. 15) (pp. 561–68). New York: Macmillan.

Eliade, M., & Couliano, I. P. (1991). *The Eliade Guide to World Religions*. San Francisco: Harper.

Ensminger, A. H., Ensminger, M. E., Kolande, J. E., & Robson, R. K. (1983). *Foods and Nutrition Encyclopedia* (vols. 1 & 2). Clovis, Calif.: Pegus Press.

Fabrega, H., Jr., & Nguyen, H. (1992, August). Culture, social structure, and quandaries of psychiatric diagnosis: A Vietnamese case study. *Psychiatry*, 55, 230–49.

Finch, P. J., Ang, L., Eastwood, J. B., & Maxwell, J. D. (1992). Clinical and histological spectrum of osteomalacia among Asians in south London. *Quarterly Journal of Medicine*, 83(302), 439–48.

Fishlock, T. (1983). *Gandhi's children*. New York: Universe Books.

Freimer, N., Echenberg, D., & Kretchmer, N. (1983). Cultural variation: Nutritional and clinical implications. *Western Journal of Medicine*, 139(6), 928–33.

Fugita, S. S., & O'Brien, D. J. (1991). *Japanese American ethnicity*. Seattle: University of Washington Press.

Ganesan, S., Fine, S., & Lin, T. Y. (1989). Psychiatric symptoms in refugee families from South East Asia: Therapeutic challenges. *American Journal of Psychotherapy*, 43(2), 218–28.

Gardner, R. W., Robey, B., & Smith, P. C. (1985). Asian Americans: Growth, change and diversity. *Population Bulletin*, 40, 1–44.

Gerber, L. M. (1983). Gains in life expectancies if heart disease and stroke were eliminated among Caucasians, Filipinos and Japanese in Hawaii. *Social Science Medicine*, 17(6), 349–53.

Gill, P. M. (1991). Korean hemorrhagic fever: Nursing care critical to recovery. *Military Medicine*, 156(3), 131–34.

Ginseng. (1980). *Medical Letter Drugs Therapy*, 22(17), 72.

Golden, S. M., & Duster, M. C. (1977). Hazards of misdiagnosis due to Vietnamese folk medicine. *Clinical Pediatrics*, 16, 949–50.

Goodman, M. J. (1991). Breast cancer in multi-ethnic populations: The Hawaii perspective. *Breast Cancer Research and Treatment*, 18 (Suppl. 1), S5–9.

Gordon, L. W. (1987). Southeast refugee migration to the United States. In J. T. Fawcett & B. V. Carino (Eds.), *Pacific bridges: The new immigration from Asia and the Pacific Islands* (pp. 153–73). New York: Center for Immigration Studies.

Government Publication of India. (1993). *India: a dynamic democracy.* External Publicity Division, Ministry of External Affairs, Government of India.

Grippin, J. T. (1979). The Japanese American client. *Issues in Mental Health Nursing*, 2(1), 57–69.

Hau, K. T. (1993). Suicide in Hong Kong 1971–1990: Age trend, sex ratio, and method of suicide. *Social Psychiatry and Psychiatric Epidemiology*, 28(1), 23–27.

Heitzman, J., & Worden, R. L. (1996). *India: A country study.* Area Handbook Series. Washington, D.C.: Federal Research Division, Library of Congress.

Henderson, G., & Primeaux, M. (1981). *Transcultural health care.* Reading, Mass.: Addison-Wesley.

Herman, A. L. (1991). *A brief introduction to Hinduism: Religion, philosophy, and ways of liberation.* San Francisco: Westview Press.

Hoang, G., & Erickson, R. (1982). Guidelines for providing medical care for Southeast Asian refugees. *Journal of the American Medical Association*, 248(6), 710–14.

Huang, T. T. S. (1996). Personal interview at East Tennessee State University.

Hurh, W. M., & Chung, K. K. (1984). *Korean immigrants in America: A structural analysis of ethnic confinement and adhesive adaptation.* Madison, N.J.: Fairleigh Dickinson University Press.

Ignacio, L. F. (1976). *Asian Americans and Pacific Islanders: Is there such an ethnic group?* San Jose, Calif.: Filipino Development Associates.

Iso, H., Folsom, A. R., Wu, K. K., & Finch, A. (1989). Hemostatic variables in Japanese and Caucasian men: Plasma fibrinogen, factor VIIc, factor VIIIc, and von Willebrand factor and their relations to cardiovascular disease risk factors. *American Journal of Epidemiology*, 130(5), 925–34.

Jensen, J. M. (1980). East Indians. In S. Thernstrom (Ed.), *Harvard encyclopedia of American ethnic groups* (pp. 298–301). Cambridge, Mass.: Belknap Press of Harvard University Press.

Jiobu, R. M. (1988). *Ethnicity and assimilation: Blacks, Chinese, Filipinos, Japanese, Koreans, Mexicans, Vietnamese, and whites.* Albany: State University of New York Press.

Kakar, D. (1977). *Folk and modern medicine.* New Delhi: New Asian Publishers.

Kakar, D. N., Chopra, S., Samuel, S. A., & Sangar, K. (1989). Beliefs and practices related to disposal of human placenta. *Nursing Journal of India*, 80(12), 315–17.

Kamar, P. (1994, January). Interview with Pavankumar Kamar of the Embassy of India, Washington, D.C.

Katagawa, J. M. (1988). Japanese religion: An overview. In M. Eliade (Ed.), *The encyclopedia of religion* (vol. 7) (pp. 520–38). New York: Macmillan.

Kim, C. S. (1989). Attribute of "asexuality" in Korean kinship and sundered Koreans during the Korean war. *Journal of Comparative Family Studies*, 20(3), 309–25.

Kim, H. (1980). Koreans. In S. Thernstrom (Ed.), *Harvard encyclopedia of American ethnic groups* (pp. 601–6). Cambridge, Mass.: Belknap Press of Harvard University Press.

Kitano, H., Yuang, W. T., Chai, L., & Hatanaka, H. (1984). Asian American interracial marriage. *Journal of Marriage and the Family*, 46, 179–90.

Kitano, H. L. (1988). The Japanese American family. In C. H. Mindel, R. W. Haberstein, & R. Wright, Jr., *Ethnic families in America* (3rd ed.) (pp. 258–75). New York: Elsevier.

Klatsky, A. L., & Armstrong, M. A. (1991). Cardiovascular risk factors among Asian Americans living in Northern Callifornia. *American Journal of Public Health*, 81(11), 1423–28.

Kleinman, A. K. (1982). Neurasthenia and depression: A study of somatization and culture in China. *Culture and Medical Psychiatry*, 6, 177–90.

Kleinman, A. K., & Lin, T. Y. (1981). *Normal and abnormal behavior in Chinese culture*. Boston: D. Reidel.

Korean Overseas Information Service. (1979). *A handbook of Korea*. Seoul, Korea: Ministry of Culture and Information.

Kraut, A. M. (1990). Healers and strangers: Immigrant attitudes toward the physician in America—A relationship in historical perspective. *Journal of the American Medical Association*, 263(13), 1807–11.

Lan, L. V. (1988). Folk medicine among Southeast Asian refugees in the United States: Risks, benefits and uncertainties. *Journal of the Association of Vietnamese Medical Professionals in Canada*, 98, 31–36.

Lassiter, S. M. (1995). *Multicultural clients: A professional handbook for health care providers and social workers*. Westport, Conn.: Greenwood Press.

Lawson, L. V. (1990). Culturally sensitive support for grieving parents. *Maternal and Child Nursing*, 15, 76–79.

Lee, E. (1982). A social systems approach to assessment and treatment for Chinese American families. In M. McGoldrick, J. K. Pearce, & J. Giordano (Eds.), *Ethnicity and family therapy* (pp. 527–51). New York: Guilford Press.

Lee, R. N. (1986). The Chinese perception of mental illness in the Canadian mosaic. *Canada's Mental Health*, 34(4), 2–4.

Lester, D. (1992). Suicide among Asian Americans and social deviancy. *Perceptual and Motor Skills*, 75(3, part 2), 1134.

Lin, T. Y. (1983). Psychiatry and Chinese culture. *Western Journal of Medicine*, 139, 862–67.

Lock, M. M. (1980). An examination of the influence of traditional therapeutic systems on the practice of cosmopolitan medicine in Japan. *American Journal of Chinese Medicine*, 8(3), 221–29.

Lock, M. M. (1983). Cross-cultural medicine: Japanese responses to social change: making the strange familiar. *Western Journal of Medicine*, 139(6), 829–34.

Louie, T. T. T. (1976). Explanatory thinking in Chinese Americans. In P. J. Brink (Ed.), *Transcultural nursing: A book of readings* (pp. 240–46). Englewood Cliffs, N.J.: Prentice-Hall.

Lu, H. C. (1986). *Chinese system of food cures: Prevention and remedies*. New York: Sterling.

Lynch, F. (1981). Social acceptance considered. In F. Lynch & A. de Guzman, III

(Eds.), *Four readings on Philippine values* (pp. 1–68). Quezon City, Philippines: Ateneo de Manila University Press.

McKeigue, P. M., & Karmi, G. (1993). Alcohol consumption and alcohol related problems in Afro-Caribbeans and south Asians in the United Kingdom. *Alcohol-Alcohol*, 28(1), 1–10.

McKenzie, J., & Chrisman, N. (1977). Healing herbs, gods and magics. *Nursing Outlook*, 25, 326–28.

Melendy, H. B. (1980). Filipinos. In S. Thernstrom (Ed.), *Harvard encyclopedia of American ethnic groups* (pp. 354–62). Cambridge, Mass.: Belknap Press of Harvard University Press.

Miller, A. L. (1988). Japanese religion: Popular religions. In M. Eliade (Ed.), *The encyclopedia of religion* (vol. 7) (pp. 538–44). New York: Macmillan.

Miller, B. F., & Keane, C. B. (1987). *Encyclopedia and dictionary of medicine, nursing, and allied health*. Philadelphia: W. B. Saunders.

Miller, S. W., & Supersad, J. N. (1991). East Indian Hindu Americans. In J. N. Giger & R. L. Davidhizar (Eds.), *Transcultural nursing: Assessment and intervention* (pp. 436–62). St. Louis: Mosby Year Book.

Min, P. G. (1988). The Korean American family. In C. H. Mindel, R. W. Haberstein, & R. Wright, Jr. (1988), *Ethnic families in America: Patterns and variations* (3rd ed.). New York: Elsevier.

Min, P. G. (1995a). *Asian Americans: Contemporary trends and issues*. Thousand Oaks, Calif: Sage.

Min, P. G. (1995b). Korean Americans. In P. G. Min (Ed.), *Asian Americans: Contemporary trends and issues* (pp. 199–231). Thousand Oaks, Calif.: Sage.

Molnar, S. C. (1983). *Human variation: Races, types and ethnic groups* (2nd ed.). Englewood Cliffs, N.J.: Prentice-Hall.

Moon, S. G. (1974). Ancestor worship in Korea: Tradition and transition. *Journal of Comparative Family Studies*, 5(2), 71–87.

Morrisey, S. (1983). Attitudes on aging in China. *Journal of Gerontological Nursing*, 9(11), 589–93.

Muecke, M. A. (1983). In search of healers: Southeast Asian refugees in the American health care system. *Western Journal of Medicine*, 139(6), 835–40.

Niklasson, B. S. (1992). Hemorrhagic fever with renal syndrome, virological and epidemiological aspects. *Pediatric Nephrology*, 6(2), 201–4.

Nishi, S. M. (1995). Japanese Americans. In P. G. Min (Ed.), *Asian Americans: Contemporary trends and issues* (pp. 95–133). Thousand Oaks, Calif.: Sage.

Nomura, A. M., Lee, J., Kolonel, L. N., & Hirohata, T. (1984). Breast cancer in two populations with different levels of risk for the disease. *American Journal of Epidemiology*, 119(4), 496–502.

Nyrop, R. F. (1986). *India: A country study*. Foreign Area Studies. Washington, D.C.: American University.

Orque, M. S., Bloch, B., & Monrroy, L. S. A. (1983), *Ethics in nursing care: A multicultural approach*. St. Louis: C. V. Mosby.

Overfield, T. (1985). *Biological variations in health and illness*. Reading, Mass.: Addison-Wesley.

Palmore, E. (1975). *Honorable elders: A cross-cultural analysis of aging in Japan*. Durham, N.C.: Duke University Press.

Park, C. B., Yokoyama, E., & Tokuyama, G. H. (1991). Medical conditions at death among Caucasian and Japanese elderly in Hawaii: Analysis of multiple causes of death, 1976–78. *Journal of Clinical Epidemiology,* 44(6), 519–30.

Patibandla, R. S. (1994, January). Interview with Roa Srinivasa Patibandla, an East Indian graduate student from Bombay attending East Tennessee State University.

Peterson, M. R., Rose, C. L., & McGee, R. I. (1985). A cross-cultural study of Japanese elders in Hawaii. *International Journal of Aging and Human Development,* 21(4), 267–79.

Peterson, R. (1978). *The elder Filipino.* San Diego, Calif.: Camponile.

Reizian, A., & Meleis, A. I. (1987). Symptoms reported by Arab-American patients on the Cornell Medical Index (CMI). *Western Journal of Nursing Research,* 9(3), 368–84.

Rajamani, J. (1994, January). Interview with Jayant Rajamani, an East Indian graduate student from Madras attending East Tennessee State University.

Ratnaraj, M. (1994, January). Interview with Madhavi Ratnaraj, an East Indian graduate student from Bangalore attending East Tennessee State University.

Rawl, S. M. (1992). Perspectives on nursing care of Chinese Americans. *Journal of Holistic Nursing,* 10(1), 6–17.

Rose, P. A. (1978). The Chinese American. In A. L. Clark (Ed.), *Culture, childbearing, health professionals* (pp. 54–63). Philadelphia: F. A. Davis.

Ross-Sheriff, F. (1991). Adaptation and integration into American society: Major issues affecting Asian Americans. In S. M. Furuto, R. Biswas, D. K. Chung, K. Murase, & F. Ross-Sheriff (Eds.), *Social work practice with Asian Americans* (pp. 45–64). Newbury Park, Calif.: Sage.

Rumbaut, R. G. (1995). Vietnamese, Laotian, and Cambodian Americans. In P. G. Min (Ed.), *Asian Americans: Contemporary trends and issues* (pp. 232–70). Thousand Oaks, Calif.: Sage.

Rutledge, P. J. (1992). *The Vietnamese experience in America.* Indianapolis: Indiana University Press.

Sarin, A. V. (1985). *India: An ancient land, a new nation.* Minneapolis, Minn.: Dillon Press.

Seward, J. (1972). *The Japanese.* New York: William Morrow.

Sheth, M. (1995). Asian Indian Americans. In P. G. Min (Ed.), *Asian Americans: Contemporary trends and issues* (pp. 169–98). Thousand Oaks, Calif.: Sage.

Shimizu, H., Ross, R. K., Berstein, L., & Yatani, R. (1991). Cancers of the prostate and breast among Japanese and white immigrants in Los Angeles County. *British Journal of Cancer,* 63(6), 963–66.

Shon, S. P., & Ja, D. Y. (1982). Asian families. In M. McGoldrick, J. E. Pearce, & J. Giordano (Eds.), *Ethnicity and family therapy* (pp. 208–28). New York: Guilford Press.

Sodetani-Shibata, A. E. (1981). The Japanese American. In A. L. Clark (Ed.), *Culture and childrearing* (pp. 96–138). Philadelphia: F. A. Davis.

Spector, R. E. (1991). *Cultural diversity in health and illness.* New York: Appleton-Century-Crofts.

Stauffer, R. Y. (1991). Vietnamese Americans. In J. N. Giger & R. E. Davidhizar (Eds.), *Transcultural nursing: Assessment and intervention* (pp. 403–34). St. Louis: Mosby Year Book.

Stavig, G. R., Igra, A., & Leonard, A. R. (1988). Hypertension and related health issues among Asian and Pacific Islanders in California. *Public Health Reports*, 103(1), 28–37.

Summerfield, J. (1991). *Fodor's China* (12th ed.). New York and London: Fodor's Travel Publications.

Sutherland, J. E., Avant, R. F., Franz, W. B., Monzon, C. M., & Stark, N. M. (1983). Indonese refugee health assessment and treatment. *Journal of Family Practice*, 16, 61–67.

Tagaki, C., & Ishisaka, T. (1982). Social work with Asian-and Pacific-Americans. In J. Green (Ed.), *Cultural awareness in the human services* (pp. 138–44). Englewood Cliffs, N.J.: Prentice-Hall.

Taylor, R. L. (1990). *The religious dimensions of Confucianism*. New York: State University of New York Press.

Tienda, M., & Angel, R. (1982). Headship and household comparison among blacks, Hispanics and other whites. *Social Forces*, 61, 508–31.

Tien-Hyatt, J. L. (1987). Keying in on the unique care needs of Asian clients. *Nursing and Health Care*, 8(5), 268–71.

Tran, P. (1990). *Living and cooking Vietnamese: An American woman's experience.* Dallas, Tex.: Taylor Publishing.

Tran, T. V. (1988). The Vietnamese American family. In C. H. Mindel, R. W. Haberstein, & R. Wright, Jr. (Eds.), *Ethnic families in America: Patterns and variations* (3rd ed.) (pp. 276–99). New York: Elsevier.

U.S. Bureau of the Census (1990). *Statistical abstracts of the United States.* Washington, D.C.: U.S. Government Printing Office.

U.S. Immigration and Naturalization Service. (1950–1964). *Annual report.* Washington, D.C.: U.S. Government Printing Office.

U.S. Immigration and Naturalization Service. (1979–1992). *Statistical yearbook.* Washington, D.C.: U.S. Government Printing Office.

Vance, A. R. (1991). Filipino Americans. In J. N. Giger & R. E. Davidhizar (Eds.), *Transcultural nursing: Assessment and intervention* (pp. 279–401). St. Louis: Mosby Year Book.

Williams, R. B. (1988). *Religions of migrants from India and Pakistan.* New York: Cambridge University Press.

Wollnofer, H., & von Rottauscher, A. (1972). *Chinese folk medicine*, trans. M. Palmedo. New York: American Library.

Wong, B. (1985). Family, kinship, and ethnic identity of the Chinese in New York City, with comparative remarks on the Chinese in Lima, Peru, and Manila, Philippines. *Journal of Comparative Family Studies*, 16(2), 231–53.

Wong, M. G. (1995). Chinese Americans: In P. G. Min (Ed.), *Asian Americans: Contemporary trends and issues* (pp. 58–94). Thousand Oaks, Calif.: Sage.

Yanagisako, S. J. (1985). *Transforming the past.* Palo Alto, Calif.: Stanford University Press.

Yanagishita, M., & Guralnik, J. M. (1988). Changing mortality patterns that led life expectancy in Japan to surpass Sweden's, 1972–1982. *Demography*, 25(4), 611–24.

Yano, K., McCarthy, L. J., Reed, D. M., & Kagan, A. (1987). Postmortem findings in sudden death and non-sudden death among Japanese-American men in Hawaii. *American Journal of Medicine*, 86(6), 1037–44.

Yeatman, G. W., & Dang, V. V. (1980). Cao Gio (coin rubbing). *Journal of the American Medical Association*, 244, 2748–49.

Yu, E., & Liu, W. T. (1980). *Fertility and kinship in the Philippines*. South Bend, Ind.: University of Notre Dame Press.

Yu, E. S. H. (1986). Health of the Chinese elderly in America. *Research on Aging*, 8(1), 84–109.

Yu, Eui-young. (1983). Korean communities in America: Past, present, and future. *Amerasia Journal*, (10), 23–52.

5

Haitian Americans

The small Caribbean Republic of Haiti, located in the West Indies, shares the island of Hispaniola with Dominica. Haiti (area about 10,714 square miles), a little larger than the state of Maryland, occupies the western third of Hispaniola. Although Dominica and Haiti lie in close proximity, they are quite different culturally. Haiti is bounded by Dominica on the east, the Atlantic Ocean on the north, and the Caribbean Sea on the west and south. South America lies to the south, the island of Jamaica is to the west, and Cuba lies to the northwest of Haiti. Because Haiti is near the equator, temperatures are usually high year round. Haiti experiences a tropical climate similar to that of the other Caribbean islands (Chaney, 1987; Hunter, 1996–1997).

GENERAL CHARACTERISTICS

Population in the United States

About 290,000 Haitian Americans live in the United States, constituting 0.1% of the U.S. population (U.S. Bureau of the Census, 1992). Most Haitians have settled in New York and Florida, their ports of entry. High concentrations of Haitian Americans are found in New York City, Chicago, and Miami. The Edison–Little River section of northeastern Miami has become known as Little Haiti. Although they tend to live in close proximity to West Indians, the majority of Haitians identify themselves primarily as Haitians and secondarily as Caribbeans or West Indians (Buchanan, 1980).

In Haiti, Haitians experience cultural and social distinctions but majority status. In the United States, they experience racism and minority status;

thus, race rather than culture becomes the overriding factor of identification in American society. They are stigmatized on several accounts: being both black and foreign; being of suspected illegal status; and having a homeland that is the poorest nation in the Western Hemisphere. Haitian Americans cope with racism either by allying with African Americans, or by isolating themselves through adherence to French or Creole languages and culture (Buchanan, 1980).

Haitians speak Creole universally, but only a small percentage (about 2–5%) fluently speak French, the official language, considered very prestigious. The language spoken by an individual reinforces the socioeconomic differences that separate the educated elite and growing middle class from the less-educated lower class (Buchanan-Stafford, 1987). Creole is a composite of several languages: French, Indian, African, English, and Spanish. Despite the higher status accorded to the speaking of French, Creole remains the popular language of Haitians and is spoken and/or understood by all classes (Cosgray, 1991; Romain, 1978). Thus, a number of Haitian Americans are trilingual—fluent in Creole, French, and English—and many in contact with Cubans in Miami are learning Spanish, making them quadrilingual (Mohl, 1985).

Immigration

Most Haitian Americans are descendants of West African slaves who were brought to Haiti by France after Columbus discovered the island of Hispaniola in 1492. Through the efforts of important Haitians like Toussaint L'Ouverture, Haiti gained its freedom from France in 1804 and became the first "black republic" in the world. However, under the harsh dictatorship of the Duvaliers since 1957, Haiti has experienced massive oppression and poverty (Schiller et al., 1987).

Haitian Americans are a relatively new immigrant group to the United States. Haitian immigration waves did not begin until after World War II. A major migration of Haitians occurred after François Duvalier ("Papa Doc") came into power in 1957. Duvalier's political rivals and opponents who became targets of the dictator's notorious executioners (the *ton ton macoutes*), were the first to leave Haiti. They were immediately followed by members of the elite classes, mostly mulattos who were strongly tied to international trade. These upper-class immigrants were political refugees. They spoke French, sent their children to European schools, tried to maintain French colonial practices, and generally did not associate with members of the lower economic classes. Middle-class migrants followed shortly after the elites (Schiller et al., 1987).

A second major exodus occurred when Jean-Claude Duvalier ("Baby Doc") took over the power after his father's death in 1971. These immigrants were the "boat people," who were mainly peasants and semiskilled workers. They fled from Haiti to escape poverty and political oppression.

Unlike the upper-class immigrants, who were able to flee with their entire families, these poorer individuals often migrated without intact family units. These lower-class immigrants retained more African practices and spoke Creole instead of French.

Between 1967 and 1984, Haitians came to the United States from all areas of Haiti. Some held legal visas, some had student visas, and undetermined numbers became undocumented aliens. Because undocumented immigrants were considered responsible for the high unemployment rate in the United States, the INS (Immigration and Naturalization Service) detention policy detained these boat people in camps, many for almost a year and took legal action to deport them. Numerous organizations—the Haitian Fathers, the National Council of Churches, the Emergency Civil Liberties Union, and the Congressional Black Caucus, among others—worked diligently to assist the "boat people." In 1980, they were given entrant status, with the right to work, receive an education, and obtain financial assistance (Lassiter, 1995; Leavitt & Lutz, 1988).

BRIEF HISTORY

The island of Hispaniola, discovered by Columbus in 1492, was ceded to France in 1697. By 1533, after the extermination of the Indians by the Spanish, large numbers of African slaves had been imported, and their descendants now populate the country. Following the French Revolution, the slaves gained their freedom and Haiti declared its independence on January 1, 1804, with General Jean-Jacques Dessalines as the self-proclaimed emperor. Following his assassination in 1806, the country became divided under General Henri Christophe (as king) in the north, and Alexander Pétion (as president) in the south and west. After Pétion died, in 1881, and Christophe committed suicide, in 1820, Jean-Pierre Boyer united the country. Haiti and the eastern part of the island, later to become the Dominican Republic, were united between 1822 and 1844. Between 1915 and 1934, Haiti was occupied by the United States.

In 1957, Dr. François Duvalier was elected president for life. He died in 1971 and was succeeded by his son, Jean-Claude Duvalier. General Henry Namphy formed a Council of Government after Jean-Claude fled the country in 1986. In January 1988, Leslie Manigat was elected president; but Namby again seized power in June 1988, only to be deposed in September, 1988, and replaced by the military government of Lieutenant. General Prosper Avril. Father Jean-Bertrand Aristide was elected president in December 1990.

On September 30, 1991, President Aristide was deposed by a military junta and exiled abroad; but due to international diplomatic pressure, he was reinstated as president in June 1993 and scheduled to return on October 30. However the military prevented United Nations forces from landing in Haiti on October 11 and 13, and the United Nations and Organization of American States missions were expelled by the junta on July 11, 1994. Consequently, on September 15, President Clinton demanded that the junta step down; and two days later, former President Carter flew to Haiti to negotiate its removal. On September 19, 20,000 U.S. troops moved into Haiti in an uncontested occupation, and President Aristide returned to office on October 15, 1994. A United Nations peacekeeping force took over from the U.S. military on April 1, 1995, with all forces scheduled to leave by April 30, 1996 (Hunter, 1996–1997).

HAITIAN FAMILY

The Haitian family is usually extended and patriarchal in Haiti and in America. Lower-class one-parent families tend to be matriarchal.

After becoming established in America, new immigrants are morally obligated to send for other family members, although it may take several years for an entire family to become reunited in the United States. This vast kinship network, spanning two countries, perpetuates the extended family system. Haitian Americans generally maintain contact with family in Haiti by sending remittances and/or visiting on vacation or for special occasions, particularly during Carnival time and for funerals. Sometimes children are sent to Haiti to be cared for by relatives and educated in Haitian schools. This practice frees Haitian American parents to work and save toward the purchase of a home and at the same time provides the children with a preferred education, which focuses on the French language, Christian principles, and Haitian customs (Laguerre, 1984; Leavitt & Lutz, 1988).

The Haitian family is usually a very close-knit and supportive group. In a study by Lassiter (1988), most Haitian informants described their families as strict, rigid, and protective. One informant added that there was "little touching and verbal expressions of affection among her family members." However, togetherness and communication were characteristic of most Haitian families. Similar to other ethnic groups, family behavior is a function of socioeconomic status or social class.

Some Haitian American communities in New York are divided with respect to social class and color, legacies of their colonial slave-based past. *Klass* is the term that some Haitians use to designate social categories on the basis of wealth, family name and ancestry, education, and complexion. These divisions constitute a social hierarchy brought from Haiti and reinstituted in the United States (Buchanan, 1983; Cosgray, 1991).

Settlement in the United States has had little or no effect on the sex roles of Haitian men and women. The home is frequently considered the Haitian woman's domain, and she has limited interest in community affairs, whereas the man's domain is outside the house (Leavitt & Lutz, 1988). Laguerre (1984) noted that some Haitian women in New York tended to be more assertive and independent than they were in Haiti. One factor responsible for this change may be a woman's ability to achieve economic independence in America. Consequently, the gender roles in many Haitian American families have tended to become less traditional and more egalitarian.

Laguerre (1984) identifies four types of marriages and household organizations:

1. *Mariag de goudin.* For the purpose of becoming eligible for resident status, a middle-class or upper-class Haitian living in the United States marries a lower-class individual who is a citizen or has a resident visa.

2. *Mariag residans.* Two Haitians of similar social status marry when only one has resident status.

3. *Mariag bay bous.* Marriage is contracted between a person with resident status and a person in Haiti, frequently arranged by the kin.

4. *Bon mariag.* Marriage is arranged for a couple, both of the same status, before they migrate to America or after residence, for the purpose of establishing a relationship and a family.

The first three unions are for purposes of immigration, to facilitate entry into the United States; the fourth type is the only one entered into for the purpose of forming a household. Another type of union, not legally recognized in the United States, is the consensual union; it generally has difficulty remaining intact after migration (Laguerre, 1984).

Although Haitian families demonstrate signs of assimilation into American culture, many aspects of their culture remain strong in the United States. For example, Haitian food and music are prevalent in Little Haiti, Haitian women dress in colorful native dress especially on Sundays, and the area is painted in bright colors. As in Little Havana (the Cuban area), there are frequent gala festivals, celebrations, and parades that display a flavor of the old country. The family serves many important functions, ranging from maintaining customs and perpetuating the culture to facilitating the chain migration process (Mohl, 1985).

Childrearing

As usually both Haitian American parents work, day care must be provided for their children. These children are usually cared for by other Haitian women who live nearby. Haitian mothers prefer this arrangement because they believe that community child-care facilities have inflexible hours, do not offer personalized care, and are too expensive (Leavitt & Lutz, 1988).

Although Haitian parents are usually extremely loving and affectionate with their children, they are also very strict and authoritarian. Childrearing may be shared by siblings as well as parents. Children are taught to show unquestioned obedience to their elders. Children do not usually ask their parents questions about intimate subjects such as sex, because this would be disrespectful (Cosgray, 1991). Some parents tend to employ physical punishment, the same disciplinary method used by their parents in Haiti. Haitian American parents generally do not like professional counseling and/ or assignment to parenting groups. They feel that other individuals from diverse cultural groups view children's behavior from a different perspective. One way of dealing with a child whom parents feel they cannot control is to send the child to Haiti to live with kin (Fouron, 1983).

Some Haitian American children face adaptation difficulties in the United States because they are torn between two cultures. Their peers encourage them to become Americanized, while their families try to maintain Haitian cultural traditions. Generally these children elect to speak English even at home, while their parents continue to speak Creole or French. Most American-born children have become socialized to mainstream American culture and, unlike their parents, have little interest in returning to Haiti. Some adult Haitian American children who are successfully employed show little enthusiasm for contributing money to fulfill their parents' economic obligations in Haiti or to bring kin and friends to America. This practice sometimes causes intergenerational conflicts (Fouron, 1983; Lassiter, 1995).

Socialization

Some Haitian Americans who adhere to the principles of social class may attempt to perpetuate this traditional class system in the United States, based on wealth, language, and color. However, many other Haitian Americans believe that a good education and professionalism can elevate one's social class, regardless of ancestry. Comportment and proper behavior are important indicators of one's class. Proper behavior includes good manners, modulated speaking voice, avoidance of public scenes, refraining from profanity, and appearing neat and clean at all times. Friends should be carefully selected, keeping in mind the expression, "Birds of a feather flock together." Improper behavior is considered an embarrassment to one's family and upbringing and may reflect on one's parents' ineffectiveness as disciplinary agents (Buchanan, 1983; Buchanan-Stafford, 1987).

I interviewed 24 Haitian Americans in New York, asking them to describe their personality. Most described themselves as "a nice person"; no one offered a negative self-description, except for expressions of shyness. A larger percentage of the women (69%) than the men (38%) described themselves as "shy and quiet." On the other hand, more men (38%) than women (25%) indicated a need for solitude. Frequent statements were "I like to be alone to think things over," "I seldom feel lonely," and "I enjoy being alone." I found the Haitian Americans more reluctant than other groups (e.g., West Indian Americans and African Americans) to participate in the interviews. Haitian-American men were more reluctant than the women. They appeared to be very private people who were not prone to reveal personal information to a stranger (Lassiter, 1988). Delusions were often related to voodoo religious beliefs. It was also noted that aggression was seldom directed toward others and that hyperactivity was usually more noisy than destructive. It was further noted that Haitians rarely commit suicide (Lassiter, 1995).

NUTRITION

The Haitian American community is able to maintain many of its cultural dietary traditions through local food stores, bakeries, and restaurants that supply favorite Haitian foodstuffs. Haitian music is frequently enjoyed by the family during the evening meal. Because of the work schedules in America, the main meal is often the evening meal. In Haiti the heavy main meal is usually enjoyed around midday, followed by a light evening supper (Laguerre, 1984).

A typical meal of a middle-class Haitian American family is similar to that of other Caribbean families. The meal might consist of a peas and rice mixture, fried plantains, corn, a meat (chicken, beef, pork, or goat) marinated in a spicy Creole sauce, avocado, and orange or papaya juice. Haitian food is usually highly seasoned (Laguerre, 1984). Harwood (1981) noted that Haitian American clients have difficulty maintaining therapeutic dietary restrictions. This can poses serious concerns in the treatment of diabetes, cardiovascular disorders, and gastric ulcers.

Favorite Haitian American foods are rice, beef, goat, chicken, fish, okra, sweet potatoes, pumpkin, sugar cane, breadfruit, plantains, kidney beans, biscuits, and cassava bread. Favorite fruits and nuts are avocados, cashew nuts, coconuts, mangoes, bananas, grapefruit, limes, pineapples, and star apples (Cosgray, 1991).

Some Haitian Americans classify foods in terms of hot and cold, unrelated to temperature. Some foods that are considered very cold are avocado, coconut, and mango. Examples of cool foods are orange juice, cane syrup, and tomato. Coffee, nutmeg, and rum exemplify very hot foods, and eggs and grapefruit juice are classified as warm foods. Several foods are considered neutral, neither hot nor cold: breadfruit, cabbage, coconut candy, fish, goat meat, pigeon peas, plantain, white and brown rice, and kidney beans (Harwood, 1981; Laguerre, 1984; Lassiter, 1995).

RELIGION

Similar to many other Caribbean cultures, some Haitian Americans recognize the coexistence of two religions. Catholicism is usually considered the religion of Haiti. In America, the Catholic church with services now offered in French and Creole (since 1966) plays an important supportive role in Haitian American communities. Some Haitian Americans affiliate with Protestant denominations: Baptist, Episcopal, Seventh Day Adventist, and Pentecostal (Leavitt & Lutz, 1988).

Voodoo

Haiti's second religion is Voodoo (Voudou, Voudoun, Vudun). Voodoo is a religion based on beliefs in the *loa*, the gods that form the vodoun pantheons, and their natural relationship to humans and the universe. Devotees of voodoo believe that all things serve the *loa* and are thereby extensions and expressions of the gods. People who practice voodoo may be Christians. In their belief, the religions can coexist; one is not replaced by the other (Metraux, 1972).

African in origin, voodoo is an informal religion, practiced by autonomous groups and manifested by ceremonial rituals. Groups of adherents perpetuate and preserve these practices under a priest (*ongan, houngan*) or priestess (*mambo*). As there is no church, gatherings usually occur at the home or sanctuary (*hunfo*) of the ongan or mambo. Here believers worship supernatural beings (*lwa, loas, mysteres*, saints, or angels).

The voodoo religion is based on the belief of practitioners, or *protégés* as they are called, that a human is composed of a material or physical body and an invisible spiritual or psyche energy force. This invisible spirit (similar to the concept of soul) gives life to matter. When this spirit withdraws permanently, death is said to occur. This spirit or soul that exists in each human is the energy that activates the mind for all thought processes and motivates behavior (Cosgray, 1991; Shannon, 1997).

Believers in voodoo perceive life in the universe in terms of a hierarchy. God is on the primary level and humans, God's first creation, are on the second level. Deities, Catholic saints, and loa or spirits that govern human affairs, occupy the third level. The loa (spirits of the dead) and protégés (believers) exist in an intimate relationship of interdependence. Protégés acknowledge the loa in regular ceremonies during which food and offerings are presented. The loa, in return, protect their protégés. Thus humans and spirits coexist in the universe in symbiotic relationships (Cosgray, 1991; Deren, 1970; Shannon, 1997).

Possession occurs when a human soul is displaced by a loa, with the possession described as the loa "riding" or "mounting" the human, who then goes into a trance. The person being mounted is called a *cheval* (or horse); thus, when a loa takes possession he mounts the devotee. The *cheval* is usually a member of a group involved in a religious Voodoo ceremony. Possession does not mean that the individual can communicate with the spirit; instead, the person is merely a vehicle though which the spirit can reveal itself. The loa could be protecting the devotee from misfortune, curing an illness, preventing suffering, or removing the devotee from a dangerous situation.

When a person is possessed, the loa enters the devotee like a blow to the nape of the neck or the legs. The cheval's muscles tense, followed by spasms of the spine. When these violent movements cease, the loa takes full control of the devotee's body, actions, and expressed attitudes, which become different from those usual for the person. During this special ceremony, led by houngans or mambos, or both (who are able to identify the possessing loa) and enhanced by ritualistic songs and dances, possession is viewed as a highly positive experience. Therefore the possessed person is considered privileged (Cosgray, 1991; Deren, 1970; Laguerre, 1984; Shannon, 1997).

Voodoo flourished in Haiti because it was flexible and adaptive to people living close to nature. There was no need to keep records, because voodoo rituals, songs, and stories were passed down from generation to generation by elders through word of mouth. Certain symbols that are drawn are known to represent particular spirits. Thus, voodoo encompasses a set of unwritten beliefs and unique practices dealing with the spiritual forces of the universe for the purpose of helping individuals interact more effectively with their environments (Cosgray, 1991; Leyburn, 1966).

Although some Haitian Americans may practice voodoo, it is impossible to ascertain the number of practitioners in the United States for at least two reasons. First, many Haitian Americans from the middle and upper classes are generally unfamiliar with voodoo. Second, those Haitian Americans who are believers are reluctant to admit it because of the stigma attached to voodoo (Cosgray, 1991; Lassiter, 1988, 1995; Shannon, 1997).

HEALTH BELIEFS AND PRACTICES

The central Haitian folk concept of illness is that disease is a disruption of the balanced state of the blood. Traditionally, various types of internal and external disruptions have been identified. For example, fright (*sezisman* in Creole, *saisissement* in French) is a system disruption caused by shock such as bad news or a threat to one's well-being. It is believed that *sezisman* causes blood to rush to the head, resulting in partial blindness, headaches, and temporary mental illness. It is thought that lactating mothers are particularly susceptible to this phenomenon (Laguerre, 1984).

Illness may cause shame for some Haitian Americans. Serious illness is discussed only with family members and close friends. In Haitian culture, illness should be accepted heroically. Traditionally it has been believed that an individual must be strong because psychological weakness will allow the illness to dominate the body. Public displays of weakness are not condoned. Thus, placing a client in a wheelchair may indicate serious illness publicly displayed. This routine hospital practice may elicit negative emotions in some traditional Haitian American clients (Laguerre, 1984).

Similar to many people from other traditional cultures, some Haitians may perceive disease as caused by factors external to the body, such as "cold" or "hot" air or foods, "gas," and spirits. Traditional Haitian Americans may perceive disease as divided into two broad categories: natural illness and supernatural illness. Natural illnesses are those with familiar symptoms and are generally of short duration. The most dangerous types of illness are believed to be caused by irregularities in the blood, which include the following:

- *San cho* (hot blood) provokes a high fever. Blood becomes hot when one is nervous or involved in intellectual activities and during physical activity or sleep. A woman's body is believed to be hot during the postpartum period, and diet is given to balance this state. The blood is said to be cold as a result of malaria when the body is quiet and at rest.

- *San cle* (thin blood) causes pallor. The blood becomes thick in the case of fright (*sezisman*) or in hypertension.

- *San febel* (weak blood) causes physical or mental weakness.

- *San jo-n* (yellow blood) indicates the presence of bile in the blood.

- *San noa* (dark blood) indicates terminal illness (Harwood, 1981; Laguerre, 1984).

Gaz (gas) causes pain and anemia. Gas may enter the body through the ears, causing headaches, or through the mouth, causing stomachaches. It may move to other parts of the body and cause pain in the back, shoulders, and/or extremities. Avoidance of leftover foods is also thought to prevent gas.

Some believe that illness is caused by an imbalance of hot and cold elements, especially in foods. Foods are classified as hot or cold. Therefore, a food or medicine of the opposite category would be used to treat a person in a cold-hot system (Harwood, 1981; Leavitt & Lutz, 1988).

Diseases of supernatural origin are believed to be caused by angry spirits. As previously mentioned in the discussion of voodoo, spirits and believers are interdependent. Ceremonies are held periodically to honor one's spirits, and the spirits in turn provide protection. Some believe that disease may occur if the protégé fails to honor the spirits properly and periodically, and illness becomes the punishment. Voodoo priests are the primary sources for diagnosis and treatment of supernatural diseases. Thus voodoo is both a religion and a therapeutic system (Cosgray, 1991; Laguerre, 1984).

Traditionally it has been believed that since the postpartum period is the most crucial period for the mother, she must keep warm, drink special teas, and take warm baths containing therapeutic leaves. These activities are considered essential for the cleansing and restoration of her natural state.

In addition, some believe that she must take a cold bath followed by self-induced vomiting in order to complete the cleansing process at about one month postpartum, (Jeanty, 1989). Some Haitian Americans may believe that the postpartum woman is susceptible to the entrance of gas after birth; after delivery, she is encouraged to wear a tight belt around her waist to prevent the gas from entering her body. Gas can be treated with a special tea made from garlic, mint, and cloves or by eating such solid foods as plantain and corn. The hot tea and foods classed as "heavy" stimulate the intestinal tract to expel gas (Snow, 1985).

Traditionally it has also been believed that the milk of a nursing mother can be displaced or spoiled by the mother's emotions. Consequently, family and friends try not to provoke a lactating mother into losing her temper, because this could result in harm to herself and her baby. Some believe that milk may rise to the mother's brain and cause acute headache, postpartum depression, and/or psychoses. Also, the danger exists that if the milk mixes with the mother's blood it could poison the nursing baby (Snow, 1985).

Another traditional belief is that of the wandering womb, a displaced womb or uterus, which is believed to occur during the early postpartum period. Because the womb and the baby are said to have established a strong relationship over a period of nine months, it is thought that the deserted womb may wander around the body in search of its lost occupant. This wandering womb may travel into any part of the mother's body. Symptoms such as weakness, dizziness, and confusion, which are experienced by many women during the postpartum period, are believed to be caused by this displaced womb wandering around looking for its lost inhabitant. Traditionally, in rural Haiti, a skilled midwife would perform a series of massages to return the uterus to its proper place (Harwood, 1981; Lassiter, 1995; Snow, 1985).

Common Diseases

During the period between November 1991 and April 1992, approximately 18,000 Haitian migrants received medical care and medical screening required for entry into the United States. The most common diseases found were:

Fever/malaria	35%
Otis media, URI	10%
Measles	6%
Pneumonia	4%
Varicella	4%

Cellulitis   2%

Filariasis   2%

Malaria was the most common disease noted among Haitian immigrants. As required by the Immigration Act of 1990, the medical staff performed tests for syphilis, HIV, and tuberculosis on the migrants and found the following percentages of these conditions among the immigrants:

Syphilis   5%

HIV positive   7%

Tuberculosis   5%

(U.S. Department of Health and Human Services, 1993).

AIDS

Because of unproven statements about AIDS in Haiti, some sources in the United States promoted fear and a stigma about AIDS in the Haitian population and prevented Haitians from donating blood. The Haitian American physician Guy Durand declared that the discovery of AIDS, unique in the history of modern medicine, has resulted in major confusion and irrationality, published by both the professional and lay press. He stated, "Never before in modern medicine has a pathological condition been linked to a nationality" (1984, p. 17).

In spite of the faulty research and the improbability of the connection, the Centers for Disease Control (CDC) in Atlanta included Haitians among the high-risk groups for AIDS until the Haitian category was finally dropped on April 8, 1985 (Lawless, 1986). The CDC later stated that "The Haitians were . . . the only groups that were identified because of who they were rather than what they did" (Woodford, 1985, p. 5C).

BELIEFS ABOUT DEATH AND DYING

Haitian Americans who practice voodoo believe in the symbiotic existence of humans and spirits of the dead. Some believe that if a child's soul is captured and placed in a bottle, that person will live until that bottle is broken. Some believe that zombies are doomed to live after death because they were cursed by an enemy. If one strongly believes this, one might request that after death one's body parts be buried in separate graves, to avoid becoming a zombie (Cosgray, 1991). Haitians who adhere solely to Catholicism endorse beliefs about death and dying in keeping with the doctrines of the Catholic church (Lassiter, 1995).

REFERENCES

Buchanan S. H. (1980). Scattered seeds: The meaning of the migration for Haitians in New York City. Unpublished doctoral dissertation, New York University.

Buchanan, S. H. (1983). The cultural meaning of class for Haitians in New York City. *Ethnic Groups*, 5(1 and 2), 7–29.

Buchanan-Stafford, S. (1987). Language and identity: Haitians in New York City. In C. R. Sutton & E. M. Chaney (Eds.), *Caribbean life in New York City: Sociocultural dimensions* (pp. 202–17). New York: Center for Migration Studies of New York.

Chaney, E. M. (1987). The context of Caribbean migration. In C. R. Sutton & E. M. Chaney (Eds.), *Caribbean life in New York City: Sociocultural dimensions* (pp. 3–14). New York: Center for Migration Studies of New York.

Cosgray, R. E. (1991). Haitian Americans. In J. N. Giger & R. E. Davidhizar (Eds.), *Transcultural nursing: Assessment and intervention* (pp. 465–88). St. Louis: Mosby Year Book.

Deren, M. (1970). *Divine horseman: Voodoo gods of Haiti*. New York: Chelsea House.

Durand, G. (1983). AIDS: Fallacy of a Haitian Connection. *Bulletin de l'Association des Medecins Haitiens a l'Atranger*, 19(9), 17–20.

Fouron, G. (1983). The black dilemma in the U.S.: The Haitian experience. *Journal of Caribbean Studies*, 3(3), 242–65.

Harwood, A. (1981). *Ethnicity and medical care*. Cambridge, Mass.: Harvard University Press.

Hunter, B. (1996–1997). *The Statesman's Year-Book: A statistical, political and economic account of the states of the world for the year 1996–1997* (133rd ed.). New York: Chelsea House.

Jeanty, M. (1989). Personal communication at Logansport State Hospital, Ind.

Laguerre, M. S. (1984). *American odyssey: Haitians in New York City*. Ithaca: Cornell University Press.

Lassiter, S. M. (1988). Coping as a function of culture and socio-economic status for Haitians and Africans. Unpublished study, Adelphi University, New York.

Lassiter, S. M. (1995). *Multicultural clients: A professional handbook for health care professionals and social workers*. Westport, Conn.: Greenwood Press.

Lawless, R. (1986). Haitian migrants and Haitian-Americans: From invisibility into the spotlight. *Journal of Ethnic Studies*, 14(2), 29–70.

Leavitt R., & Lutz, M. E. (1988). *Three immigrant groups in New York City: Dominicans, Haitians, and Cambodians*. New York: Community Council of Greater New York.

Leyburn, J. G. (1966). *The Haitian People*. New Haven: Yale University Press.

Metraux, G. (1972). *Voodoo in Haiti*. New York: Schocken Books.

Mohl, R. A. (1985). An ethnic "boiling pot": Cubans and Haitians in Miami. *Journal of Ethnic Studies*, 13(2), 51–74.

Romain, J. B. (1978). Cultural values: Identification, dangers, lines of action. *Cultures*, 5(3), 90–109.

Schiller, N. G., DeWind, J., Brutus, M. L., Charles, C., Fouron, F., & Thomas, A.

(1987). All in the same boat? Unity and diversity in Haitian organizing in New York. In C. R. Sutton & E. M. Chaney (Eds.), *Caribbean life in New York City: Sociocultural dimensions* (pp. 182–201). New York: Center for Migration Studies of New York.

Shannon, T. S. (1997). An introduction to Vodoun. Available online at (http://www.vmedia.com/shannon/voodoo/intro.html. Also at voodoo/possession. html.

Snow, J. (1985). *Common health care beliefs and practices of Puerto Ricans, Haitians and low-income blacks living in New York/New Jersey area*. Contract #120–83–0011, Region II. Prepared by the National Health Service Corps, Dept. of Health and Human Services. John Snow Public Health Group, Inc.

U.S. Bureau of the Census (1992). *Statistical abstracts of the United States*. Washington, D.C.: U.S. Government Printing Office.

U.S. Department of Health and Human Services/Public Health Services/CDC. (1993). Health Status of Haitian Migrants: U.S. Naval Base, Guantanamo Bay, Cuba, November 1991–April 1992. *Morbidity and Mortality Weekly Report*, pp. 138–40.

Woodford, C. (1985, April 10). Haitian immigrants no longer listed as high-risk group for contracting AIDS. *Gainesville Sun*, p. 5C.

6

Hawaiian Americans

Hawaii is the only American state that is an island and is not a part of North America. The Hawaiian Islands, having a land area of 6,423 square miles, lie in the North Pacific Ocean, about 2,090 nautical miles southwest of San Francisco. Hawaii has a renowned subtropical climate, with little year-round temperature variation. Summers average about 78 degrees Fahrenheit and winters about 72 degrees Fahrenheit, although snow is not uncommon on some of the high mountain peaks during winter. Hawaii's economy is based mainly on its sugar cane and pineapple crops, livestock, fisheries, and outstanding tourism.

OVERVIEW

The chain of 136 named Hawaiian islands and islets (covering an area the size of Connecticut and Rhode Island combined) were originally formed by volcanoes on the ocean floor. The Hawaiian Islands contain seven major and eight minor inhabited islands. The major islands are Hawaii (4,028 square miles), Maui (727 square miles), Oahu (600 square miles), Kauai (552 square miles), Molokai (260 square miles), Lanai (141 square miles), Niihau (70 square miles), and uninhabited Kahoolawe (45 square miles) (Hunter, 1996–1997).

Hawaii, often called the "Big Island," was formed by five volcanoes, of which two are presently active. Today, the bubbling lava and fire fountains of Mauna Loa and Kilauea attract thousand of visitors. Hawaii's major crop is sugar cane.

Maui is sometimes called the "Valley Island" because many canyons cut through the two dormant volcanic mountains that form the island. Maui's major crops are sugar cane and pineapples.

Oahu is often known as the "Gathering Place" because about 80% of the Hawaiian population reside there, and it is the most frequently visited island. Oahu's two mountain ranges are separated by a wide valley of sugar cane and pineapple plantations. Oahu's dazzling white sand beaches and natural harbors (including Honolulu's famous Waikiki Beach) are among the finest in the world. Puuloa, better known as Pearl Harbor, lies on the southern coast, west of Honolulu. Pearl Harbor, one of the best natural harbors in the world, contains about ten square miles of navigable coral free water behind a mile-wide harbor entrance. Honolulu, the state capital, is on the island of Oahu (Russell, 1994).

Kauai is often called the "Garden Island" because of its beautiful tropical greenery, lush vegetation, and gardens of exotic flowers. Because of the high annual rainfall over the years, rivers have worn the volcanic rock forming the colorful canyons of Waimea, reminiscent of Colorado's Grand Canyon.

Molokai, often called the "Friendly Island," boasts of its friendly welcome to visitors. Part of the island has dry plateaus conducive to cattle ranching, while the fertile soil of its central plains supports numerous pineapple plantations.

The entire island of Lanai is one big pineapple plantation owned by the Dole Company. Thus Lanai is called the "Pineapple Island."

Niihau is often called the "Forbidden Island" because it is privately owned and not open to the public. It is almost entirely covered by huge cattle ranches. Because of its comparative isolation, it is one of the few places in Hawaii where the people still speak the Hawaiian language.

Kahoolawe, the smallest island, is dry and barren. Because there are no inhabitants, the U.S. military uses it for ammunition testing (Aylesworth & Aylesworth, 1988; Beechert, 1991; Russell, 1994).

Population

During the 1990 U.S. Census, Hawaiian Americans numbered 1,108,229, or 0.1% of the American population, an increase of 15 % since 1980. Their population estimate for 1993 was 1,171,592 (Hunter, 1996–1997; U.S. Census Bureau, 1990). There are almost 100,000 Hawaiians living on the American mainland (Na Mamo, 1996).

Pacific islanders include Polynesians (Hawaiians, Samoans, Tongons), Micronesians (Chamorros), and Melanesians (Fijians). Hawaiian Americans comprise an exceptional variety of cultural and ethnic groups. The major Hawaiian groups, in descending population numerical order, are Caucasians, Japanese, Filipino, Hawaiian, Black, Chinese, and Korean. Intermarriage between the races is common; 43% of all Hawaiian marriages are of mixed cultures (Hunter, 1996–1997). In the 1990 U.S. census, Hawaiians reported over 145 ancestries, of which the major were (in descending numerical order) Portuguese, German, English, Irish, and Italian.

Language

Today, most Hawaiians speak English. The Hawaiian language is spoken by only about 2,000 individuals. Hawaiian is spoken exclusively in some private preschools to preserve the culture by teaching children their native language (Na Mamo, 1996; U.S. Bureau of the Census, 1990).

HISTORY

Pre-European Contact

Anthropologists believe that several thousand years ago Hawaiian ancestors, called Polynesians (people from many islands), traveled by canoes between the many islands of the Pacific, particularly Tahiti, Raitea, and Hawaii. Some believe that the Hawaiian islands were named after a Polynesian chief called Hawaii-loa; yet others think that the name was derived from Hawaiki, the Polynesian homeland to the west. About 1000 A.D. the canoe voyages gradually terminated with the growth of a dominant culture in Hawaii.

A unique society emerged that was totally isolated from outside influence and structured itself in a manner similar to medieval Europe with class levels such as a ruling class (*ali'i*), priests or experts (*kuhuna*), commoners (*maka'ainana*), and slaves (*kauwa*). Social status was inherited through bloodline. The society was highly organized and disciplined under a strict *kapu* (meaning "restriction," "separation," and "forbidden") system that established definite roles and relationships among the people, the gods, and nature. In a subsistence economy, the people lived in harmony with the land, observing environmental control and balance of natural resources.

Post-European Contact

Although other explorers may have visited the islands, the first official report of a landing was by Captain James Cook of the British Royal Navy in January 1778. He named the area the Sandwich Islands for the Earl of Sandwich, England's First Lord of the Admiralty. Cook traded with the natives, who were friendly, perhaps because they thought he was a god. He found a well-organized society ruled by chiefs, one of which was Kamehameha, who later became the sole ruler of Hawaii island after a ten-year war that began in 1782. Cook was killed in 1779 in a conflict with the Hawaiians. The Europeans' great impact on aspects of Hawaiian culture caused several subsequent events.

First, the introduction of iron implements (knives and nails), explosives, and cannons helped chief Kamehameha to gain control of all the islands except Kauai and Niihau, that preferred to keep their chief, Kaumualii. However in 1810 the two islands accepted Kamehameha as their leader. The European presence gradually changed the harmonious Hawaiian society from one of subsistence for daily needs to one based on trade with foreigners for the acquisition of material goods.

Second, the introduction of new diseases for which the natives had no immunity and their folk practitioners (*kahuna*) had no treatments, devastated the Hawaiian population. Major diseases were chicken pox, measles, smallpox, influenza, the plague, leprosy, and venereal diseases (STDs). In 1853, the Hawaiian people experienced a major smallpox epidemic. Thus, as a result of diseases introduced by the Europeans, the native population decreased from 300,000 at Cook's arrival to only 50,000 one hundred years later.

Third, in 1820, the first company of missionaries under the auspices of the American Board of Commissioners for Foreign Missions arrived to convert the natives to Christianity. The Christian invasion significantly impacted on the Hawaiian society: The church replaced the traditional religious system; many of the missionaries' descendants eventually dominated the business community; and the missionaries put the Hawaiian language into print and began a system of schooling for the natives. Many Hawaiian songs reflect a hymnal quality, such as the popular "Hawaii Aloha," written by a missionary, Lorenzo Lyons, who was inspired by an old hymn, "I left it all with Jesus." Today, religion permeates the lives of most Hawaiians.

Fourth, in 1819, after Kamehameha's death and his son, Liholiho, became king, the *kupu* system (the foundation of Hawaiian life) was overturned by the influx of new ideas. However, in 1874, King Kalakaua (called the "Merry Monarch") revived many of the old Hawaiian customs, including traditional music and the hula (meaning "dance" in Hawaiian), that the missionaries had forced previous kings to prohibit. During his reign, the custom of wearing grass skirts, imported from Samoa, began. At the same time sugar cane and pineapples (from a special strain of Jamaican pineapples) were cultivated on a large scale, and Hawaii prospered.

Upon the death of Kalakaua in 1891, his sister Liliuokalani became queen, but she was deposed in 1893 after a bloodless revolution led by nine Americans, two Britons, and two Germans, backed by the U.S. Marines and Navy. Relieved of their leaders, the Hawaiian people felt a loss of their identity, as well as many aspects of their heritage, to economic supremacy. In 1894, the Republic of Hawaii (largely under the control of American businessmen) was formed, and Judge Sanford B. Dole became the president. In August 1989, the islands were formally annexed to the United States and in June 1900 were constituted as the Territory of Hawaii. In 1917, before the United States entered World War I, the construction of the naval base at Pearl Harbor began. The Japanese attack on Pearl Harbor that sank the battleship USS *Arizona* on December 7, 1941, motivated the U.S. entry into World War II. Two regiments of the Hawaiian National Guard were called into action during the war. After the war, flourishing Hawaii desired to become a state of the union, and in March of 1959 statehood was granted. Effective August 1959, Hawaii became the fiftieth state (Aylesworth & Aylesworth, 1988; Beechert, 1991; Hunter, 1996–1997; McDermott, Tseng, & Maretzi, 1980; Russell, 1994).

Over the years several cultural groups had migrated to Hawaii. In 1823, skilled Chinese workers arrived to set up sugar mills, followed by a second group in 1852. The first group of Japanese arrived in 1868, and the first Portuguese in 1878. A group of Germans arrived in 1881. Korean immigration began in 1903, followed by Filipinos in 1906. Between 1920 and 1930, Hawaii experienced a sharp rise in Caucasian immigration, especially of members of the U.S. armed forces. And finally Vietnamese, Hmong, Laotian, and Cambodian refugees arrived, between 1975 and 1978. Despite Hawaii's high cost of living, migration to the islands continues, including retirees, individuals arriving to work in technology and communication industries, and others seeking a less stressful lifestyle (McDermott, Tseng, & Maretzi, 1980).

FAMILY

Traditional Families

Because of their small population, Native Hawaiians have been an ethnic group inadvertently incorporated in the label "Asian and Pacific Islanders." However they are a unique people indigenous to the Hawaiian islands, originally living in an isolated geographical location, and bearing a record of oppression and displacement under colonial intervention.

Many of the words in the Hawaiian language convey strong emotional feeling, such as *aloha* (love), *'aina* (land), and *kuku* (grandparents); but the word *'ohana* is very special and means extended family. *'Ohana* is derived from *'oha* (taro plant), brought to Hawaii by the original Hawaiians. The plant, having survived fierce tropical storms, devastating effects of salt water, and intense equatorial heat, remained a staple in the diets of many natives. Similar to the potato, the parent taro plant sends out rootlets from which other plants develop. Hence, the analogy of extended family members connected by genetic roots to the parents. Traditional Hawaiians have perceived the family as the center of all relationships in which a support system is taken for granted. In the *'ohana*, individuals are taught their responsibilities, appropriate behavior, consideration of other's needs, respect for *kupuna* (elders), and the true meaning of *aloha* as love among family members.

Traditional Hawaiians have had a great love for children, regardless of legitimacy or illegitimacy, for they viewed a house without children as one without life. Consequently both legal and informal adoptions (*hanai*) were common within the community. In ancient Hawaiian families, the firstborn, or *hiapo*, was given to the grandparents: In the case of a boy, to the paternal grandparents, or if a girl, to the maternal grandparents. Through this act of *hanai* ties were extended; rather than losing his or her parents, the child was afforded a more intense relationship with the grandparents. Although today, firstborns are no longer given to grandparents, the term *hanai* still denotes feelings of love and fondness related to foster parents and other child-care providers (McDermott, Tseng, & Maretzi, 1980).

Another traditional Hawaiian family practice is known as *ho'oponopono*, or family conference, practiced daily in ancient Hawaii before colonial contact. Later the missionaries prohibited the practice because of its inherent spiritualism. The purpose of *ho'oponopono* was to restore and maintain good relationships among family members and supernatural spirits. All family members participated in the conference led by a senior member (healer, father, mother, or grandparent). Family members were given the opportunity to discuss any problems on a daily basis. Based on a strong belief in spiritualism, the *ho'oponopono* process begins with a prayer of communication with God and family spirits for assistance. The first phase of the process involves assessment (*kukulu kumuhana*) and prioritizing (*mahiki*) of problems presented by family members. The second phase entails discussion of the problems. The third phase, resolution (*mihi*), beginning after all discussion is completed, calls for forgiveness, release of any negative feelings (*kala*), and the reestablishment of family cohesiveness. Thus, *ho'oponopono* is an important traditional process that maintains the integrity of the family unit through prayer and sharing in order to prevent and/or resolve problems.

Certain values are basic to this traditional family-centered problem-solving practice. Love and affection, mutual regard, and caring describe the values of *aloha*, that also speaks to the common bond of humanity and the interrelatedness of each individual with family and the spiritual world. *Aloha* was first used to describe the love between mother and child. Another important cultural value inherent in the process is *lokahi*, meaning unity, agreement, and harmony (Mokuau, 1990).

Modern Families

Today there are probably fewer than 3,000 pure Hawaiians. Most Hawaiian Americans are offspring of intermarriages, having become the statistical norm. Hawaii is probably the most multiracial society in the world. About 50% of Hawaiians on the island are Caucasian, often called *haole*; newcomer Caucasians from the mainland are called *malihinis*. Asians form another major portion of the Hawaiian population. Although the Asian cultures have retained focal points of their identity such as temples, ceremonies, and language schools, they have also absorbed other influences. Although tensions may occasionally erupt between the cultures and between the settled and the newcomers, the relaxing of ethnic boundaries is a distinct phenomenon throughout Hawaii.

Pidgin, a speech form developed from several languages spoken on the island, has became commonly used by most residents (including the Caucasians), creating a pidgin culture and a sense of multicultural Hawaiian unity. Modern Hawaiian families may demonstrate any of the behaviors discussed in the chapters on Asians and African Americans or other cultures. However in all groups, except perhaps the Caucasian, the extended family plays a central role, in which the individual is viewed as an interdependent part of the family network and affiliation is more important than individualism. Caucasians also value the family but tend to face the world more as individuals. The continuing intermarriage may eventually blur distinguishing cultural values and concepts of family (Fong & Mokuau, 1994; McDermott, Tseng, & Maretzi, 1980; Mokuau, 1991).

Socialization

Hawaiian American socialization emphasizes group affiliation rather than individual competitive achievement. Many Hawaiians enjoy working with friends to prepare a luau (Hawaiian feast) or helping a friend with home or car repairs. Hawaiian work teams are highly productive because commitment is most intense when the objective is to enhance human relationships rather than acquire individual wealth or promote personal achievement. Many Hawaiian Americans will honor commitments to friends, help a person in need, or engage in situations of cooperative fellowship, even in the face of personal material deprivation.

Hawaiian Americans often believe that a home should be a place to facilitate interpersonal interactions, not one that distracts from comfort by ostentatious furnishings. Consequently, they avoid showing off, so that even individuals of high income may maintain a relatively low level of material comfort.

Also, some Hawaiian Americans may downplay the significance of things and events, perpetuating the romanticized image of the "happy-go-lucky," "easy-going" Hawaiian. The phrase "Ain't no big thing" (title of the book by Alan Howard) describes this behavior pattern. "Ain't no big thing" philosophy is a defense mechanism by which things are taken lightly in order to minimize vulnerability and consequent negative effects. Also, the philosophy requires that a person downplay any personal achievements. Boasting behavior is inappropriate; acclaim should come from acknowledgement and recognition by others. The "ain't no big thing" concept promotes a "happy-go lucky" social posture that encourages good friendships and affiliations. However, some Hawaiian Americans may downplay, deny, or avoid a serious situation and fail to confront major problems. This socialization has raised concerns by social workers and other health professionals with respect to social and medical problems such as unemployment, inappropriate family relationships, drug abuse, and illness.

A basic premise underlying Hawaiian American social life is that interactions should be harmonious and void of conflict. Because traditional Hawaiians have viewed conflict as the wrath of god, conflict management was been given high priority among family and community activities. A strategy used to maintain harmony has been to avoid confrontations. Many Hawaiian children learn early not to make demands or seek attention for recognition because this behavior only leads to their being ignored or punished. They learn to remain unobtrusive but become keenly sensitive to expressive cues or the nonverbal behavior of others (especially parents and other adults). Thus, Hawaiian Americans are socialized to react more to how something is said than to what is said. Many Hawaiian children tend to develop strong ties with their peers, beginning the practice of affiliative/friendship relationships. These relationships are generally egalitarian. Egalitarianism, among friends and within the family, is another important value of Hawaiian American socialization (Howard, 1974; McDermott, Tseng, & Maretzi, 1980; Mokuau, 1990).

NUTRITION

Cuisine in Hawaii reflects the tastes of eastern and western cultures. However, some dishes are uniquely Hawaiian, such as *poi*, a paste made from the taro root that has a slightly sour taste. Another is *laulau*, a steamed dish made of pork and fish wrapped in plant leaves. During a luau (an outdoor Hawaiian picnic), a suckling pig roasted in a pit is a feature. Other favorite foods are fruits and vegetables including their renowned pineapple, raw fish, squid and liver, taro leaves cooked in coconut cream, and *limu* (seaweed). Seaweed may be served either raw or cooked and is commonly prepared with salt, herbs, and other spices such as chili powder, ginger, and garlic (Ensminger et al., 1994; Howard, 1974).

RELIGION

In 1819, a year before the Christian missionaries arrived, the Hawaiian chiefs began destroying the temples that had been the symbols of ancient Hawaiian religion. The void was partially filled by the missionaries (Calvinists, Catholics, and Mormons), who encouraged conversion to Christianity. Yet some Hawaiians who still quietly worship *aumakua* (traditional family spirits) believe that their traditions have been violated by the development of geothermal energy on the "Big Island," the military's damage of Kahoolawe Island, and the desecration of ancestral graves in order to build resorts and highways (Na Mamo, 1996).

Many Hawaiian Americans are highly spiritual and perhaps in closer communication with their inner or unconscious lives than individuals of many other cultures. Some use dreams to help understand human and group behavior. Their belief in and use of dreams is similar to the psychology and philosophy of Carl Jung, a Western psychoanalyst.

Many Hawaiian Americans believe in a strong connection between natural and supernatural forces. Some Hawaiians strongly believe in the Christian expression, "God is everywhere," and actually experience the Presence in concrete symbols encountered in every day life. Thus, their spirituality/religion, requiring special behavioral responses to symbols, is a part of daily life. Some Hawaiians attest to psychic experiences, others identify with the Christian teachings and or with the traditional *aumakua*, and yet many ascribe to a combination of both Christian and traditional religions. Beliefs about death and dying are related to their religions (McDermott, Tseng, & Maretzi, 1980).

HEALTH

Beliefs and Practices

Traditional Hawaiian Americans have held a holistic concept of health: mind and body, nature and humans, are inseparable. In like manner, their approach to therapy has been holistic, using spiritualism and natural herbs for healing purposes. Today, because many Hawaiians no longer have faith in the "old ways," some young Hawaiian doctors and nurses are attempting to incorporate traditional healing techniques into their modern practices (Na Mamo, 1996).

Common Diseases

Native Hawaiians, the indigenous people of the Hawaiian Islands, have a 34% higher death rate than the total population of the United States. Thus, Native Hawaiians have the highest mortality rate of the five major ethnic groups (Caucasian, Japanese, Native Hawaiian, Chinese, Filipino) living in Hawaii. The Native Hawaiian overall heart disease rate is 44% higher, cancer rate 39% greater, cerebrovascular disease 31% higher, and diabetes mellitus 22% greater, than rates for the overall United States population. The mortality rate from these diseases is higher in full-blooded

Hawaiians than in mixed Native Hawaiians. Full-blooded Native Hawaiians have the highest death rate from heart disease in the United States (177% higher than that of the total U.S. population). They also have the highest mortality rate for diabetes in the nation (588% higher than that for the total U.S. population) (Aluli, 1988, 1990).

Over 60% of Native Hawaiians (62.8% of the women, 65.5% of the men) reported being overweight, with 44.6% severely overweight. For comparison, all U.S. cultures combined indicate an overweight rate of 25.6% and a severely obese rate of 9.3%. Native Hawaiians have the highest prevalence of obesity in Hawaii, which is 2.3 times greater than the prevalence for the state. Thus, the rate of obesity-related diseases is higher for Native Hawaiians than for any other ethnic group in the nation. Obesity in Native Hawaiians may be due either to the lower energy expenditure of modern lifestyles or to a preference for Western foods that are high in fat, cholesterol, and calories and low in fiber, or a combination of both. To date, there is little information to substantiate the causes of Native Hawaiian health problems in the scientific literature (Aluli, 1991).

Often diabetes and hypertension among Native Hawaiians are uncontrolled, with many individuals unaware that they have a health problem. Perhaps the "ain't no big thing" philosophy may come into play here. Consequently, in addition to a high death rate for heart diseases, Native Hawaiians also experience higher mortality rates for hypertension and diabetes, as well as cancer, cerebrovascular disorders, and accidents than all other Hawaiian ethnic groups (Curb et al., 1991).

Cigarette smoking was noted for 42% of males and 34% of female Native Hawaiians (Aluli, 1991). Also, leprosy, believed to have been imported to the United States by refugees from Indochina between 1978 and 1988, is found in certain isolated communities of Hawaii (as well as Texas, Louisiana, and possibly California), with no evidence of transmission to other United States populations (Mastro, Redd, & Breiman, 1992; Mokuau, 1990).

Health Care

To date, Hawaii is the only state to have implemented health insurance for over 95% of its population. This State Health Insurance Program (SHIP), initiated in 1991, provides nearly universal health insurance coverage for Hawaiians. The system mandates employers to provide insurance for all who work at least 20 hours per week, places controls on costly health care facilities, and provides government assistance through Medicaid for those not covered through employment. However, there remains a great need for prevention awareness, primary care, and health education programs for Native Hawaiians (Baumgartner, Grossmann, & Fuddy, 1993; Neubauer, 1993; Lewin, 1994).

CONCLUSION

Hawaiians are a beautiful, warm, and friendly people who welcome visitors with long fresh flower wreaths called *leis*, placed around the neck with a greeting of "Aloha," the same word used for goodbye. Hawaii is believed to be the most popular honeymoon site in the world. The thousands of tourists to Hawaii year round enjoy many attractions including hula dancing, Hawaiian guitar music, beautiful exotic flower gardens, lava fields and volcanoes, sandy beaches, surfing on the rolling waves, pineapple at the Dole factory, and lavish Hawaiian luaus.

REFERENCES

Aluli, N. E. (1988). *The Moloka'i heart study*. Honolulu: American College of Physicians.

Aluli, N. E. (1991). Prevalence of obesity in a Native Hawaiian population. *American Journal of Clinical Nutrition, 53*(6, Supp.), 1556s–60s.

Aylesworth, T. G., & Aylesworth, V. L. (1988). *Let's discover the states: The Pacific, California and Hawaii*. New York: Chelsea House.

Baumgartner, E. T., Grossmann, B., & Fuddy, L. (1993). *Journal of Health Care for the Poor and Underserved, 43*, 194–202.

Beechert, E. D. (1991). *Honolulu: Crossroads of the Pacific*. Columbia: University of South Carolina Press.

Curb, J. D., Aluli, N. E., Kautz, J. A., Petrovitch, H., Knutsen, S. F., Knutsen, R., O'Conner, H. K., & O'Conner, W. E. (1991). Cardiovascular risk factor levels in ethnic Hawaiians. *American Journal of Public Health, 81*(2), 164–67.

Eliade, M., & Couliano, I. P. (1991). *The Eliade guide to world religions*. San Francisco: HarperCollins.

Ensminger, A. H, Ensminger, M. E. Konlande, J. E., & Robson, J. K. (1994). *Foods and nutrition encyclopedia* (2nd ed.) (Vol. I), pp. 578–83. London: CRC Press.

Fong, R., & Mokuau N. (1994). Not simply "Asian Americans": Periodical literature review on Asians and Pacific Islanders. *Social Work, 39*(3), 298–305.

Howard, A. (1974). *Ain't no big thing*. Honolulu: University Press of Hawaii.

Hunter, B. (1996–1997). *The Statesman's Year-Book: Statistical and historical annual of the states of the world for the year 1996–1997* (133rd ed.). New York: St. Martin's Press.

Lewin, J. C. (1994). Reflections on national health care reform based on Hawaii's experience. *American Journal of Surgery, 167*(2), 227–31.

Mastro, T. D., Redd, S. C., & Breiman, R. F. (1992). Imported leprosy in the United States, 1978 through 1988: An epidemic without secondary transmission. *American Journal of Public Health, 82*(8), 1127–30.

McDermott, J. F., Jr., Tseng, W. S., & Maretzi, T. W. (1980). *People and cultures of Hawaii: A psychocultural profile*. Honolulu: John A. Burns School of Medicine and the University Press of Hawaii.

Mokuau, N. (1990, December). A family-centered approach in Native Hawaiian culture. *Families in Society*, 71(10), 607–12.

Mokuau, N. (1991). *Handbook of social services for Asian and Pacific Islanders*. Westport, Conn.: Greenwood Press.

Na Mano (1996). *Hawaiian people today*. Available online: http://www.lava.net/namamo/mamochap.html#farm.

Neubauer, D. (1993). State model: Hawaii: A pioneer in health system reform. *Health Affairs Millwood*, 12(2), 31–39.

Russell, W. (1994). *Hawaii: Islands in the sea*. Vero Beach, Fla.: Rourke.

U.S. Bureau of the Census (1990). *Statistical abstracts of the United States*. Washington, D.C.: U.S. Government Printing Office.

7

Native Americans

America is the homeland of Native Americans, who were the first Americans. The literature uses the terms "American Indian," "Indian," or "Native American"; but because the group encompasses hundreds of different cultures, individuals prefer to be referred to by tribal affiliation when possible. Some people of other cultures have argued that anyone born in America can rightfully be called a native American (Hirschfelder, 1995). However, "Native American," currently the preferred term, is used for most of this chapter's references. "Indian" is retained when the group must be distinguished from other native groups.

The Native American population (including Eskimos and Aleuts) numbers slightly less than two million or 1,959,000 and represents 0.3% of the American population in the 1990 Census. This indicates an increase of 38.7%, as compared to the white population increase of 3.9%, between 1980 and 1990. According to the 1990 Census, the largest number of Native Americans (over 369,000) identified themselves as Cherokee. Since the census uses self-identification, many individuals may have claimed Cherokee ancestry whether or not they were affiliated with the tribe (Finger, 1991). Actually, the Navajo constitute the largest federally recognized tribe in the country. Although the Census Bureau lists 465 tribes, Native Americans claim affiliations to over 500 tribes. Half of the population identifies with the largest tribes which include the Navajo, Cherokee Chippewa, and the Sioux (O'Hare, 1992).

Oklahoma has the largest Native American population in the United States. The following indicates the areas having the largest Native American population:

Oklahoma	252,400
California	242,000
Arizona	203,500
New Mexico	134,400
Alaska	86,000
Washington	81,500
North Carolina	80,150

The Native American population in California cities has increased rapidly in recent years, suggesting an influx of reservation Indians to California urban areas. Today here are 300 separate and distinct land areas in the United States (5% of the country) that are occupied by Native American groups. Reservations range in size from small settlements or *rancherías* of a few acres in California to the Navaho reservation of 15–16 million acres in Arizona, Utah, and New Mexico. This Navaho reservation occupies an area the size of West Virginia. Also, there are several small communities of Native Americans in the eastern states, such as the Paugussets in Connecticut, the Shinnecocks on Long Island, the Mattaponys in Virginia, and the Eastern Cherokee in the mountains of North Carolina. Although these eastern groups demonstrate a high degree of acculturation into the white society, many have retained their cohesiveness, their traditional culture and values, and their sense of Indianness (Josephy, 1991; Viola, 1990).

More than 300,000 Native Americans who live on or near reservations are eligible to participate in programs offered by the Bureau of Indian Affairs. By treaty, the Bureau's jurisdiction includes 301 separate Indian land units (reservations, communities) and 35 groups of scattered off-reservation land sites. The Bureau of Indian Affairs, also called the Office of Indian Affairs, is a government agency that provides public services to Native Americans. The bureau, created in the early nineteenth century, serves in a guardianship role, by combining the functions of all other federal agencies, state governments, counties, municipalities, and even private organizations. Today more than half of the bureau's 9,500 employees are of Indian descent (Grant, 1994; Josephy, 1991).

HISTORY

Origins and Early Settlements

Native Americans are of Asian descent. It is theorized that the first Native Americans, who were subarctic hunters, probably entered North America by way of Beringia. Until some 12,000 years ago, Beringia was a large land mass extending from Siberia into Alaska and northwest Canada; therefore Alaska was geographically a part of Siberia. Changes in weather and sea levels over many years caused water to cover much of Beringia, changing it to what we now know as the Bering Strait. Geologists believe that the land bridge was exposed for two long periods, once between 75,000 and 45,000 years ago and again from about 25,000 to 14,000 years ago. Consequently, theory has it that the original Indians either walked over the frigid land mass of Beringia or crossed in boats through the Bering Strait over 25,000 years ago (Fagan, 1987).

As these migrants moved farther south, they settled in all areas of North and South America and had to make adjustments to a wide variety of geographical environments. These varying adjustments produced a broad spectrum of Indian cultures. The following sections will briefly discuss the major early settlement areas and the general lifestyles and name some of the areas' tribes. Please note that these are original sites, not necessarily the location of all these tribes today. The nations of the Arctic are considered in chapter 3, entitled "Alaskan Americans" (Fagan, 1987; Viola, 1990).

Indians of the Northwest

Perhaps over 8,000 years ago, the early peoples that settled on the Northwest Coast included the Haidas, Kwakiutls, Tlingits, Bella Coolas, Nootkas, Klallams, Chinooks, and Hupas. These tribes developed complex stable societies. They practiced distinct social-class levels based on ancestry; they had slaves and practiced *potlatch*, a giveaway ceremony indicative of social status. They lived in underground pit houses or wooden houses with totem poles in front to indicate status. Early clothing usually consisted of cedar-bark loincloths and elaborate basketwork hats. They also fashioned beautiful garments from the wools of goats and husky dogs. Their comfortable abundant lifestyle was facilitated by easily obtainable food, fish from the sea, and game from the surrounding forests. These early tribes became excellent woodworkers and boatmen who crafted totem poles, elaborate houses, and boats from the region's great evergreens. The first whites to reach the Northwest were Russian traders during the eighteenth century. Spanish and English traders arrived toward the end of the century.

Indians of the Plateau

Early Native Americans tribes that settled in the Plateau areas included the Nez Perces, Spokans, Yakimas, Lilooets, Thompsons, Shuswaps, Chilcotins, Colvilles, Okanogans, Klickitats, and Klamaths. The early peoples who occupied this area 11,000 or more years ago became fishermen, foragers, and hunters. Fish, especially salmon, became their major food along with deer and other game. They did not farm or make pottery, but they became highly skilled in making beautiful baskets, mats, and other useful objects. Early clothing consisted of skins, feathered headdresses, and ornamentation, and houses were usually leather-covered tipis. Plateau youths often acquired guardian spirits through a vision quest to a lonely place. It was believed that throughout a lifetime a person possessed one or more guardian spirits, which could be animals, natural forces, or inanimate objects.

Early in the eighteenth century the horse reached parts of the middle and upper Columbia Basin, introduced by some of the Plains peoples who had earlier acquired horses from the Spanish settlers. Since over the centuries people from many regions had interacted at central trading stations, many of the Plateau peoples had been influenced by neighboring cultures. Thus in 1805, Lewis and Clark (the first white men recorded to have reached the Plateau area) found sharp lifestyle differences among the inhabitants. For example, there were the horse-riding Indians of the middle Columbia area and the canoe-using people of the western part of the region.

Indians of the Plains

To many non-Indians, the early tribes who settled over 5,000 years ago in the North American Plains became the most familiar, based on the stereotypes passed down by white history writers. Writers and dramatists described them as the hard-riding buffalo hunters and warriors of the nineteenth century. For more than a thousand years before the coming of whites, many Plains tribes lived in semipermanent farming villages where agriculture and hunting provided their principle sources of food. The many Plains Indians, tribes that were semiagricultural included the Arikaras, Pawnees, Wichitas, and Arapahos. The nomad tribes of the Plains travelled constantly in pursuit of the buffalo, using dogs to help transport their tents and belongings. Rather than farming or fishing, the subsistence of the nomad tribes was based solely on the products of the buffalo. These buffalo hunters utilized every part of the buffalo, with no waste. They used the buffalo skins for their tepees, clothing, and blankets. They braided the buffalo hair to make ropes. They used the hoofs for glue, the bones for weapons and household implements, and the stomachs as drinking vessels. They used the dung for fuel and the horns for ceremonials. The meat was eaten or dried in the sun, to be ground into flour for storage. The Blackfoot, Hidatsas, Algonquian Cheyennes, Kiowas, Comanches, and Apaches were among the Plains tribes that depended on the buffalo.

The introduction of horses by the Spanish settlers transformed many Plains tribes from farmers to buffalo hunters. By the last half of the eighteenth century almost every Plains tribe in both the eastern and western regions of the Plains owned horses. Indians became expert horsemen, which transformed their lives. Mobility greatly improved, hunting became more successful, and other tribes such as the Cheyenne and the Sioux readily traveled to the Plains. Although the acquisition of horses had a positive effect in that it increased contacts between tribes, the negative result was that horses facilitated tribal warfare, mainly caused by territorial conflicts.

Also, horses revolutionized the warfare methods of the Plains inhabitants so that they became formidable defenders against attacks by the settlers. The fierce resistance of the nomadic Plains tribes gained a number of victories for the Indians. One important victory was the defeat of General Custer at the Little Bighorn in 1876. But eventually, due to the persistent force and firepower along with the slaughter of the buffalo herds by the non-Indians (depriving the Indians of their subsistence), the Plains tribes, no longer able to resist, surrendered and were assigned to reservations by the American government.

Indians of the Northeast

About 12,000 years ago the Northeast Woodlands was the place of settlement for early Native American tribes who became hunters, fishers, and farmers. Land was fertile, and there was an abundance of wild game in the forests and fishes in the lakes and streams. The use of *wampum* (a medium of exchange like "money") had become widespread in this area before the white settlers arrived. *Wampum* were bits of sea shells that had been cut, drilled, and strung into beads and worn as necklaces or belts. Also, a long-stemmed pipe called the *calumet* had been widely used as an important element in councils and religious ceremonies. These tribes included the Iroquois, Pennacooks, Nipmucs, Massachusets, Wampanoags, and Mohegans. The League of the Iroquois became powerful between 1644 and 1700. The organization developed a complex system of government from which many of the democratic concepts reflected in the U.S. Constitution originated.

Indians of the Southeast

Also about 12,000 years ago, the early tribes that settled in the southeastern United States included the Creeks, Yamasees, Seminoles, Apalachees, Alabamas, Choctaws, Chickasaws, Timucuas, Tunicas, and Cherokees. The southeastern nations usually enjoyed an abundance and variety of food. They raised many crops, such as corn, beans, melons, and tobacco. Fishing and game hunting were also common occupations. The Choctaws, Chickasaws, Creeks, Cherokees, and Seminoles formed "The Five Civilized Tribes." This name was applied to the group by the American government in the nineteenth century because of their more rapid adaptation to the white man's civilization than other tribes. However, as an expanding nation of settlers coveted Indian lands, in the 1830s, the U.S. government forced the Indians to relocate to new areas west of the Mississippi. By the mid-1840s only relatively small pockets of Indians, including some Cherokees in the North Carolina mountains, remained in the Southeast.

Indians of the Great Basin and California

Many of the early Native American tribes that settled in the Great Basin, across Utah and Nevada (about 10,000 years ago), developed a desert culture. These individuals often used caves for dwellings and traveled frequently in search of seasonal foods. Great Basin tribes did not farm; instead they became gatherers, collectors, hunters, and, along river shores, fishermen. Their major diet consisted of grasshoppers, prairie dogs, lizards, birds, and rabbits. They lived in temporary dwellings made of grass or bushes and excelled in the making of baskets. They wore light clothing fashioned from desert plants and wore rabbit fur in the winter. Peoples of the Great Basin included the Utes, Gosiutes, Chemehuevis, Paviotsos, Monos, Kawiisus, and Washos.

California was a bountiful area that attracted diverse groups. The great variety and accessibility of food made it possible to acquire food surpluses and fostered the development of a rich social lifestyle. Acorns from the many oak trees were used to make flour. In addition there was an abundance of fish from the streams and the ocean, as well as wildlife from the forests. Among the early tribes of California were the Hupas, Tolowas, Yukis, Pomos, Karoks, Patwins, Costanoans, and Serranos.

Indians of the Southwest

Some of the largest and best-known tribes today in the United States live in the Southwest. The area comprises Arizona and parts of New Mexico, Utah, Colorado, and Texas. These tribes were often called Pueblos, named after their flat-roofed multistoried houses, that were made of sundried adobe or stone. They became expert at making fine pottery and weaving cotton cloth. The prehistoric Mogollon, Hohokam, and Anasazi (the "Old Ones") tribes are the ancestors of the present-day Pueblos. The Anasazi are believed to be the ancestors of the present-day Hopi and Zuni people. The ancestors left a rich culture. They had cultivated beans, corn, squash, and cotton, domesticated the turkey, and developed the art of basketmaking. The nomadic Navajos and Apaches moved from the north into the region about 1400 A.D.

Some of the early Apache tribes were strong and hardy nomads who had developed a fearsome reputation as raiders, often raiding areas far from their own home territory for horses, cattle, and other goods. The word "Apache" was derived from a Zuñi word meaning "enemy." Navajo will be discussed later on in the chapter (Farrer, 1991; Finger, 1991; Josephy, 1991; Snipp, 1989; White, 1980; Worton, 1974; Viola, 1990).

After Columbus

Columbus arrived at the New World in 1492. Believing that he had reached the Indies, he named the natives "Indios," who became known as American Indians. Columbus described the Indians as affectionate, gentle, and friendly. Colonists perceived them as childlike, naive people. Instead, the Indians' behavior pattern actually personified a secure people who were so comfortably aware of their own identity that they had no problems accepting outsiders to join them (Dooling & Smith, 1992).

Columbus and the other newcomers were primarily interested in establishing authoritative control over the natives and then transforming them into the image of the white man. At the Quincentenary, a remark by J. T. Goombi, a Kiowa, and first vice president of the National Congress of American Indians (NCAI), sums up the attitude of peoples whose ancestors had lived in this country for centuries before Columbus. He remarked that 500 years ago Columbus washed up on Indian shores, "and there went the neighborhood" (Major, 1992).

Prior to the end of the eighteenth century, there was no nationally established policy for interaction with the Indians, simply because the American nation had not yet come into existence. Likewise, since the Indians had not established political or social unity among themselves, they were not prepared to confront the various Europeans. By 1871 most of the tribes had signed treaties ceding most of the ancestral territories to the U.S. government in exchange for reservations and welfare. The government placed Indian children in distant boarding schools, often forcefully removing them from their families and the elders who were the major teachers and preservers of traditional culture. In addition, the government forbade the practice of native traditional ceremonies on the reservations.

Federal officials had decided that reservations were necessary to decrease the contact between Indians and non-Indians. Thus land purchases between tribes and colonists or states could not be made without the approval of the federal government. However this no-contact policy was complemented by a removal-if-necessary policy. So as the colonists insisted on pressing west into Indian lands, Indians were removed from their homelands to areas farther west. Today, the largest number of Native Americans live in the West, with the highest population in Oklahoma. However, only about 25% of Native Americans now live on reservations (U.S. Bureau of the Census, 1990; Healthy People 2000, 1990; Josephy, 1991; Pommersheim, 1995; Snipp, 1989; Viola, 1990; J. R. Finger, personal communication, May 17, 1996).

Languages

Although an estimated 206 indigenous languages still survive in the United States, many are spoken only by a dwindling number of elders.

Many Indian languages were lost when the federal government forced Native American children to go to boarding schools. The Cherokees created the first written Indian syllabary. Other written language alphabets include those of the Navajos, Sioux, and Seauoyas (Crawford, 1992).

During the 1980s, a group of tribes including the Navajo, Red Lake Band of Chippewa, Northern Ute, Arapahoe, Pasqua Yaqui, and Papago attempted to halt the language erosion. The group adopted official language policies that mandated the teaching of their languages in their schools. Currently, the Ojibway language, or the Algonquian stock, is probably the most widely spoken in North America (Copway, 1995; Hirschfelder, 1995; Crawford, 1992).

Forcing Native Americans to speak English, called coercive anglicization, has isolated many Native Americans from cultural resources essential to their self-definition. For this reason, speaking one's tribal language is extremely important to many tribal systems because information about their past, the spiritual and natural world concepts, and their religion and ceremonials has been passed down by tribal language (Crawford, 1992).

Recent Indian Protests

Since 1492, Indians have been on the defensive fighting for their lives, their homes, their land, their societies, and their religion. Anti-Indian violence had become rampant throughout the country amid false promises and broken treaties by the government. The situation had resulted in frustration and a feeling of helplessness among the Indian population. Consequently, in November of 1969, a group of Indians, mainly students of nearby colleges in San Francisco, seized Alcatraz Island and occupied it for a year and a half. The seizing of Alcatraz ushered in a new era of pan-Indianism and served as the stimulus for later Indian rights demonstrations and takeovers (Viola, 1990). Throughout 1970 and 1972, angry Indians enacted protest demonstrations. In 1972, several Indian groups formed an auto caravan to Washington, calling it the "Trail of Broken Treaties." The originally planned peaceful endeavor resulted in a forceful takeover of the Bureau of Indian Affairs building for almost a week. Ultimately, the impact of these events and similar protests stimulated the interest of non-Indian Americans in Native American culture and motivated improvements in federal-Indian relations.

Some improvements included allowing the Indians on reservations jurisdiction over their children and protecting Indian rights to practice their traditional religion. Also, the government provided the tribes with programs to help improve the economic and social conditions of their people. In addition, the government provided some opportunities for Indians who had obtained professional education and skills in the cities to obtain well-paying jobs. Presently, many tribes and individuals are using litigation to argue for sovereignty, treaty rights, protection of tribal resources and rituals, and Indian civil rights. Several of these litigations have won notable victories in the federal courts (Josephy, 1991; Viola, 1990).

The Quincentenary

The Quincentenary, October of 1992, marked the 500th anniversary of the arrival of Columbus. The National Congress of American Indians (NCAI) presented the Native American perspective in a program on the lawn of the Capitol, in Washington. The purpose of the Quincentenary was to make a statement to the American people that Native Americans have indeed survived 500 years of Europeans attempting to exterminate, assimilate, and redefine their identities. Although some Native Americans viewed the Quincentenary as an occasion for mourning, many thought of it as an opportunity to disseminate positive information, including an accurate Native American history in order to challenge ethnic stereotypes and negative images (Major, 1992).

Other objectives of the Columbus Quincentenary included fundraising for a variety of worthy causes, building international brotherhood, and promoting tourism. Concurrent programs, geared to reflect America's diversity, also highlighted Jewish American, Latin and Hispanic American, Italian American, and other American cultures (Bovet, 1992).

NAVAJO AMERICANS

Navajo call themselves *Diné*, meaning "us, the people, distinct from anyone else." Archaeologists believe that the Navajo migrated from Canada or Alaska about 500 years ago and became the most recent residents of the Southwest. The Navajo language is related to a group of languages known as the Athapaskan family. This group of languages was named after Lake Athapaska in Canada and is still spoken today by some subarctic Indian groups. Since the Navajo are also related linguistically to the Apache, linguistics have theorized that the Navajo and the Apache were once a single group, that separated after migration. In the northern regions, the Navaho depended on wild game, fishing, and wild plants for survival. Their early homes, called *hogans*, were circular dwellings made of logs and earth. They usually lived in small, loosely organized groups. As Navajo migrated to the Southwest, they readily adapted to changes in food and clothing in the warmer temperatures.

In the Southeast, the Navajo were most influenced by the peoples known today as the Pueblos, who had arrived in the Southwest about 900 years earlier. The Pueblos lived in villages along the Rio Grande in what is now New Mexico and also in several isolated locations on the Colorado Plateau. The Navajo and the Pueblo lived together, intermarried, and shared technology, folklore, crafts, and conflicts with the Spanish. Although the Navajo adopted some Pueblo features such as farming techniques, pottery making, and weaving, they retained the essential Athapaskan language. The Navajo also interacted and intermarried with the Hopi of northern Arizona. By the 1500s the influence of the Spanish colonists was evident, as the Navajo learned to grow peaches, potatoes, and wheat and to raise cattle, sheep, and horses. By the late 1700s, sheep raising became a central aspect of Navajo life. Traditionally, the wool was used by Navajo women to weave blankets. By the 1800s, Navajo blankets and rugs had become desirable trade and sale items. The Navajo were culturally flexible, willing to learn from others, and able selectively to adopt beneficial features from other societies (Farrer, 1991; Hall, 1994; Iverson, 1990; Mander, 1991).

At the end of the Civil War, Colonel Kit Carson forcefully rounded up about 9,000 Navajo and marched them to Fort Sumner, New Mexico (Bosque Redondo), where they were confined. During this march in 1864, known as the "Long Walk," covering 250–300 miles, many Navajo resisters were killed. Internment at Bosque Redondo was brutal and inhuman, and many Navajo died from disease and starvation. After Navajo representatives signed a treaty with the government in 1868, the Navajo were allowed to return to a portion of their traditional territory within the boundaries of the four sacred mountains. The four sacred mountains that mark the boundaries of traditional Navajo territory are San Francisco Peak (or Abalone Shell Mountain) on the west, Blanka Peak (Dawn or White Shell Mountain) on the east, Mount Taylor (Blue Bead or Turquoise Mountain) on the south, and La Plata Mountain (Obsidian Mountain) in the north (Hall, 1994; Iverson, 1990; Mander, 1991).

By the twentieth century, Navajo life showed significant signs of improvement. In 1921, Standard Oil found oil on Navajo land. During the middle 1950s, large oil and gas fields were found near an area called Four Corners. Money obtained from oil and uranium deposits greatly enhanced the Navajo economy. During the 1950s, the Navajo made numerous improvements in reservation life. A tribal college scholarship program was initiated. The *Navajo Times*, a newspaper written in English and circulated throughout the reservation, was established. In 1958, the Navajo Forest Products Industries (NFPI) was established, and the following year the Navajo Tribal Utilities Authority (NTUA) was founded. By 1969, the Navajo believed that they possessed the financial resources and the determination to take charge of their own destiny. Thus, through a tribal council, they began to refer to themselves as the Navajo Nation.

The Navajo People

From 1933 to 1937, the famed anthropologist Edward T. Hall lived and worked on Navajo and Hopi reservations in Arizona. He was able to observe and record many cultural behavioral characteristics of the two groups. Hall found that many Navajo were objective and nonjudgmental thinkers; they were very adaptable and readily able to absorb other people into their society. He observed that many Navajo tended to avoid eye contact during an encounter or conversation, as a show of respect. Some Navajo would enter a room quietly, unobtrusively, and with ease so as not to disturb the air, making one's entrance subtle and harmonious. The Navajo handshake was often gentle (not firm) and held for a while to sense the emotional tone of the other person. Hall noted that many Navaho avoided asking questions because they believed that questioning is not as effective as looking and listening when one wants to gain information. This aspect of his association with the Navajo motivated Hall's later work in nonverbal communication (Hall, 1994).

Catherine Hanley, a registered nurse who has worked with Native American patients for many years in Arizona and is presently continuing her work in Oklahoma, has recorded several observations of Navajo behavior. Many of Hanley's observations were similar to those mentioned by Hall. In addition, Hanley noted that some Navajo were present-time oriented. Thus time was casual and relative to needs that must be accomplished in a present-time frame, and so some Navajo homes had no clocks. She further observed that some Navajo are considered more "being" oriented than "achievement" oriented, which means that some Navajo perceived individuals as being more important than possessions, wealth, or material things (Hanley, 1991).

Navajo Beliefs and Practices

Traditionally, the basis of Navajo belief system is centered around the Navajo word *hozho*, that summarizes the ultimate goal of the Navajo world. *Hozho* represents a combination of many ideas, including beauty, goodness, and harmony. Traditionally, some Navajo have perceived health as not limited to one's physical body but also involving harmony with one's family, natural environment, and community, as well as with supernatural forces. Some individuals have held the belief that health and religion are inseparable in the Navajo world, forming a strong link between traditional religion and healing ceremonies. Along with the good and beauty of the world, traditional beliefs have acknowledged the coexistence of evil elements. Therefore, many Navajo ceremonies have been designed to prevent or eliminate these evil influences. Examples of such ceremonies include the Blessingway, the Kinaalda, and the healing Nightway.

The Blessingway

The Blessingway rite may be performed in variations for different purposes. For example, the rite may be used to protect sheep herds, to bless a new marriage, to assist through childbirth, or to guard a warrior or soldier in battle. The ceremony usually involves participants praying and singing over a period of one day and two nights.

The Kinaalda

The Kinaalda, a version of the Blessingway, is usually a four-day ceremony performed for Navajo girls at puberty. Because traditionally girls would marry shortly after puberty, this was a premarriage blessing. Traditionally, the Kinaalda ceremony provided the young girl with the opportunity to learn from older women about the expectations of an adult, a good mother and wife, a strong person, and a good weaver.

The Nightway

The Navajo Nightway is a healing practice during which a sick individual attempts to reharmonize, reorder, and rebalance his/her relationships with another and/or with the universe. Traditionally, the belief has been that symptoms of illness manifest when relationships are out of balance. The Nightway chant (Chantway) is led by a properly prepared Medicine man, knowledgeable about the intricate and detailed practices. Unlike the Shaman, who has a "gift," the Medicine man does not necessarily have a "gift"; but he must apprentice for years, memorize details of esoteric chants, songs, prayers, and sandpainting techniques, and also abide by rigid behavioral restrictions.

The purpose of a Nightway sandpainting is to create a beautiful masterpiece that will attract holiness (the Holy People) to bless the proceedings. Traditional belief has held that the Holy People who retreated to the caves, mountains, and sacred places after 1000 A.D. can be attracted to help humans. Because the physical permanency of the sandpainting is not of value to the Navajo, the sandpainting is considered only a means to an end. Consequently, the sandpainting is destroyed after the ceremony, usually at dusk. The purpose of the Nightway ceremony, with the use of sandpaintings, chants, prayers, and order, is to present a perfect and beautiful situation that will attract holiness to bless and restore balance for the healing of a sick individual (Faris, 1990; Hanley, 1991).

The Number Four

Traditionally, four has been an important number for the Navajo, as for many other Native American tribes. It has served as a reminder of the four seasons, the four directions, and the four sacred mountains that mark Navajo land. The four sacred mountains have provided a sense of security for some traditional Navajo. Some believers in the sacredness of the mountains would keep among their possessions four small sacs of earth, one from each of the mountains (Iverson, 1990).

The Navajo Family

The basic family structure is usually nuclear. The traditional Navajo society has been matrilineal, in which women have had strong, influential positions in all phases of life, including economic, political, and religious areas. Although traditional married couples have usually built their homes near that of the wife's mother, the husband often maintained strong ties to his mother's family. Extended families, composed of husband, wife, and unmarried children as well as married daughters and their husbands and children, usually lived near each other, forming a cooperative unit that shared economic resources and worked together in farming and house-building. Two or more extended families, bonded together by marriage ties, might also have lived in close proximity as cooperative units. Today the unit is called an "outfit," consisting of from 50 to 200 persons. The outfit usually accepts the informal leadership of the male or female head of the most prominent family. Decisions related to policy are determined by unanimous agreement at public meetings attended by both sexes.

Navajos are also divided into several matrilineal clans, generally named for specific locations. Although clans may reside in areas distant from each other, the clan maintains specific functions. For example, the clan regulates certain activities: One must not marry into the clan of one's mother or father; men may not converse with their mothers-in-law; and brothers and sisters must avoid physical contact and restrict their speech to each other (Farrer, 1991; Grant, 1994; Iverson, 1990; Hall, 1994; Josephy, 1991; Mander, 1991).

Today, the Navajo live on the largest reservation in the United States, where they reside in dispersed settlements rather than in towns or compact villages. Currently, Navajo are well known for their sandpaintings, blankets, rugs, silver with turquoise jewelry ("western jewelry"), and their gambling establishments. Today Navajo culture is in transition. With changes in educational levels, employment, and environment, the Navajo are assimilating more into the dominant American culture, which may be causing conflict with some proponents of tradition and the "old ways" (Hanley, 1991; Viola, 1990).

CHEROKEE AMERICANS

The Cherokee people call themselves *Ani Yunwiya*, which means "principal people" or "real people." It is believed that, nearly 10,000 years ago, the forefathers of the Cherokee entered through Alaska and settled in North and South America. By their defeat of the Creeks and expulsion of the Shawano, the Cherokee claimed all lands from upper Georgia to the Ohio River, including the rich hunting grounds of Kentucky. At the time of European contact, the Cherokee Nation was established in the Southeast, in the Appalachian mountain regions of Carolina and Georgia. Linguistically the Cherokee are of the Iroquoian stock. Thus, linguistics have assumed that the Cherokee and Iroquois are probably related. Both tribes have been known for their superior height and robust stature. The Cherokee language developed into three dialects, which corresponded roughly to the major geographical divisions (lower or eastern, middle, and western) of the Cherokee settlements. The *Elati* dialect, which is now essentially extinct, was from the areas that are now northwestern South Carolina and northeastern Georgia. The other dialects are *Kituhwa*, spoken by settlements of western North Carolina and still spoken by the majority of Cherokee of Qualla Boundary, and *Atali* or *Otali*, spoken in East Tennessee and Oklahoma.

Recorded history began for the Cherokee in 1540, with the arrival of DeSoto in search of gold. The early settlers had not yet penetrated into the interior when they arrived at the Cherokee location in the Southeast. Sustained contact with the Europeans did not occur until later in the seventeenth century. By the early 1700s, the deerskin trade became a successful enterprise for the Cherokee. In exchange for deerskins, the Cherokee received ammunition, guns, metal knives, axes, gardening equipment, beads, clothing, and rum. The guns and ammunition proved to be the most important trade items because they not only facilitated hunting for skins but also improved the effectiveness of warfare. However, in 1738, smallpox, for which the Cherokee had no treatment or natural immunity, was brought into the Carolinas by the settlers. The epidemic killed nearly half of the Cherokee population within a year. In 1776, the Cherokee were driven into the Smokies, and their homes, crops, and livestock were destroyed by settlers.

By 1820, the now well-acculturated Cherokee developed a republican form of government modeled after the U.S. government. Some Cherokee demonstrated a desire for instruction and education. After years of hard work and several failures, a Cherokee named Sequoyay (of white and Indian parentage) completed the Cherokee syllabary (alphabet). The alphabet was approved by the Cherokee chiefs in 1821 and became the only alphabet to be developed by one person alone. The syllabary greatly enhanced Cherokee development. Numerous Bible translations, hymnals, and schoolbooks have been printed in the Cherokee syllabary. In 1828, the first newspaper, the *Cherokee Phoenix*, was printed in both English and Cherokee. During the nineteenth century, the Cherokee and the Choctaws, Chickasaws, Creeks, and Seminoles were named the "Five Civilized Tribes." The colonists ascribed this name to the group because they had adapted to the white man's civilization more rapidly than other tribes (Finger, 1991; King, 1979; Mooney, 1982; Nichols, 1986; Sharpe, 1991).

However, the government was determined to drive the Cherokee out of the East. A sad result of this endeavor was the notorious "Trail of Tears."

In the winter of 1838–1939, President Andrew Jackson ordered the removal of the Cherokees (a total of 16,000 people) and their relocation to Oklahoma, west of the Mississippi. During the long trip across to Oklahoma, pushed by government troops, over one-quarter of the Indians died of disease, starvation, and hardship. A few years later one soldier commented that although he had fought in the Civil War and seen men slaughtered by the thousands, the Cherokee removal was the most brutal and cruelest work he had ever seen (Greene, 1994).

A small group of Cherokee that was able to escape the drive hid in the North Carolina mountains where their descendants, the Eastern Cherokees, still reside. Greene (1994) describes in graphic detail the story of one of the groups who escaped to the mountains. The soldiers who had burned Cherokee homes and destroyed their crops were ordered to shoot any Indians who refused to leave for the West. So small groups of Cherokee hid in mountain caves and slept wherever they could find shelter. They had no warm clothing for the winter climate and no food. All their food, stored for these lean winter months, had been left behind during their hurried escape from the soldiers. Without weapons to defend themselves, they were exposed to the many wild animals such as mountain lions, wolves, bears, and snakes. Some individuals who went into the forest in search of food disappeared and were never seen again. Several mothers killed and buried their own children to prevent the suffering of the young and imminent death. Although, historic records establish that about 4,000 Cherokee died during the removal west, there remains no estimate of the high numbers who died in the mountains of exposure, illness, starvation, and wild animals (Greene, 1994).

Finally, in the years 1843–1861, Will Thomas purchased land for the Cherokees remaining in North Carolina; and because Indians were not permitted to purchase land at that time, the deeds were held in trust for them. In 1876, Qualla Boundary (Reservation) was formed, and the Cherokee lands were secured. The Cherokee have since paid for the land in U.S. dollars and prefer that their territory be called "Quallah Boundary" rather than a reservation (J. W. Greene, personal communication, June 2, 1996). Qualla Boundary comprises 56,573 acres of extremely mountainous regions (Smoky Mountains) in western North Carolina, located adjacent to the Great Smoky Mountain National Park (Finger, 1991; King, 1979; Mooney, 1982; Nichols, 1986; Sharpe, 1991). The following discussion will focus on the Eastern Cherokee Band.

The Cherokee Family

Similar to several other traditional Native American tribes such as the Hopi, Iroquois, Huron, Apache, Susquehanna, and Navajo (to name a few), many Eastern Cherokee families have been extended, matrilocal, and matrilineal. Eastern Cherokee families are still essentially matrilineal (R. J. Crow, personal communication, June 1, 1996; Finger, 1991). Interestingly, some of the basic concepts of the traditional Native American family system have been reformulated and reintroduced into American society by participants of the recent feminist movement (Allen, 1992).

Unlike the typically dispersed Navajo units, Cherokee tend to live in villages. Eastern Cherokee towns or settlements consist of individual cabins or frame houses that are small nuclear dwellings in close-knit communities. There are seven Cherokee Clans: Wild Potato, Bird, Long Hair, Blue, Paint, Deer, and Wolf, with seven mother towns that serve as clan headquarters. Some communities have developed a lifestyle similar to that of the Appalachian white residents of the nearby mountain areas. The Eastern Cherokee communities differ in their adherence to traditional concepts and practices because of their varying levels of acculturation (Allen, 1992; Finger, 1991; Josephy, 1991).

Beliefs and Practices

Recently (June 1–2, 1996) I attended an Indian Festival at Sycamore Shoals Historic Center in Tennessee that featured the Eastern Band of Cherokee. I had the opportunity to interview several leading members of the tribe, including John Greene, noted author and archaeologist, Richard Crow, the Cherokee goodwill ambassador, and Morningstar, a dancer. I also listened to interesting and informative lectures on Cherokee religion by Dr. Michael Abram (director of the Cherokee Heritage Museum and Gallery), Cherokee archaeology by John Greene, and Cherokee culture and dance by Richard Crow. Cherokee storytelling was presented by Fred Bradley.

The Cherokee have been religious people. Through the generations, stories have been passed down about spiritual beings who created the earth, sun, and stars. Traditional belief has held that the one supreme being was called *Yowa*, a name so sacred that only certain priests were permitted to speak it out loud. After *Yowa*, the creator, had formed the earth, he left the sun and moon to govern the world and allocated fire and smoke to accept and deliver messages. Therefore one must pray over fire, allowing the smoke, that acts as a messenger, to convey the prayers up to the sun, moon, or god. Some traditional individuals believed in spirits and the afterlife. Archaeologists discovered favorite articles buried with the deceased, perhaps for use in their afterlife (J. W. Greene, personal communication, June 2, 1996). Some traditionalists believed that after death the spirit exits through the head and hovers over the house and then revisits the individual's previous places of residence. Suicide souls hover over the earth forever. Therefore traditional Cherokee rarely, if ever, committed suicide (M. Abram, personal communication, June 1, 1996).

Traditionally, a priest was selected during childhood for complex religious training, including the use of herbs and sacred quartz crystals for religious ceremonies. Crystals were used to make predictions. Dancing and singing were forms of prayer. Instead of wine, the Cherokee sacrament was tobacco.

However, most of the Cherokee ceremonies and religious practices no longer exist today. Although a small number of individuals may still practice some aspects of traditional religions in conjunction with Christianity, most only perform ceremonies for tourists who visit the reservations. Currently, many Eastern Cherokee are affiliated with the Baptist religion. Perhaps because some traditional Cherokee had practiced daily purification rituals of immersion in water to counteract evil and ensure group survival, their attraction to that denomination could be related to the Baptist religion's practice of baptism by immersion. However, churches of many Christian denominations now exist on Qualla Boundary (Finger, 1991; Sharpe, 1991).

The Number Seven

Seven is a sacred number to the Cherokee people. Traditionally, seven women served as counselors for the government. Traditional council houses were seven sided, with sections of seats for representatives of the seven clans. Some Cherokee conceptualized life in seven dimensions. In addition to the four directions, of north, east, south, and west, there were also upper, center, and lower dimensions. The upper world was ruled by birds, the lower world by insects and rattlesnakes, and the center world by animals. Traditional Cherokee observed seven festivals, six of which were performed each year and the seventh, once every seven years. The ceremonies consist of the First New Moon of Spring in March, Green Corn in August, Ripe Corn in September, Great New Moon in October, Friendship or Atonement in November, Bouncing Bush Feast in September, and the Chief Dance every seventh year (M. Abram, personal communication, June 1, 1996; Sharpe, 1991).

The People

The current chief of the Eastern Cherokee is a woman, Joyce Dugan. As people the Eastern Cherokee have been described as peaceful and law-abiding, kind, generous, hospitable, and self-reliant. Today, the Cherokees are noted for their skillful and intricately woven baskets and their beadwork jewelry, pottery, and exquisite wood carvings. Many Cherokee experience a fairly comfortable lifestyle, similar to that of some of their white neighbors. Cherokee wear mainstream American clothing. According to Crow (R. Crow, personal communication, June 1, 1996), Cherokee are not fancy dressers like some of the traditional Plains Indians. They may adorn regalia to entertain tourists (Finger, 1991; Mooney, 1982).

Today, although some Eastern Cherokees have small farms where they produce corn and tobacco and are expert craftspeople, their major livelihood is derived from tourism and Cherokee Bingo Extravaganzas. Casino gambling was introduced by the Bureau of Indian Affairs against the wishes of many Cherokee (J. W. Greene, personal communication, June 2, 1996). Tourism has had a twofold influence on today's Cherokee identification. It has provided the Indians with a profitable access to modern America, while at the same time motivating a continued awareness of their Cherokee identity and the necessity to maintain knowledge of traditional ways, at least for the sake of the tourists (Grant, 1994; Finger, 1991; Viola, 1990).

NATIVE AMERICAN THEMES

Acknowledging the diversity of Native American cultures, the literature has noted certain central themes that apply to a significant number of Native Americans. A traditional theme for some tribes has been that life is infused with spiritual forces that connect humans with all other living forms, and thus there is no clear distinction between the spiritual and the material worlds. The two worlds have been viewed as different expressions of the same reality, life having both spiritual and material manifestations that are mutually interchangeable. Thus mind, spirit, and matter are not separate entities, but one and the same. Therefore some Native Americans have believed that there is no separation between humans and the environment; nature and humans are of equal value and exist in harmony and unity (Allen, 1992; Brown, 1992a).

Another basic traditional theme for some Native Americans has been the belief that life is a series of relationships that are central to the tribal system. These relationships are always expanding outward from the immediate family, to the extended family to the clan, to the tribe, and finally to the environment and the universe. All creatures are viewed as equal and related; unlike non-Indian thought, there is no hierarchical ladder that perceives man (not woman) on the highest rung, but land, trees, and animals on the lowest level (Allen, 1992).

Traditional Native American belief has held that there is an equal relationship between people and their land; so that one's environment (Place) becomes a reflection of one's soul. Thus, to some Native Americans, there is an identification or internalized bonding with their Place. Some individuals have believed that because the environment affects humans and humans affect the environment, most activities should be directed toward maintaining this mutual reciprocal relationship (Cajete, 1995).

Associated with the belief of relationships is the theme of reciprocity, that means if one takes away or receives, one must give back. If humans take care of the land, the land will take care of them, because the forces of life move in a circle.

This introduces another important traditional theme, the traditional belief that all forces of the world work in cycles or circles. For example, the sun, sky, moon, and earth are circles; birds' nests are circular; the greatest force of the wind moves in a circle; the process of breathing is circular, and life is a circle. Some traditional Native Americans have perceived the biological interdependence of life as continuous, circular activity, representing a perfectly balanced and complete circle in which nothing is wasted or lost (Allen, 1992; Cajete, 1995; Josephy, 1991).

Traditionally, some Laota Native Americans have held the belief that young children and old people relate especially well because the young child has recently arrived from the "Great Mysterious" (*Wakan Tanka*) to which the old person will soon return. Consequently, in a circular time sequence, they are close together, resulting in a naturally strong attraction between children and their grandparents (Brown, 1992a).

Childrearing

Most Native American families consider a child a blessing and of equal status to any other member in the extended family regardless of age. Traditionally, childrearing was not only the responsibility of the immediate family but also the responsibility of clan and other tribe members. Except for the first six years, when the child learned from the mother, training of the child was often assigned to an uncle, an aunt, or grandparents. Traditionally, the father was rarely assigned as a tutor because it was believed that the relationship between the father and child was too personal to cultivate an objective learning atmosphere (Shield, 1995; Tafoya, 1995).

Some traditional mothers have been quite permissive, allowing the child to explore and experience the environment. At an early age the child was taught the importance of harmony with the environment and that all forms of life were sacred. These ideas were later reinforced by special ritual ceremonies and rites of initiation (Buckley, 1992). Traditionally, children have been expected to learn by observing and listening to adults, especially the elders. Thus, important life concepts could be learned best by observing, listening to the Storytellers, and through the experience of personal successes and failures (Benedict, 1995: Pelletier, 1995).

Traditionally, some Native Americans have viewed education as a lifelong process rather than a destination. Education has been conceptualized as the sum total of learning acquired through interaction with one's environment, family, and community members. Education in traditional societies was informal and primarily aimed at preparing the child to survive in the world (Okakok, 1995; Tafoya, 1995).

Today, the boarding school system established by the federal government having ended in the middle of the twentieth century, Native American children attend elementary schools on the reservations or neighboring public schools. According to the Richard Crow, Eastern Cherokee Ambassador of goodwill, "Approximately half of the residents of the Eastern Cherokee reservation are educated" (R. Crow, personal communication, June 1, 1996; Finger, 1991).

Values

Traditional Native American values have embodied the concepts of respect, sharing, interdependence, and harmony. Families have emphasized cooperation instead of competition, and generosity and compassion rather than materialism (Whirlwind Soldier, 1995).

Elderly

Traditionally, many Native American children have been taught to respect their elders. It has been believed that as children are bridges to the future, elders are bridges to the past and that, therefore, both are important to complete the circle of life. Some elders have had the responsibility of instructing and guiding the younger members of the tribe. Also many elders have been expected to remember the past and to preserve their Indian heritage. An Apache imperative for moral behavior is to honor and care for the elders because only old people have lived long enough to know all things. Consequently, no proper family would allow its old members to experience need or to live alone (Allen, 1992; Farrer, 1991; Lamb-Richmond, 1995).

RELIGION

Native American tribal culture reflects their religious beliefs. While some tribes conceptualized a Supreme Being, others did not. Many Plains Indians believed in *Wakan Tanka*, the Great God or Great Mysterious; and the Mojave conceptualized the *Mayavilya*, who was born from the union of earth and sky, as their Supreme Being. Most tribes held some belief about the creation of the world. The Poma of California attributed creation to a god, *Madunda*; the Five Civilized tribes attributed it to *Breath-Holder* or *Master of Breath*; and the Pueblos believed that the earth was created by *Thought Woman* or the *Spider grandmother*. Traditional religious beliefs held by some Native Americans accept the coexistence of numerous spirits, gods, and goddesses. Most of the gods and goddesses were represented by the shapes of animals, familiar in the territory of the particular tribe. Gods were believed to dwell in such places as mountains, rivers, woods, lakes, lightning, rainbows, and so on. In conjunction, some Native Americans have depended on various rituals and ceremonies that serve to support and intensify their beliefs. Shamans, the central figures in rituals, ceremonies, divine experiences, and healings, have been considered religious specialists (Eliade & Couliano, 1991; White, 1980).

Some Northeastern Indians have believed that a sacred power, being either good or evil, dwelled in certain things and could communicate with humans. The Algonquins called this power *Manitu*, the Huron called it *Oki*, and it was known as *Orenda* by the Iroquois. Many Indians of the Southeast Coast, such as the Cherokee, have believed in witchcraft and counteractive rituals. The practice of all-night vigils at the home of a recently deceased person may reflect a traditional Cherokee desire to protect the dead from witches (Eliade & Couliano, 1991; Finger, 1991).

Today many Native Americans have adopted the Christian faith, although several tribes maintain knowledge about their religious rituals and ceremonies. Some practice both Christianity and their traditional religion. For example, the Native American Church is a widespread religion that incorporates Indian beliefs and elements of Christianity. An important rite of this religion is the eating of peyote (a nonaddictive substance obtained from the mescal cactus). Peyote produces hallucinations to help induce contact with the supernatural during religious ceremonies (Josephy, 1991; Viola, 1990).

Rituals and Ceremonies

The Vision Quest

A traditional ritual, central to the lives of Plains Indians, has been the "Vision Quest" or "Guardian Quest." Before a person retreated on a vision quest, he or she experienced a ritualized preparation that included the rites of the purifying *sweat lodge* in addition to instructions from qualified elders. During the sweat lodge ritual, a group of individuals (usually males) would dance and sing while whipping themselves with twigs under intense heat created by heated stones. The sweat lodge was intended to purify the warrior or visionary. Once the visionary was alone at the distant place, the sacred experience would be revealed in the form of an animal or a power of nature, at which time a special message was conveyed to the individual in a vision. This vision, that would act as a guide throughout the individual's life, could also stimulate some artform or serve as the origin of special powers (such as those of a Shaman) and/or introduce guardian spirits. Native Americans differentiate between hallucinations and visions. A hallucination is a fantasy, perhaps a result of wishful thinking, while a vision is the objective perception of spiritual facts manifested in the physical (Brown, 1992b; Buckley, 1992; Eliade & Couliano, 1991).

Smoking the Peace Pipe

Traditionally the calumet, or peace pipe, has been a highly sacred object to Native Americans from the East Coast to the Rockies. Some of the reasons for smoking the calumet (performed in a circular seated group) have been to seal a peace pact, to bring about good weather for travel or ideal conditions for hunting, to bring rain, to replace evil with good, or to assure victory in warfare. The ritual of smoking the calumet demonstrates the importance of relationships while also achieving a sense of purification (Brown, 1992b; Grant, 1994).

The Sun Dance

The highest religious expression of the Plains Indians has been the Sun Dance. Some of the tribes that perform the Sun Dance include the Arapaho, Cheyenne, Siksika, Cree, Dakota, Assiniboin, Mandan, Crow, Pawnee, and Ute. Sun Dance ceremonies have been based on the affirmation that only through suffering and sacrifice can one attain sacredness. The ceremony honors all life and its source in order that life may continue in its cycle. The Sun Dance, often a four-day ceremony, has usually been held during the full moon in June. The participant, who must fast throughout the ceremony, dances and blows a whistle made from a hollow bone of an eagle's wing. In traditional practices, the dancer was attached to a central pole by a string connected to a stick that pierced two holes cut in his chest muscles. The participant, scantily clad, danced while looking at the sun from sunrise to sunset until he could free himself by tearing out his flesh. Some participants collapsed from pain, hunger, and exhaustion. Today the Sun Dance is generally held only as a ceremony, without the torture and hardships (Brown, 1992b; Grant, 1994; Viola, 1990).

The Powwow

The *powwow* originally was a term applied to feasts, dances, and public meetings of Indians prior to a grand hunt, a war expedition, or a council. Later, when clans held councils to decide special matters, the occasion was called a powwow. Today, every summer, thousands of Native Americans participate in weekend powwows across the United States and Canada. Participants, ranging in age from two to eighty-two, dressed in splendid, colorful, full tribal regalia, dance to the rhythm of drumbeats and sing in Native American languages. In keeping with the belief that the circle represents equality, all powwow activities revolve around a drum located at the center of an arena (Grant, 1994; Livingston, 1992).

The powwow is one of the most visible expressions of Indianness today. It serves as a social gathering, a family reunion, a celebration of heroes, and an occasion for spiritual renewal. The protocol and full regalia are intended to keep the tradition of the ancestors alive for future generations. Powwows include Native Americans of all tribes, clans, and divisions. The tribes also invite non-Indians to enjoy a uniquely American cultural experience, glimpsing the private world of Native Americans without infringing on sacred ceremonies. Oklahoma's Red Earth Festival is the largest powwow in the United States. Beginning with an opening-day parade through downtown Oklahoma City, the festivities include dance and drum competitions, fashion shows, art exhibits, and a film festival (Viola, 1990).

INTERMARRIAGE

Over the generations, intermarriages have occurred between Native Americans and the colonists. In the western areas of former French colonial dominion, the Ottawa, Potawatomi, Chippewa, and Sioux have had extensive intermarriage with the French. The French spouses tended to move into the tribe and assume tribal practices; thus, except for French Catholicism, the French had minimal cultural influence on the tribes. Today one may readily observe the overpowering influence of the Spanish/Mexican culture that engulfed the Indians of the Southwest to form a strong Mexican ethnic group. Intermarriage between Indians and Anglos has greatly enhanced Native Americans' acculturation into mainstream American culture. Individuals of mixed blood have long dominated the political affairs of the "Five Civilized Tribes," and many famous Oklahoma politicians are mixed-blood Native Americans.

Marriage between tribes became a dynamic experience after Native Americans were settled on reservations. Tribal intermarriage has resulted in the fusing together of similar tribal behaviors and a strengthening of an Indian heritage consciousness. The effect of this tribal fusion has been a recent emergence of a national sense of pan-Indianism (Deloria, 1992; Finger, 1991).

SOCIOECONOMIC STATUS

Generally, Native American income and educational levels tend to be low, with about one in four individuals living below the poverty level (Healthy People 2000, 1990). Fourteen percent of Native American adults aged 18–24 are currently enrolled in college. Of this age group, 53.8% are high school graduates or higher, and 39% have bachelor's degrees (U.S. Bureau of the Census, 1990).

Native Americans living in metropolitan areas usually have better employment opportunities than those individuals in non-metropolitan areas and reservations, where earnings are 81% that of metropolitan Native Americans (Snipp & Sandefur, 1988). The unemployment rate on reservations ranges from 65–80%; one-third of the residents exist below the poverty level (Udall, 1990).

NUTRITION

The diets of Native Americans often vary with the wild foods that are available in their areas of residence and any affordable commercial foods.

For example, Native Americans in the Northwest eat a variety of seafood, whereas inhabitants of the inland mountainous areas eat more dried meats and freshwater fish. The diets of tribes in the Southwest are similar to those of Mexican Americans, consisting of such favorites as tortillas, refried beans (frijoles refritos), and fried bread (sopapillas).

Today, the daily meals of many Native Americans may consist of a blend of traditional and American foods. Complete traditional meals are usually served on special occasions and generally incorporate foods that have a religious or ceremonial significance. Some favorite traditional foods include maize or Indian corn, fry bread, piki bread, corn soup, chili stew, acorn bread, smoked salmon eggs, deer meat, and the fruits, leaves, and roots of wild plants (Allen, 1992; Ensminger et al., 1994).

Native American diets have become Americanized, as have many other ethnic food patterns during the processes of acculturation and assimilation. It is believed that dietary and nutritional change is a major factor in the changing pattern of Native American diseases. Recently, a nature writer, Gary Paul Nabhan, investigated how the loss of traditional crops affected the health of Native Americans in the Southwest. He observed that since about 1940, when Native Americans started consuming store-bought, Anglo foods, they have suffered from several diseases previously unknown to them. Today, Southwestern Native Americans have the highest incidence of diabetes in the world, whereas their traditional foods such as mesquite, cholla cactus buds, prickly pear fruit and pads, and chia seeds were believed to actually delay the release of sugar into the bloodstream (Goodstein, 1993).

HEALTH

In general the Native American population, on and off reservations, is young, with a median age of 23, as compared to the median of 32 and older for the total United States population. The reason for the youthfulness of their population is that a large proportion of Native Americans die before the age of 45. Leading causes of Native American deaths are unintentional injuries (such as motor vehicle accidents that are usually alcohol related), cirrhosis of the liver, homicide, suicide, pneumonia, and complications of diabetes. Heart disease, cancer, and stroke are not among the major causes of death, probably because these are generally diseases of old age. However, many Oklahoma Native Americans are heavy smokers and show a lung cancer rate that is twice as high as that for the total United States population. A high incidence of obesity among Native Americans contributes to the high rate of diabetes (Healthy People 2000, 1990; Young, 1994).

In certain areas, especially in Oklahoma, a high rate of alcohol-related deaths are reported. Homicide and suicide are often alcohol related. The high rate of alcohol abuse extends into the future generations in the form of fetal alcohol syndrome. It has been estimated that 95% of Native American families are in some way affected by a family member's alcohol abuse. However, continuing progress is being made by the Indian Health Service as well as by individual tribes in improving the health status of Native Americans (Healthy People 2000, 1990; Young, 1994).

NATIVE AMERICAN IMPACT ON AMERICAN CULTURE

It has generally been accepted that acculturation occurs in both directions when two societies are in prolonged contact. Thus, even a subjugated people can have an important impact on their conquerors' culture.

Native Americans selected most of the sites now occupied by great American cities, and they plotted the trails now occupied by highways, railways, and canals. Thousands of cities, states, mountains, lakes, rivers, and other geographical sites have Indian names. Familiar cities with Indian names include Chattanooga, Chicago, Kalamazoo, Miami, Milwaukee, Muncie, Omaha, Oshkosh, Spokane, Schenectady, Seattle, Tucson, and Wichita. Americans today use many Native American inventions such as canoes, toboggans, cigars, cigarettes, hammocks, ponchos, parkas, and moccasins. The rubber ball and game of lacrosse were adopted from Native American games. Americans drive Pontiac and Jeep Grand Cherokee cars and ride in trains named "Hiawatha" and "The Chief" (Josephy, 1991; Worton, 1974). In addition Native Americans have enriched the English language with their names for animals (e.g., chipmunk, cougar, moose, opossum, raccoon, skunk, woodchuck) and trees (e.g., hickory, pecan, persimmon, tamarack). American athletic teams are named "Black Hawks," "Braves," "Redskins," and "Warriors" (Josephy, 1991; Worton, 1974).

Native Americans have had a significant influence on American literature, as exemplified by Longfellow's *Hiawatha* and Cooper's *Last of the Mohicans*. Many other famous authors have written stories with Indian themes. Early movies did not portray Native Americans in a positive light. However, recently, the screen has presented some sympathetic and dignified portrayals in such movies as *Broken Arrow, Devil's Doorway, Cheyenne Autumn*, and *Dances with Wolves*. Some Native Americans who were extremely pleased with *Dances with Wolves* expressed the feeling that the movie had nourished an intense sense of pride in their "Indianness" (Allen, 1992; Worton, 1974)

Americans have learned much from selected Native American concepts. The concept of democratic government, reflecting the equality of individuals, universal suffrage for women and men, and respect for the diversity of individuals, was practiced by some Native American tribes before Columbus arrived. The Indian shamans gave attention to an individual's mental health as well as physical illness, in order to place the person in balance with the environment or universe. Today, popular concepts of health define good health as appropriate adaptation to or interaction with one's environment. Recently psychosomatic medicine has become attentive to the Indian concept of mind and body interaction. Today, environmentalists are turning to the traditional Indian land rites based on the concept that "we are not outside nature, but of it" (Josephy, 1991, p. 33). During recent years conservationists and environmentalists are seeing the value in the Indian lesson that we must learn to live with nature, rather than try to conquer it (Josephy, 1991).

And finally, Native Americans have served the country in both world wars. During World War II, Navajo Marine "code talkers" helped maintain the security of American troops by transmitting orders in their tribal languages. Thousands of Native Americans served in Korea and Vietnam, and over 12,500 fought in the Gulf War (Allen, 1992; Viola, 1990).

SUMMARY AND CONCLUSIONS

Whether Spanish, English, French, or American, colonists of foreign heritage strived to eradicate "Indianness" from the Indians, if not to eliminate Indians altogether. The conquistadors conquered the Indians. The colonists fought them and confiscated their lands. Missionaries christianized them. Epidemics of European disease destroyed them. And the American government tried to Americanize them. Today, however, Native Americans have survived as a unique and progressive group within American society.

Native Americans' ethnicity is attributed less to racial and cultural homogeneity than to historical and political factors. Native Americans are a large group of diverse people who occupy land areas rather than a nationalistic consciousness with historic homogeneous roots. Native American tribes have managed to keep their identities as distinct national groups, maintaining a traditionalism that provides a recognizable identity (Deloria, 1992).

Native Americans have separate laws that deal with tribal and Indian rights. Native Americans are a distinct group with legal standing and entitled to certain privileges from the federal government. Native American protests were distinct from other American group protestors, for example Native Americans carefully kept their concerns separate from those of African Americans and chose not to participate in the civil rights movements of the 1960s (Finger, 1991).

Many Native Americans who have married into other cultures or have left the reservation and intermingled with other ethnic groups in urban areas have become exposed to different values. In the process of assimilation away from the tribe, many of these individuals have experienced a sense of being an ethnic minority. Thus, the future of Native Americans may be toward a rapidly increasing acculturation, but a much slower assimilation.

REFERENCES

Allen, P. G. (1992). *The sacred hoop: Recovering the feminine in American Indian traditions*. Boston: Beacon Press.

Allen, P. G. (1995). Family is a matter of clan membership. In A. Hirschfelder (Ed.), *Native heritage: Personal accounts of American Indians, 1790 to the present* (pp. 18–19). New York: Macmillan.

Benedict, E. (1995). Through these stories we learned many things. In A. Hirschfelder (Ed.), *Native heritage: Personal accounts of American Indians, 1790 to the present* (pp. 111–12). New York: Macmillan.

Bovet, S. R. (1992). Columbus Quincentenary events reflect America's diversity. *Public Relations Journal*, 48(11), 22.

Brown, J. E. (1992a). Becoming part of it. In D. M. Dooling & P. Jordan-Smith (Eds.), *I become a part of it: Sacred dimensions in Native American life* (pp. 9–20). San Francisco: Harper.

Brown, J. E. (1992b). Sun Dance. In D. M. Dooling & P. Jordan-Smith (Eds.), *I become a part of it: Sacred dimensions in Native American life* (pp. 241–45). San Francisco: Harper.

Buckley, T. (1992). Doing your thinking. In D. M. Dooling & P. Jordan-Smith (Eds.), *I become a part of it: Sacred dimensions in Native American life* (pp. 36–52). San Francisco: Harper.

Cajete, G. A. (1995). Ensoulment of nature. In A. Hirschfelder (Ed.), *Native heritage: Personal accounts of American Indians, 1790 to the present* (pp. 55–57). New York: Macmillan.

Copway, G. (1995) The Ojibway language. In A. Hirschfelder (Ed.), *Native heritage: Personal accounts of American Indians, 1790 to the present* (pp. 63–64). New York: Macmillan.

Crawford, J. T. (1992, September 30). Coercive anglicization has taken more from Native Americans than a set of linguistic skills. *Chronicle of Higher Education*, 39(6), B5.

Crow, R. (1996, June). Interview with Richard Crow, Eastern Cherokee Ambassador of good will. Sycamore Shoals Indian Festival, Elizabethton, Tenn.

Deloria, V., Jr. (1992). American Indians. In J. D. Buenker & L. A. Ratner (Eds.), *Multiculturalism in the United States: A comparative guide to acculturation and ethnicity* (pp. 31–52). Westport, Conn.: Greenwood Press.

Dooling, D. M., & Jordon-Smith, P. (1992). *I become a part of it: Sacred dimensions in Native American Life*. San Francisco: Harper.

Eliade, M., & Couliano, I. P. (1991). *The Eliade guide to world religions*. San Francisco: Harper.

Ensminger, A. H., Ensminger, M. E., Konlande, J. E., & Robson, J. R. K. (1994). *Foods and nutrition encyclopedia* (vol. 2) (2nd ed.). Boca Raton, Fla.: CRC Press.

Fagan, B. M. (1987). *The great journey: The peopling of ancient America*. New York: Thames & Hudson.

Faris, J. C. (1990). *The Nightway: A history and a documentation of the Navajo ceremonial.* Albuquerque: University of New Mexico Press.

Farrer, C. R. (1991). *Living life's circle: Mescalero Apache cosmovision.* Albuquerque: University of New Mexico Press.

Finger, J. R. (1991). *Cherokee Americans: The Eastern Band of Cherokees in the Twentieth Century.* Lincoln and London: University of Nebraska Press.

Goodstein, C. (1993). People: Seeding the desert. *Amicus Journal,* 15(5), 16–19.

Grant, B. (1994). *Concise encyclopedia of the American Indian.* New York: Wings Books.

Greene, J. W. (1994). *The narrative of Little Wolf.* N.P.: John W. Greene.

Hall, E. T. (1994). *West of the thirties.* New York: Doubleday.

Hanley, C. E. (1991). Navajo Indians. In J. N. Giger & R. E. Davidhizar (Eds.), *Transcultural nursing: Assessment and intervention* (pp. 215–38). St. Louis: Mosby Year Book.

Healthy People 2000. (1990) *National health promotion and disease prevention objectives.* DHHS Publication No. (PHS) 91–50212. Washington, D.C.: U.S. Department of Health and Human Services, Public Health Service.

Hirschfelder, A. (1995). *Native heritage: Personal accounts of American Indians, 1790 to the present.* New York: Macmillan.

Iverson, P. (1990). *The Navajos.* New York: Chelsea House.

Josephy, A. M., Jr. (1991). *The Indian heritage of America.* Boston: Houghton Mifflin.

King, D. H. (1979). *The Cherokee Nation: A troubled history.* Knoxville: University of Tennessee Press.

Lamb-Richmond, T. (1995). Dear Wunneanatsu. In A Hirschfelder (Ed.), *Native heritage: Personal accounts by American Indians, 1790 to present* (p. 121). New York: Macmillan.

Livingston, L. C. (1992). The American Indian Powwow: Tribal splendor. *Dance Magazine,* 66(6), 45–50.

Major, M. J. (1992). Dancing to a different drummer: How Native Americans view the Columbus Quincentenary. *Public Relations Journal,* 48(11), 20–23.

Mander, J. (1991). *In the absence of the sacred: The failure of technology and the survival of the Indian Nations.* San Francisco: Sierra Club Books.

Mooney, J. (1982). *Myths of the Cherokee and sacred formulas of the Cherokees.* Nashville, Tenn.: Charles and Randy Elder.

Nichols, R. L. (1986). *The American Indian: Past and present* (3rd ed.). New York: Alfred A. Knopf.

O'Hare, W. (1992). America's minorities: The demographics of diversity. *Population Bulletin,* 47(4), 2–47.

Okakok, L. (1995). Education: A lifelong process. In A. Hirschfelder (Ed.), *Native heritage: Personal accounts by American Indians, 1790 to the present* (pp. 122–24). New York: Macmillan.

Pelletier, W. (1995). Learning through listening. In A. Hirschfelder (Ed.), *Native heritage: Personal accounts of American Indians, 1790 to the present* (pp. 105–6). New York: Macmillan.

Pommersheim, F. (1995). *Braid of feathers: American Indian law and contemporary tribal life.* Los Angeles: University of California Press.

Sharpe, J. E. (1991). *The Cherokees past and present: An authentic guide to the Cherokee People*. Cherokee, N.C.: Cherokee Publications.

Shield, P. (1995). I tried to be like my mother. In A. Hirschfelder (Ed.), *Native heritage: Personal accounts of American Indians, 1790 to the present* (pp. 97–99). New York: Macmillan.

Snipp, C. M. (1989). *American Indians: The first of this land*. New York: Russell Sage Foundation.

Snipp, C. M., & Sandefur, G. D. (1988). Earnings of American Indians and Alaska Natives: The effects of residence and migration. *Social Forces*, 66(4), 994–1008.

Tafoya, T. (1995). The old ways teach us. In A. Hirschfelder (Ed.), *Native heritage: Personal accounts of American Indians, 1790 to the present* (pp. 113–15). New York: Macmillan.

Udall, M. K. (1990). Legislation to reauthorize the Indian Alcohol and Substance Abuse Prevention Treatment Act of 1986. *Congressional Record*. Daily edition (March 22), pp. 788–789.

U.S. Bureau of the Census. (1990). *Statistical reports of the United States*. Washington, D.C.: U.S. Government Printing Office.

Viola, H. J. (1990). *After Columbus: The Smithsonian chronicle of the North American Indians*. Washington, D.C.: Smithsonian Books; New York: Orion Books.

Whirlwind Soldier, L. (1995). We must encourage the use of our language. In A. Hirschfelder (Ed.), *Native heritage: Personal accounts of American Indians, 1790 to the present* (pp. 82–85). New York: Macmillan.

White, J. M. (1980). *Everyday life of the North American Indian*. New York: Holmes & Meier.

Worton, S. N. (1974). *The first Americans*. Rochelle Park N.J.: Hayden Book Company.

Young, K. T. (1994). *The health of Native Americans: Toward a bicultural epidemiology*. New York: Oxford University Press.

8

Puerto Rican Americans

The Commonwealth of Puerto Rico is an island of 3,426 square miles, approximately 100 miles long and 35 miles wide, located southeast of Miami. The island is bounded by the Atlantic Ocean on the north and the Caribbean Sea on the south. The capital of Puerto Rico is San Juan. The climate is tropical.

Puerto Ricans are a blended Creole population of Spanish whites, mestizos, native Indians, and African strains, which gives their society a unique polychromatic distinctiveness. The official languages of Puerto Rico are Spanish and English, but Spanish is more popular. Thus, Puerto Ricans may speak Spanish, English, or Spanglish, a combination (Márquez, 1995).

Puerto Rican individuals number 2.7 million, constituting 1.1% of the American population (U.S. Bureau of the Census, 1992). Hispanic individuals represent 9% of the American population. The following percentages indicate the relative position of each Spanish-speaking group within the total Hispanic population:

Mexicans	53.3%
Central and South Americans	10.8%
Cubans	6.6%
Puerto Ricans	
in Puerto Rico	14.8%
on mainland U.S.	9.9%
Other Hispanics	4.5%

The Puerto Rican population on the mainland has increased between

18% and 28% since 1980, which makes Puerto Ricans the fastest-growing ethnic group on the mainland United States (Rodriquez, 1994).

OVERVIEW

History

Columbus arrived at the island of Puerto Rico on his second voyage in 1493. The island was called Boriquen and inhabited by Arawak-Taino and Carib Indians. The island's historical heritage extended back at least 5,000 years before the arrival of Columbus. Puerto Rico became a colony of Spain in 1508, after the arrival of Ponce De Leon, when the island's name was changed from Boriquen to Puerto Rico. Sugar production was introduced, and African slaves replaced the Arawaks as laborers on the growing sugar plantations. As the colonizers expanded further north and south beyond Mexico, Puerto Rico was made a *presidio*, or strategic military outpost, with San Juan heavily fortified to defend the larger empire (Márquez, 1995).

The nineteenth century was marked by explosive population and economic growth, world market integration through plantation production (especially sugar and coffee), increased slave imports from Africa, and increased immigration from the Spanish Canary and Balearic islands and from many foreign countries. However, the final century of Spanish rule witnessed a strengthening of national consciousness and popular unrest. Radical national agitation and insurrection occurred on September 23, 1868, but despite its failure, the day became symbolic as the Declaration of Puerto Rican Independence Day. The years between this *Grito de Lares* and 1898 led to the collapse of Spanish colonization in Puerto Rico. In 1898, after the American victory in the Spanish-American War, Puerto Rico was ceded to the United States. An independence movement grew; in 1917, under the Jones Act, Puerto Ricans were granted U.S. citizenship. This meant that all Puerto Ricans would experience the rights and duties of American citizens, except they need not pay federal income taxes and could not vote in national elections unless they lived on the U.S. mainland. They were now free to travel between their homeland and mainland America (Sánchez-Ayéndez, 1988; Márquez, 1995).

During the early years of American domination there was emphasis on agricultural production of export crops, especially sugar, preferred over coffee by the United States market. The decreased demand for coffee weakened the economy for most coffee plantation owners and led to an exodus of unemployed coffee growers from the inland mountainous areas (where coffee was grown) to coastal sugar cane fields and urban tobacco factories.

Between 1928 and 1940, the island of Puerto Rico suffered the devastating effects of world depression. In 1951, after World War II, "Operation

Bootstrap" was established to help improve the Puerto Rican economy. The concept was to industrialize Puerto Rico by encouraging investments by foreign companies, mainly American, with benefits of low wages and tax incentives. This also fostered the development of Puerto Rico's tourism industry. In 1952, the island became the Commonwealth of Puerto Rico with its own constitution.

Initially there was notable economic improvement in areas such as education, housing, drinking water, and transportation facilities. However, the industries became increasingly capital intensive, with little long-term commitment to the development of the island. Increased population growth on the island and displacement from traditional labor positions resulted in a growing number of Puerto Ricans that could not be accommodated in the island's new industrial system. Also, the decreasing number of jobs required specialized skills. Consequently, many displaced workers migrated to the mainland (Columbia Electronic Encyclopedia, 1994; Sánchez-Ayéndez, 1988; Márquez, 1995; Rodriquez, 1994; Scarano, 1994).

Migration

Puerto Ricans migrated to the mainland United States for various reasons, for example, to improve their economic status, to seek a better life as an American, to join family members already living on the mainland, and to satisfy an adventurous spirit (Rodriguez, 1994). Political and economic ties between Puerto Rico and the mainland United States helped encourage migration. Some incentives were tax breaks granted to mainland firms for doing business in Puerto Rico, the open borders, citizen status, low-cost and accessible air travel, education ties to the mainland, and military opportunities available for Puerto Rican men and women. In the military, Puerto Ricans fought as Americans in World Wars I and II. The first American troops to reach the Yalu River during the Korean War were members of the all–Puerto Rican 65th Infantry Regiment. Puerto Ricans participated heavily and had very high casualty rates in the Vietnam War. Some of the first Americans to sacrifice their lives in the Gulf War and in the Somalian rescue mission were Puerto Ricans (Lamberty & Garcia Coll, 1994b).

Although Puerto Ricans had migrated to New York in the early nineteenth century, the bulk of the migration occurred after the United States takeover in 1898 and may be categorized into three major phases. The first phase consisted of the "pioneers," who arrived between 1900 and 1945 and settled in New York. Also during this period, contract industrial and agricultural laborers arrived and settled in communities outside New York. The first immigration contract group from Puerto Rico after the United States takeover went to Hawaii. However, most of these laborers returned to Puerto Rico at the end of their contract period. Migration was facilitated after 1917, when Puerto Ricans became American citizens.

The second phase of migration, known as the "great migration," occurred between 1946 and 1964. At this time the largest groups arrived and settled in the established Puerto Rican communities of East Harlem and the South Bronx of New York City. Although settlements extended to New Jersey, Connecticut, and Chicago, the bulk of Puerto Rican society continued to reside in New York.

The third and last phase of migration occurred from 1965 to the present and is often called the "revolving door" migration because it has involved a fluctuating pattern back and forth as well as greater dispersion to other parts of the United States, namely, New Jersey, eastern Pennsylvania, and Massachusetts (Rodriquez, 1994).

By 1980, Puerto Rican settlements had expanded to establish some presence in almost every state of the Union, including Hawaii. This immigrant community has grown to include over one-third of the island's total population. New York City still has the largest concentration of Puerto Ricans in the United States, numbering 896,763 in 1990, or 33% of the 2.7 million Puerto Ricans living in mainland America. The population on the island of Puerto Rico numbers 3.8 million (*Columbia Electronic Encyclopedia*, 1994; Falcón, 1995; Hispanic Americans, 1992).

As a result of this bicultural, binational nature, the "new" Puerto Rican's place has been both here and there, between one and the other, with no point of termination. Some Puerto Ricans feel caught up between two worlds, or *entremundos*. The two worlds refer to their island and the mainland United States and to the need to speak two languages, Spanish and English. Some individuals may feel marginal or alienated from one or both worlds (Martinez, 1994). This allegiance to two worlds could be problematic if the individual's lifelong dream is to return to Puerto Rico, thus preventing a sense of settling down in mainland America (Hispanic Americans, 1992; Márquez, 1995).

FAMILY

Traditional Family

Puerto Ricans place high value on family (*la familia*) unity. Family ties and relationships are usually intense. The diversity in family structure is strongly related to location and socioeconomic status. Traditionally, Puerto Rican families have been patriarchal with an extended structure. After the 1960s, the term *modified extended* has best described the family structure of many Puerto Ricans on the mainland United States. The extended and modified family structures have been most prevalent among poverty-level individuals usually residing in ethnic communities of the inner cities. Relocating individuals to public housing separates extended family members because the placements are made based on request priority and availability, rather than on family grouping. Consequently, family members could be sent to public housing units scattered throughout different parts of the city, thereby breaking up strong kinship ties (Mencher, 1995).

Traditionally, the extended family has included not only those related by blood or marriage but also children adopted formally or informally (*hijos de crianza*), grandparents, and grandchildren, as well as members of the *compadrazgo* system. This system involves the relationships among children, godparents, and coparents. Children's sponsors at baptism become godparents (*padrinos*) to their godchildren (*ahijados*) and coparents (*compadres*) with their parents. The functions of the godparents are to offer the children security and provide assistance in times of crisis. The function of the coparents, who may be other than the godparents, is to assume responsibility for the care of children when the natural parents are unable to do so, for whatever reason. A special group of friends may also form a part of the kinship network. Thus, the expression "my friend who is like family" (*como de la familia*) signifies a special friend whose expected intimacy, obligations, and support are similar to those of kin of the family unit.

Puerto Ricans may have a large number of relatives and friends who are available for coping with economic, social, health, and emotional problems. However, they perceive degrees of responsibility on a continuum within the kin structure. Consanguinal kin are more obligated to provide assistance than other kin. The major consanguinal unit includes parents, children, grandparents, grandchildren, siblings, and their families (Garcia-Preto, 1982; Sánchez-Ayéndez, 1988).

Nuclear Family

The nuclear family includes the conjugal unit of parents and children, with weak bonds to the extended family. Middle-class Puerto Rican nuclear families tend to show less group identity and interdependence than extended family members. Higher degrees of acculturation by middle-class Puerto Rican on the mainland United States have emphasized competition and upward mobility and fostered the American concept of feminine independence. Thus many middle-class Puerto Rican husbands tend to exercise less authority over their wives than do lower-income husbands. Although the nuclear family is somewhat isolated and lacks extensive close family networks for support, the Puerto Rican immigrant working class in America has viewed this family structure as a symbol of progress. The relatively small Puerto Rican upper class is characterized by its nuclear family structure, its wealth, and its almost complete acculturation into the "ideal" American life style (Sánchez-Ayéndez, 1988; Torruellas, 1995; Vásquez-Nuttall & Romero-García, 1989).

Single-Parent Family

Recent census data indicate that the percentage of Puerto Rican families headed by females is 38.9%, compared to the national figure of 16.5% for all female-headed households (U.S. Bureau of the Census, 1990). The female-headed family is most prevalent among poverty-level families. Some Puerto Rican women have been able to obtain jobs more readily than their husbands, posing a threat to the traditional concept of male dominance and male authority and challenging the male's dignity and self-esteem. A conflict of values and expectations may have been a significant causative factor in the divorce and separation rate among Puerto Ricans on the mainland (Mencher, 1995; Sánchez-Ayéndez, 1988).

Socialization and Family Values

Kindly keep in mind that there may be differences in cultural beliefs and values among people of the same ethnic group and/or those living in the same community or country. Traditionally, Puerto Rican girls have patterned their modes of behavior after their mothers, female extended family members, and teachers. In mainland America the definition of gender-appropriate behavior has caused some conflict with traditional cultural beliefs. For instance, on the island young Puerto Rican girls were taught to be passive and dependent, whereas mainland behavior patterns encouraged them to be more assertive and independent.

Traditionally, as Puerto Rican women had been socialized to assume the major responsibility for the family household, a formal education was not considered a priority for women. Domestic work for wages or at home became women's primary work. When they entered the labor market, they worked well in the garment industry (sewing, embroidering, etc.), that has been a traditional source of employment for Puerto Rican women on the island and the mainland United States through the 1960s (Chamarro, 1994; Vásquez-Nuttall & Romero-García, 1989).

Traditionally, when the women married and became mothers, they preferred to stay home and focus their energies on developing and maintaining the family. However, this desire to stay home was conditioned by a gender socialization based on patriarchal values that ascribed decision making and authority to the husband. With this ideology of male dominance, female education was further discouraged. So traditional women have been viewed as "of the home" (de la casa), while men have belonged "to the street" (de la calle), proudly maintaining their roles of primary household providers and family protectors.

Family Values

In Puerto Rican culture, the traditional view of women comes from *Marianismo*, that uses the Virgin Mary as a role model. The concept of maleness is referred to as *machismo*. Maleness is associated with virility, sexual aggressiveness, fearlessness, and an ability to be the primary provider and protector of the family (García-Preto, 1982; Sánchez-Ayéndez, 1988).

Prioritizing the family is highly important for most Puerto Ricans. For many, the family may direct their life style by focusing on the values of dignity (*dignidad*), respect (*respeto*), and mutual help (*ayuda mutua*). The concept of personalism (*personalismo*) is a value that stresses individualism and highlights personal qualities that promote internal feelings of worthiness regardless of external or worldly success or failure.

Respect among Puerto Ricans is strongly related to age hierarchy. Respect for elders is based on their status as an older adult and not on their activities or power within the family or community. Children relate to others according to their age, sex, and social class. Respect for authority is strongly emphasized.

The values of mutual assistance and reciprocity are norms that do not require equal exchanges among family members. Family interdependence is perceived as positive, and therefore individuals expect and readily ask for assistance with no detriment to their self-esteem.

Familism, the value of family unity is sustained through close family ties demonstrated by keeping in touch regularly and frequently attending family holiday celebrations and special occasions. Occasions such as weddings and funerals draw many kin together and strengthen family ties (Sánchez-Ayéndez, 1988; Torruellos, 1995).

Puerto Rican emphasis on kinship and dependence on the group are reflections of Taino Indian characteristics. Value placed on preserving a peaceable demeanor is similar to the Taino concept of tranquility. Many aspects of Spanish culture such as pride and dignity, Catholic worship of saints, belief in an afterlife, and a strong sense of family obligation, blended well with the Taino Indian culture and thereby formed the basis of the Puerto Rican value system (Garcia-Preto, 1982).

Today many urban Puerto Rican Americans, both in Puerto Rico and on the mainland United States, are experiencing new social structures and adopting different values that may influence their behavior patterns. Thus traditional Puerto Rican family roles may not necessarily determine social behavior, for many of these roles have been supplemented and sometimes replaced as a result of acculturation. The relatively high rate of out-group marriage has also affected Puerto Rican cultural family values. A recent report by the Latino National Political Survey indicated that 40% of mainland-born Puerto Rican Americans marry Anglos (Cole, 1993). However, traditional cultural values are usually maintained by some first-generation and elderly Puerto Ricans and those individuals who are among the un-acculturated (Mahard, 1989; Padilla, 1995). Acculturation is usually determined by the language spoken. A more precise measure would be to consider the individual's degree of involvement in mainland United States cultural activities as well as distinctive Puerto Rican cultural behaviors, that would indicate degrees of biculturalism. Then one could examine biculturalism in light of the growing appreciation for cultural diversity in the United States (Cortes, Rogler, & Malgady, 1994).

Childrearing

Puerto Rican children are loved and enjoyed, and this affection is demonstrated verbally and nonverbally. Generally, Puerto Rican mothers often smile with and keep close proximity to their children. There is frequent eye contact, hugging, and touching.

Although childrearing patterns differ by socioeconomic class and region, some patterns are almost standard for most Puerto Ricans, especially on the island. Traditionally the sexes have been separated. Girls have experienced restrictions in dress, conduct, freedom, and social associations. In contrast, boys have been less restricted. Acceptable boys' behavior included sexual aggressiveness, physical conflicts, drinking, and rare requirements to perform household duties. Thus traditionally, boys have been characterized as active or restless (*desinquieto*) and daring (*atrevido*), while girls have been viewed as quiet, submissive, dependent, and nondaring. In a recent study, Porrata (1995) found that adolescent Puerto Rican girls scored relatively low on "toughness."

Traditionally, both boys and girls have been expected to obey, submit to, and respect their parents. The father has been the prime disciplinarian who, although not present all day, would lay down a code of behavior and if necessary inflict corporal punishment for disobedience. This punishment was especially severe for the boys. Fathers have generally shown leniency toward their daughters. In the case of a fatherless family, the extended family would provide backup authority members to maintain the discipline. However, in the nuclear family, common after migration, family members often were not available to help. Consequently, the Puerto Rican woman who had been socialized into a role of love and nurturing and to observe distinct differences between the sexes was ill prepared to assume a firm disciplinary role in the absence of a husband. Thus some single mothers have experienced difficulty in disciplining their children. Some of these Puerto Rican mothers tended to be inconsistent, some too strict and others too lenient, fearful of losing the love of their children (Borrás, 1989).

Although a number of Puerto Rican children on the mainland have lived in racially and ethnically segregated urban communities, many have shown a unique characteristic of "resiliency," the ability to bounce back or recover from problems. Some Puerto Rican children may have experienced many stressors and insults, and some may not have had the opportunity to develop fully their innate potential due to social and political forces beyond their control. However, most Puerto Rican children grow up to be competent adults (Lamberty & Garcia Coll, 1994a).

Puerto Rican Elderly

Many of the Puerto Rican elderly living on the mainland United States were born in Puerto Rico and migrated here as part of the large migration wave after World War II. Despite a relatively lengthy period of residence on the mainland, the elderly population is largely unacculturated; the women are less acculturated than the men (if acculturation is mainly determined by language spoken). Elders tend to maintain a strong Puerto Rican identity and may express nostalgia for their island home. Many Puerto Rican elders have demonstrated a preference for using the Spanish language and may thus rely on translators, who are most often their adult daughters. The strength of family ties, respect for the elderly, and the philosophy of mutual help have made the extended family a major resource for elderly Puerto Ricans.

SOCIOECONOMIC STATUS

Poverty has been the most potent factor limiting the options and shaping the life choices of many Puerto Ricans. Researchers (Meléndez, Rodriquez, & Figueroa, 1991; Gurak & Falcón, 1990) have attempted to identify the various social and economic factors that influence the Puerto Rican poverty rate. Many believe that the contraction of the unskilled labor market in the northeastern states, where most Puerto Ricans live, has had a devastating effect on Puerto Ricans employment. Puerto Ricans who had come to the mainland to work in the disappearing industries generally had limited education and were ill prepared to find other kinds of work. This situation often led to family dissolution and other problems. Generally, the major causes for the poverty rate were found to include the following: a decline in manufacturing since the 1960s; discrimination in the labor market; failure of the public schools to educate minority children; high rate of family breakups; a pattern of circular migration between Puerto Rico and the mainland United States; and selective migration of the poorest Puerto Ricans to the mainland (Torruellas, 1995). Middle-class Puerto Ricans who move back to the island decrease the number of economic role models and political leaders for those who remain on the mainland. Therefore, Ramón Daubón of the National Puerto Rican Coalition has noted that "there is no distinctive middle-class Puerto Rican neighborhood in the United States" (Hispanic Americans, 1992, p. 944).

NUTRITION

The basic ingredients of Puerto Rican diets are rice, legumes, and *viandas*. *Viandas* mainly include green banana, green plantain, ripe plantain, yellow sweet potato (*batata amarilla*), white sweet potato (*batata blanca*), breadfruit and cassava. *Viandas* are usually boiled and served hot with oil, vinegar, and codfish. *Sofrito* is a basic sauce often used in cooking, made of tomatoes, onions, garlic, thyme and other herbs, salt pork, green pepper, and fat. Favorite Puerto Rican fruits include acerola, grapefruit, guava, mango, orange, papaya, and pineapple. Some individuals enjoy a strong coffee with milk (*cafe con leche*). The major sources of energy and nutrients in the Puerto Rican diet are rice and *habichuelas* (beans) and salsa (Block et al., 1995; Ensminger et al., 1994).

HEALTH

Common Folk Diseases

Folk diseases are categorized as hot or cold, but treatments may be classed as hot (*caliente*), cold (*frio*), or cool (*fresco*). Cold conditions are treated with hot remedies, while hot diseases are treated with cold or cool remedies. Examples of cold conditions are arthritis and menstruation. The common cold exemplifies a cool condition. Hot conditions include constipation, diarrhea, pregnancy, ulcers. Cool medications and herbs include bicarbonate of soda, milk of magnesia, and tobacco, while hot medications include aspirin, castor oil, penicillin, and vitamins. A similar classification is noted for foods. Some cold foods are avocado, banana, and coconut. Cool foods include barley, whole milk, chicken, and honey. Among the foods classed as hot are alcoholic beverages, chocolate, coffee, and garlic.

Susto is a common folk disease, characterized by sudden fright causing shock, and is treated by rest and relaxation. Another folk disease, *empacho*, is believed to occur when a ball of food adheres to the stomach, causing cramps. It is treated by massaging the abdomen, rubbing the spine, and administering medications. The common folk condition known as evil eye (*mal de ojo*) is manifested by a sudden unexplained illness in a healthy adult or child caused by the powers of a strong person's psyche on a weaker person. *Mal de ojo* may be prevented by the wearing of a special charm, most often placed on babies. Some Puerto Ricans believe in spirits and spiritualism and that conditions caused by evil spirits and forces should be treated by a spiritualist medium. *Botanicas* are special stores in the Puerto Rican community that sell products such as roots, herbs, beads, sprays, ointments, candles, incense, and potions often prescribed by spiritualists.

Folk diseases are treated in various ways. One method is through the use of *Santeria*. Santeria is a Latin American religious belief system that blends Roman Catholic principles and African Yoruba tribal beliefs and practices. Yoruba slaves, brought to the Caribbean during the eighteenth century, associated their deities with Roman Catholic saints (*santos*); thus *Santeria* means "worship of saints." Santeria has an elaborate system of rituals and an acknowledged group of priests known as *santeros*. Individuals may call upon a *santero* not only to help in curing a disease but also to help interact with supernatural forces or to help find a job, and so forth. Santeria believers continue to worship in the traditional manner, especially in Puerto Rico, Cuba, and Brazil (Alonzo & Jeffrey, 1988; Spector, 1991).

Some Current Health Problems

Infants of Puerto Rican-born mothers have a lower risk of low birthweight but a higher risk of neonatal mortality than infants of mainland-born Puerto Rican mothers. Low-birthweight children are likely to experience multiple risks. They are more susceptible to such problems as cognitive delays, school failures, major neurosensory handicaps, plus emotional and other health disorders. Asthma is the most common chronic childhood condition. The highest prevalence of childhood asthma in the United States, both on the mainland and on the island, occurs in the Puerto Rican population. This prevalence of asthma suggests a possible hereditary factor. Folk remedies are frequently used to treat asthma. Another important condition noted in mainland Puerto Rican children is anemia, which may be related to malnutrition and/or lead ingestion in poor housing areas. Other health concerns among children include rheumatic fever and heart conditions (Engel, Alexander, & Leland, 1995; McCarton, Brooks-Gunn, & Tonascia, 1994; Mendoza, Takata, & Martorell, 1994: Pachter, Cloutier, & Bernstein, 1995).

"Attack of nerves" (*ataque de nervios*) is frequently described by some Puerto Ricans. This condition is often diagnosed as a form of anxiety disorder such as panic disorder and/or recurrent major depression and occurs more often in women than in men. *Ataque* victims may demonstrate behavior such as screaming, falling to the ground, and moving extremities wildly. Many folk practitioners believe that this condition will subside spontaneously. Some Puerto Ricans perceive a distinct difference between "nervous" behavior and *loco*. To be *loco* means to be bad and possessed of evil spirits, whereas *ataque* is simply a temporary illness (Liebowitz et al., 1994; Spector, 1991).

Significant proportions of Puerto Rican children and adults are overweight or obese with a tendency for fat to be deposited in the trunk. This finding is consistent across Hispanic groups (Martorell et al., 1994).

REFERENCES

Alonzo, L., & Jeffrey, W. D. (1988). Mental illness complicated by the Santeria belief in spirit possession. *Hospital Community Psychiatry*, 39(11), 1188–91.

Block, G., Norris, J. C., Mandel, R. M., & DiSogra, C. (1995). Sources of energy and six nutrients in diets of low-income Hispanic-American women and their children: Quantitative data from HHANES, 1982–1984. *Journal of the American Dietetic Association*, 95(2), 195–208.

Borrás, V. A. (1989). Dual discipline role of the single Puerto Rican woman head of household. In C. T. García Coll & M. de Lourdes Mattei (Eds.), *The psychosocial development of Puerto Rican women* (pp. 200–213). New York: Praeger.

Chamarro, L. (1994). Cultural beliefs and values: Implications for graduate nursing education in the Puerto Rican community. *Journal of Cultural Diversity*, 1 (2), 41–43.

Cole, A. (1993). Diversity revisited. *Modern Maturity*, 36(4), 10–12.

Columbia electronic encyclopedia (1994). New York: Columbia University Press.

Cortes, D. E., Rogler, L. H., & Malgady, R. G. (1994). Biculturality among Puerto Rican adults in the United States. *American Journal of Community Psychology*, 22(5), 707–21.

Engel, T., Alexander, G. R., & Leland, N. L. (1995). Pregnancy outcomes of U.S. born Puerto Ricans; The role of maternal nativity status. *American Journal of Preventive Medicine*, 11(1), 34–39.

Falcón, A. (1995). Puerto Ricans and the politics of racial identity. In H. W. Harris, H. C. Blue, & E. E. H. Griffith (Eds.), *Racial and ethnic identity: Psychological development and creative expression* (pp. 193–207). New York: Routledge.

Garcia-Preto, N. (1982). Puerto Rican families. In M. McGoldrick, J. K. Pearce, & J. Giordano (Eds.), *Ethnicity and family therapy* (pp. 164–186). New York: Guilford Press.

Gurak, D. & Falcón, L. (1990). *Puerto Ricans: Breaking out of the cycle of poverty.* Washington, D.C.: National Puerto Rican Coalition.

Hispanic Americans. (1992). Why are Puerto Ricans in such dire straits? *CQ Researcher*, 2(40), 944.

Lamberty, G., & Garcia Coll, C. (1994a). Conclusion: Expanding what is known about the health and development of Puerto Rican mothers and children. In G. Lamberty and C. Garcia Coll (Eds.), *Puerto Rican women and children: Issues in health, growth, and development* (pp. 255–76). New York: Plenum Press.

Lamberty, G., & Garcia Coll, C. (1994b). Overview. In G. Lamberty and C. Garcia Coll (Eds.), *Puerto Rican women and children: Issues in health, growth, and development* (pp. 1–10). New York: Plenum Press.

Liebowitz, M. R., Salman, E., Jusino, C. M., Garfinkel, R., Street, L., Cardenas, D. L., Silvestre, J., Fyer, A. J., Carrasco, J. L., & Davies, S. (1994). Ataque de nervios and panic disorder. *American Journal of Psychiatry*, 151(6), 871–75.

Mahard, R. E. (1989). Elderly Puerto Rican women in the continental United States. In C. T. García Coll & M. de Lourdes Mattei (Eds.), *The psychosocial development of Puerto Rican women* (pp. 243–60). New York: Praeger.

Márquez, R. (1995). Sojourners, settlers, castaways and creators: A recollection of Puerto Rico past and Puerto Rico present. *Massachusetts Review*, 36(1), 94–118.

Martorell, R., Mendoza, F. S., Baisden, K., & Pawson, I. G.. (1994). Physical growth, sexual maturation, and obesity in Puerto Rican children. In G. Lamberty & C. Garcia Coll (Eds.), *Puerto Rican women and children* (pp. 119–35). New York: Plenum Press.

McCarton, C. M., Brooks-Gunn, J., & Tonascia, J. (1994). The cognitive behavioral and health status of mainland Puerto Rican children in the infant health and development program. In G. Lamberty & C. Garcia Coll (Eds.), *Puerto Rican women and children* (pp. 161–89). New York: Plenum Press.

Meléndez, E., Rodriquez, C., & Figueroa, J. (1991). *Hispanics in the labor force: Issues and politics*. New York: Plenum Press.

Mencher, J. (1995). Growing up in Eastville, a barrio of New York: A retrospective view. *Annals of the New York Academy of Sciences*, 749, 51–59.

Mendoza, F. S., Takata, G. S., & Martorell, R. (1994). Health status and health care access for mainland Puerto Rican children: Results from the Hispanic Health and Nutrition Survey. In G. Lamberty & C. Garcia Coll (Eds.), *Puerto Rican women and children* (pp. 211–27). New York: Plenum Press.

Nazario, T. (1986). Social support networks of migrant Puerto Rican women. Doctoral dissertation, Boston University.

Pachter, L. M., Cloutier, M. M., & Bernstein, B. A. (1995). Ethnomedical remedies for childhood asthma in a mainland Puerto Rican community. *Archives of Pediatric and Adolescent Medicine*, 149(9), 982–88.

Padilla, E. (1995). Retrospect of ethnomedical research among Puerto Ricans living at the margin of East Harlem. *Annals of the New York Academy of Sciences*, 749, 41–51.

Porrata, J. L. (1995). Scores on psychoticism of adolescent girls in Puerto Rico. *Psychological Report*, 73(3, part 1), 808–10.

Rodriguez, C. E. (1994). A summary of Puerto Rican migration to the United States. In G. Lamberty and C. Garcia Coll (Eds.), *Puerto Rican women and children: Issues in health, growth, and development* (pp. 11–28). New York: Plenum Press.

Sánchez-Ayéndez, M. (1988). The Puerto Rican American family. In C. H. Mindel, R. W. Haberstein, & R. Wright, Jr. (Eds.), *Ethnic families in America: Patterns and variations* (pp. 173–95). New York: Elsevier.

Scarano, F. A. (1994). Writing Puerto Rican history: The challenge of synthesis. *Social Studies*, 81(1), 16–20.

Spector, R. (1991). *Cultural diversity in health and illness* (3rd ed.). Norwalk, Conn.: Appleton & Lange.

Torruellas, R. M. (1995). Mi sacrificio bien pago: Puerto Rican women on welfare and family values. *Annals of the New York Academy of Sciences*, 749, 177–87.

U.S. Bureau of the Census. (1992). *Statistical abstract of the United States*. Washington, D.C.: U.S. Government Printing Office.

Váquez-Nuttall, E., & Romero-García, I. (1989). From home to school: Puerto Rican girls learn to be students in the United States. In C. T. García Coll & M. de Lourdes Mattei (Eds.), *The psychosocial development of Puerto Rican women* (pp. 60–83). New York: Praeger.

9

West Indian Americans

"West Indian" generally refers to people from the English-speaking Caribbean, the island colonies formerly known as the British West Indies. West Indians show cultural similarities to people of the neighboring Spanish-speaking islands of Puerto Rico, Cuba, and the Dominican Republic, as well as to French-speaking Martinique, Guadeloupe, and Haiti. Jamaica, Trinidad/Tobago, and Barbados, among the largest English-speaking West Indian islands, are addressed individually later in this chapter.

The ancestors of most West Indians were African slaves transported to the West Indies during the sixteenth century, mainly from Sierra Leone, Guinea, Ghana, the Ivory Coast, and Nigeria. The descendants of these Africans comprise about 50% to 85% of the population of the West Indies, although two-fifths of Trinidad's population and one-half that of Guyana are East Indians. Descendants of the British, French, Spanish, and Dutch settlers constitute about 5% of the West Indian population, and their languages are spoken on the islands. African, East Indian, European, and Chinese influences have produced a definite multicultural flavor to the West Indies (Chaney, 1987; Halliburton, 1994; Lassiter, 1994).

The Spanish and French had named the islands the Antilles, after the legendary Atlantic island of Antilla. The term, Antilles, has been used to distinguish the islands by size: Greater Antilles and Lesser Antilles. The Lesser Antilles have also been called the Caribbees and often divided into the Windward Islands and Leeward Islands, describing their position relative to the northeast trade winds. Political changes have caused important alterations in terminology with respect to the islands. The former British colonies of Antigua and Barbuda, the Bahamas, Barbados, Dominica, Grenada, Jamaica, St. Kitts-Nevis, Saint Lucia, St. Vincent and Trinidad and

Tobago are now independent and no longer called the British West Indies. Although the name West Indies is still used, they officially refer to themselves as the Commonwealth Caribbean.

Four island chains comprise the West Indies archipelago. The northernmost consists of the Bahama Islands, about 20 inhabited islands, stretching southeastward from Florida. The second and largest chain, extends from Cuba through Hispaniola (shared by Haiti and the Dominican Republic) and Jamaica to Puerto Rico. This chain is sometimes called the Greater Antilles because it contains nine-tenths of the 91,000 square-mile area that constitutes the over a thousand islands of the West Indies; Cuba alone covers almost half of the total land area of the archipelago. This chain has the highest mountain range of the Caribbean; the highest peak is Pico Duarte, in the Dominican Republic.

The third or eastern chain consists of two groups of small mountainous islands. One group curves north from Grenada through the miniature islands known as the Grenadines, by way of St. Vincent, Saint Lucia, Martinique, Dominica, the western half of Guadeloupe, Montserrat, and Nevis to St. Kitts and the Virgin Islands. The other group of the eastern chain, lying east of the former group, consists of low-lying coral islands including Barbados, the eastern half of Guadeloupe, Antigua, Barbuda, and Anguilla.

In contrast to the arid conditions of many of the others, the islands of the fourth chain have more lush tropical greenery. They lie off the coast of Venezuela and include Aruba, Caraçao, Bonaire, Margarita, and Trinidad and Tobago (*Collier's Encyclopedia*, 1996; Internet: Columbia University Press, 1996).

Most of the islands of the Antilles are actually the peaks of a mountain range called the Caribbean Andes that sank beneath the sea millions of years ago and therefore some of the islands are rugged and mountainous. The tropical climate and clear water beaches of the islands provide ideal tourist attractions. Tourism and the export of sugar, rum, and bauxite are the major industries of the West Indies (Anthony, 1989; Halliburton, 1994; Internet: Columbia University Press, 1996).

Population in the United States

The total number of Caribbean-born individuals residing in the United States is estimated at 1,987,000, representing 9.2% of the total American population. United States population numbers according to country of ancestry are: Jamaica, 343,000; Trinidad and Tobago, 119,000; and Barbados, 44,000; these numbers represent 1.7%, 0.6%, and 0.2%, respectively, of the total American population. Including immigrants and their offspring, there are about 700,000 West Indians in the United States. Thirty percent of the immigrants are naturalized citizens (U.S. Bureau of the Census, 1990).

West Indians are the largest black population to migrate voluntarily to the United States. Currently about 60% of their population in the United States is of the third and later generations. West Indian Americans comprise approximately 10% of the African American population (Klevan, 1990; Palmer, 1995).

Although most West Indians have settled in New York, New Jersey, and the Connecticut tristate area, sizeable numbers also reside in Los Angeles, Chicago, Atlanta, Boston, Miami, and Washington, D.C. Canada also has a notable West Indian population. Despite the geographical proximity of the West Indies to Miami, New York remains the major port of entry for West Indians. New York City has the largest Caribbean population in the world, surpassing those of Kingston, Jamaica; San Juan, Puerto Rico; and Port-of Spain, Trinidad, combined. Sutton (1987) refers to New York as the "Caribbean crossroads" of the world because it contains the most diverse mixture of Caribbean people. The greatest New York residential concentration of West Indians was in Harlem before 1940 (one-quarter of Harlem's population), but is presently in the predominantly black neighborhoods of Brooklyn from Crown Heights to Flatbush (Klevan, 1990; Sutton, 1987).

Most Caribbean groups in the United States have established communities that mirror a province of their homeland. English-speaking West Indians and Creole/French-speaking Haitians tend to reside in relatively close proximity to each other in this country. On the other hand, West Indians exhibit more residential separation from Spanish-speaking Caribbeans (Dominicans and Cubans) than do native African Americans from Puerto Ricans (Sutton, 1987).

LARGE WEST INDIAN ISLANDS

Jamaica

Jamaica lies in the Caribbean, south of Cuba, between Haiti and Central America. The terrain is mountainous, bordered by coastal plains and sandy beaches. Jamaica, located in the hurricane belt, has a damp tropical climate with variations of high temperatures on the coast mitigated by cool sea breezes and upland cooler, less humid areas. There are rain forests in the highlands, desert-like areas in the south, and an interior area (Cockpit Country) of largely unexplored limestone pits, caves, and hills covered by thick brush.

Jamaica's capital is Kingston. Other popular towns are Montego Bay, Ocho Rios, and Port Antonio. Her economy depends on agriculture (mostly sugar cane and bananas), bauxite mining (for manufacturing aluminum), and tourism. Self-government was introduced in 1944 and extended until

Jamaica achieved full independence within the Commonwealth on August 6, 1962.

Jamaica's population of over two and a half million is 75% African ethnic origin, including many of mixed race. The official language is English, although many Jamaicans speak a local dialect of African, French, and Spanish words in a unique rhythmic lilt. Anglicanism is the major religion, but some Jamaicans incorporate African rituals such as drumming and dancing in their worship. The Rastafarian religion has become popular among young people. Reggae, a dance music and lyrics, is associated with Rastafarianism. Jamaica's most popular cultural contribution to the modern world is probably reggae (Anthony, 1989; Hunter, 1996–1997). Rastafarianism and reggae are discussed further in the section on religion.

Trinidad and Tobago

Trinidad and Tobago are the southernmost islands in the Antilles chain lying off the northeast coast of Venezuela. Trinidad, the larger, is hilly, green, and humid. The tropical climate is cooled by the northeast trade winds, with a dry season extending over half the year and a wet season the other half. Pitch Lake in southwest Trinidad is the world's largest source of natural asphalt. Tobago, 21 miles northeast of Trinidad, is less densely populated than Trinidad. Little Tobago, an island off the coast of Tobago, is a well-known sanctuary for the tropical bird of paradise, an endangered species.

The population of Trinidad and Tobago is 40.8% African descent, 40.7% East Indian, 16.3% mixed races, and 2.2% European, Chinese, and others (Hunter, 1996–1997). Trinidad/Tobago's ethnic mix is attributed to Spanish, French, East Indian, African, Dutch, English, Portuguese, and Arawak cultures. Although English is the official language, Trinidadians also speak three different Creole languages, in addition to Hindi and Urdu, which are spoken by the East Indians.

Trinidad and Tobago's capital is Port-of-Spain. Its chief export crops are sugar, cocoa, and coffee and, more recently, oil and gas. Trinidad tourism is most prevalent during Carnival time in early spring. Trinidad and Tobago became an independent member state of the Commonwealth on August 31, 1962 (Anthony, 1989; Dewitt and Wilan, 1993; Hunter, 1996–1997).

Trinidad is famous for its calypso music and steel bands, best enjoyed during Carnival, the annual week-long festival of music, dancing, and parades that takes place the week before Lent. Calypso musical style originated on the west coast of Africa as *Kaiso*, a Hausa word meaning "bravo." The African musical and festival traditions, transferred to Trinidad and Tobago by slaves, are the ancestral heritage of calypso and Carnival. The early calypsos were sung in tribal tongue, *patois*, and used like the spirituals of American slaves to spread forbidden messages among themselves and to mock their owners. Later calypso songs became political, for example, the popular song of the late 1950s entitled "Federation." Others were sung in competitions ("wars") between two or more singers. A true calypsonian was a natural composer of lyric and melody and was able spontaneously to improvise a witty story on any subject as well as to insult another singer during a "war." Many of the musicians were able to fashion instruments out of scrap metal; for example, steel drums were made from old rain barrels, hammered to produce various grooves in the surfaces, that when hit with special drumsticks would resound in melodious tones.

During the 1950s calypso music became commercial, and its songs were memorized. Calypso became popular in the United States about 1953 with the songs of the Trinidadian Mighty Sparrow (e.g., "Jean and Dinah") and the ballads of the Jamaican Harry Belafonte (e.g., "Marianne"). Calypso was later transformed into soca, a combination of calypso and soul that was considered party music. Soca has never achieved the world renowned popularity of calypso and reggae (Anthony, 1989; Dewitt & Wilan, 1993).

Barbados

Barbados lies to the east of the Windward Islands. It has a dry tropical climate and generally flat terrain. The majority of Barbadians are of African ethnic origin. The capital of the island is Bridgetown. Barbados's full internal self-government was attained in 1961, and full independence on November 30, 1966.

Most Barbados farmlands are owned by corporations or large landowners. Exquisite hotels and other industries that support tourism contribute to the island's economy. Tourism is paramount to Barbados' economy. Visitors are attracted to the beautiful white beaches with clear water and colorful coral reefs that surround the island. Also, a favorite tourist attraction is Barbados' annual festival known as "Crop Over," that occurs during late August. Crop Over is a gala celebration of calypso music, dance, and festivals similar to, but on a smaller scale than, the Trinidadian Carnival.

Barbados, the most British of the Caribbean islands, is sometimes called "Little England." Traditional British customs are seen throughout the island: Harbor officials wear uniforms similar to the traditional attire of the British Royal Navy, cricket is the most popular sport, and afternoon tea is a daily ritual in many Barbadian homes (Anthony, 1989; Hunter, 1996–1997).

HISTORY

Pre-Columbian

The Caribbean had a long history before Columbus arrived. Cibony Indians from South America were probably the first inhabitants of the

Caribbean. They migrated to the island of Hispaniola, where some settled along the coast and became fishermen and others ventured inland to became hunters. The Arawaks, also from South America, followed the Cibony but settled in the Bahamas and the Greater Antilles, where they became farmers. Sometime in the 1300s, the Caribs also migrated from South America and settled in Cuba. Unlike the Arawaks, the Caribs were warlike and soon raided Arawak villages in the Greater Antilles and eventually ruled over most of their captives. Although the Arawaks (recognized as the original inhabitants of the West Indies), were eventually wiped out by the European settlers, traces of their culture are still observed in the West Indies. For example, an Arawak dish, pepperpot stew, remains a favorite. Familiar words originated from the Arawak language, such as *huracan* (hurricane), *tobaco* (tobacco), *canaua* (canoe), and *hamaca* (hammock). In addition, many translated Arawak phrases remain familiar to West Indians, such as "the thumb is the father of the fingers," "the pulse is the soul of the hand," "the rainbow is God's plume of feathers," and the term, "my heart," used by an Arawak man when referring to his wife (Halliburton, 1994).

Post-Columbian

Columbus arrived in 1492 and, believing he was in India, named the islands the West Indies. He named the inhabitants "West Indians," while he called the indigenous people of America "Indians." During his four voyages to the West Indies between 1492 and 1502, Columbus claimed each island he explored as Spanish territory; consequently, Spain ruled the Caribbean for the following 130 years. The Spanish exploited the native inhabitants and forced them into slavery, where many died of overwork but most from European diseases to which they had no immunity, such as smallpox, measles, influenza, and malaria. Almost the entire indigenous population, including the Arawaks, had died out within 150 years after Columbus's arrival. So in order to replace the dwindling numbers of native laborers, the Spanish brought the first African slaves to the West Indies in 1518.

In the early 1600s, Spain's enemies, England, France, and the Netherlands, seized many of the Caribbean islands, with the British taking most of the islands. England took possession of Barbados in 1625, seized Jamaica in 1655, and captured Trinidad in 1797 from Spain. The islands became known as the British West Indies, and the transport of slaves continued. By the 1700s the population of the West Indies had become 90% black. For over 200 years, until the 1830s, 1.5 million slaves arrived from Africa, and the slave trade remained a profitable business (Halliburton, 1994; Palmer, 1995).

Most West Indian slaves lived as families and retained their African customs. Popular slave songs mixed English and African words that non-Africans could not understand. Slaves were denied formal education and forbidden to practice their traditional religions. Converted to Christianity by the English, many worshiped a combination of Christian beliefs and African spirits. From 1640 through the early 1800s, there were many slave revolts, resulting in high British casualties but far greater slave losses. In 1760, the famous Tacky Rebellion broke out in Jamaica; and in 1816, a major revolt occurred in Barbados (Halliburton, 1994).

Because of the many insurrection problems and the pressure from an active antislavery movement in England led by William Wilberforce, a British statesman, England abolished the slave trade in 1807. Concurrently, the demand for sugar plantation labor had been decreasing as it was found that sugar could be produced more cheaply from European beets than from West Indian sugar cane. Later, a major slave revolt that erupted in Jamaica in 1831 prompted the British Parliament to abolish slavery in the West Indies. All slaves of the British Empire were free by 1838.

Many of the freedmen refused to work for the low plantation wages and left the plantations to become farmers on their own. Consequently, between 1838 and 1917, the colonial government imported laborers from Asia as indentured servants; the expression "coolie labor" referred to cheap labor from Asia, particularly India. During this time nearly 500,000 immigrants from India (then a British colony) came to the West Indies, with the greatest number arriving in Trinidad and Tobago. The interaction of these new cultures brought cultural, racial, and religious diversity to the West Indies, resulting in a unique and heterogeneous population (Halliburton, 1994; Palmer, 1995).

Because blacks constituted over 90% of the population of the British West Indies during the nineteenth century, many were allowed to perform a wide variety of jobs, in order for the society to function. Many blacks held positions as government administrators, businessmen, professionals, and craftsmen (Klevan, 1990).

MIGRATION

The post-emancipation population rose rapidly, due to falling death rates and rising birth rates. Between 1896 and 1936, the population in the West Indies outgrew the availability of jobs, so many left to find work. West Indian migration occurred in several phases. During the first phase (1835–1885), after emancipation in the British West Indies but while slavery still existed in the Hispanic Caribbean and in America, West Indians mainly migrated to other British colonies. However, West Indians began traveling to Central America in 1853 to build the Panama Canal and ten years later to help build railways in Costa Rica and Mexico. Migration during the second phase (1885–1920) was primarily to Central America and the Hispanic Caribbean. Between 1853 and 1914, about 100,000 men went to Central America to work on the Panama Canal. The expression, "Panama Man" (a successful person who had returned from working on the Canal sporting fine clothes and a bankroll) became popular in the West Indies (Halliburton, 1994, Palmer, 1995).

Although West Indians earlier had entered the United States in small numbers, the third phase, beginning about the early 1900s, saw a major surge of immigrants to America. The early West Indian immigrants held a sojourner philosophy, to earn their fortune and return to their homeland. Migration was facilitated by the United Fruit Company's development of the banana industry, because bananas could be grown on West Indian plantations now unsuitable for sugar. Banana boats transported bananas as well as passengers and marked the beginning of regular steamship travel between the Caribbean and the United States.

Because the United States Immigration and Naturalization Service recorded mulattos as West Indian but dark-skinned individuals as African, it was difficult to determine accurately the number of West Indians entering the country. However, it was estimated that 412 West Indians were admitted to the United States in 1899; the number rose to 12,243 by 1924. During the height of this immigration phase (1911–1924), 70% of all employed persons entering the United States from the British West Indies were well-educated, professional, white-collar, or skilled workers between the ages of 14 and 44, including a high percentage of mulattos.

After slavery, the freed West Indians had stressed the importance of education for their children. Teachers were permitted and even encouraged to whip children who did not pay attention and learn. Consequently, the West Indies soon achieved one of the highest literacy rates in the world, surpassing that of many European countries as well as the United States. Ninety-nine percent could read and write English as compared to the 66% of European immigrants who could read or write any language (Halliburton, 1994; Klevan, 1990; Palmer, 1995).

Immigration from the West Indies declined around the early 1920s due to the onset of the Great Depression and later because of restrictive U.S. immigration laws. Prior to 1952, residents of the British West Indies had qualified for admission to the United States under the quota for Britain (65,000 per year). The McCarran-Walter Act of 1952 discontinued West Indian migration under the British quota and allowed only 100 immigrants from each British colony per year. Thus immigration declined until the fourth phase, when there was a major surge of English-speaking Caribbean people in the 1960s. Several factors accounted for this increase in West Indian migration to the United States: the achievement of their independence from Britain beginning in 1962, the termination of migration to Britain by the 1962 British Immigration Law, and the rapid economic growth in the United States (Klevan, 1990; Palmer, 1995).

In contrast to the West Indian immigrants of the early 1960s, who were mostly well educated and skilled in their professions, a significant number of the immigrants of the late 1960s were unskilled workers and unmarried female domestic servants. Between 1962 and 1976, the majority of West Indian immigrants were women independent of male sponsorship, making the ratio of females to males, 3 to 2. According to Gordon (1981), West Indians migrated in family groups less frequently than most other immigrants to the United States. However, since 1970, the migration of entire families as well as dependent children of settled West Indians has increased, suggesting an intention to make America their permanent home (Klevan, 1990).

The American Experience

In America, West Indians became aware of discrimination based on color unrelated to social standing. They were allocated to minority status, in contrast to their majority status on the islands. They experienced double jeopardy: racism from whites and antagonism from native African Americans, intensifying their feelings of being outsiders. Although racism existed in the British West Indies, with a hierarchy from the most "superior" whites to mulattos to dark-skinned blacks, it did not prevent blacks from achieving middle-class status and receiving recognition for their accomplishments. Consequently, West Indians tended to establish close-knit communities in the United States, partly because of racial discrimination and partly because they wished to remain separate from American blacks, on whom they looked down because of their lack of education. Perhaps they did not understand that blacks in America did not have the opportunities for education and advancement (either in the South or the North) that were common on the islands. Due to this misunderstanding West Indians tended to associate only with other West Indians, and American blacks responded to this snobbery by mocking West Indians with names like "monkey chasers," "Jewmaicans," "Garveyites," and "cokneys" (Klevan, 1990, p. 44).

Many West Indian Americans worked hard and saved, becoming known for their thriftiness. Skilled individuals often had to accept menial jobs. They were driven by two major objectives: to own a house and to get an education, if not for oneself, for one's children. Thus a strong future orientation was the force behind the advancement of West Indians as a group. Those with entrepreneurial skills opened small businesses, giving rise to the popular saying in Harlem, "As soon as a West Indian gets ten cents above a beggar, he opens a business" (Klevan, 1990, p. 42). In order to assist each other and facilitate their success in a hostile environment, many middle-class West Indians pooled their resources and formed mutual-benefit and homeowners associations (Klevan, 1990).

West Indian American lawyers, doctors, and other professionals who were often excluded from practicing in white communities serviced the black community. In the early twentieth century, it was estimated that one-third of the black professionals in New York were West Indian. Although West Indians have strived to maintain their cultural identity, much of their socioeconomic success has depended on the black community as a ready market. West Indian American success has been attributed to their high aspirations, a sense of purpose for which they are willing to sacrifice, and close family and indigenous support systems. Palmer (1995) notes that the major reason for the success of the American-born West Indians is their relatively high percentage of technical and professional workers (18.8%, compared with 14.6% for whites and 8.1% for native blacks in 1980). On the whole, West Indian communities in the United States are prosperous. While the median household income of the United States was higher than that for first-generation West Indians in 1980, the median household income for individuals of West Indian ancestry exceeded the United States median by 1990 (U.S. Bureau of the Census, 1990). West Indian American achievements appear all the more remarkable because of the low expectations of blacks held by the majority population (Klevan, 1990; Palmer, 1995).

In America some first-generation West Indians remained loyal to Britain through affection for the crown or more probably to distinguish themselves from black Americans as well as to express their disapproval of America, a racist society. West Indians who arrived after 1960 have the lowest rates of naturalization compared to all other immigrant groups in the United States. Consequently, as many have been unable to vote and affect political changes, so their political influence has lagged behind their economic success.

Although many first-generation West Indians in New York have preferred to maintain their West Indianness and have held an identity separate from indigenous blacks, many have identified with civil rights issues that affect blacks in American society. By the late 1930s and 1940s, perhaps because of decreased immigration during the Depression and World War II, tension seemed to lessen between the two groups. During the civil rights movement, West Indians and native Black Americans worked together toward common goals.

American civil rights activists of West Indian descent include Marcus Garvey, a Jamaican, the first man of color to develop a mass movement, about 1916. He encouraged racial pride, to be achieved by economic self-sufficiency through alienation. He advocated a back-to-Africa movement. This idea made him unpopular with many of the black intellectuals who advocated equality within the context of white society. In 1960 Stokely Carmichael, a Trinidadian, started the Student Nonviolent Coordinating Committee (SNCC) and helped blacks to register and vote for the first time in Alabama. He was known for the slogans "black is beautiful" and "black power." Malcolm X, of Grenadan ancestry, was an outspoken leader in the 1960s. In 1964, he formed the Organization of Afro-American Unity (OAAU), that upheld his goals of black nationalism and economic self-sufficiency.

Other notable West Indian Americans include Shirley Chisholm, of Barbadian heritage, who became the first black woman elected to Congress and the first black woman to run for the presidency of the United States; General Colin Powell, of Jamaican ancestry, who served two tours of duty in Vietnam, where he won a Bronze Star for valor and a Purple Heart. Retired after success in Operation Desert Storm, he heads the American Volunteerism project, and is the polls' favorite Republican Vice Presidential candidate for 2000; and Sidney Poitier, of Bahamian heritage, who committed his acting and directing to breaking the negative stereotype of the ignorant, lazy Negro that had been perpetuated by the white minstrels. Through his efforts along with those of his colleagues, black artists are now acknowledged as more than mere song-and-dance men (Klevan, 1990; Palmer, 1995).

Many theories have been offered to explain West Indian American economic success and prosperity when compared to native American blacks. Shirley Chisholm (1970) suggested that perhaps one reason for the success of people of West Indian ancestry in New York could be that slavery was a less destructive experience on the islands than in America; families were not broken up as they were in the South. Also, on the islands social class was more important than skin color; class could intercept racial barriers (Palmer, 1995).

Model (1995) presents some other theories that explain West Indian prosperity when compared to native blacks. Cultural distinction theory explains that since blacks in the Caribbean have long held many influential positions, West Indian immigrants are less deterred by racism and thus seek the better jobs more confidently than do native Blacks. Also, the West Indians experienced more autonomy during slavery, became free earlier, and encountered fewer post-emancipation barriers than American blacks.

Traditional selective theory offers another possible reason for the outperformance of West Indians. This theory states that motivated immigrants are self-selected for positive characteristics and holds that people who migrate tend to be more ambitious, talented, and diligent than those who do not. It was noted that southern-born blacks who had migrated to the North were more successful economically than blacks born in the North. Consequently, West Indians and native black migrants were both positively selected.

Other theories related to the prosperity of West Indians suggest that differences in class perception affect the outlook and expectations of West Indians from the islands and of blacks in America. Also, white American employers were more prone to employ foreign-born Caribbean individuals than native blacks. Further, many West Indians settled in the East and West where salaries are higher; when jobs were available, many preferred wage-paying positions over entrepreneurial endeavors (Model, 1995).

FAMILY

The West Indian family has generally been patriarchal. The father/husband is usually the dominant, authoritative figure and typically holds a more traditional concept of family life than the mother/wife. Many middle-class West Indian American families have remained patriarchal, while some lower-class families have become matriarchal.

Beyond the workplace, first-generation West Indians have attempted to maintain their West Indianness, mainly through the family. Although the traditional extended family style was common in the West Indies, the typical West Indian American family structure has been a generally closed-type nuclear model designed for survival and coping in a foreign and often hostile environment. A positive aspect of this organized closed family is that it fosters a determination to achieve as well as preserves West Indian ethnic pride. A negative aspect of this closeness (sometimes aloofness from others) is that it sometimes alienates other African Americans. Alienation from African Americans along with divisions among West Indians may be related to some West Indians' emphasis on social class based on socioeconomic status and/or skin shades (Foner, 1987; Lassiter, 1994; Sutton & Makiesky-Barrow, 1987).

The major adaptive strengths of the West Indian American family have been cohesiveness and emphasis on obedience to authority, appropriate behavior, and future orientation. The family generally respects its elders, whose advice is often sought in times of emotional and physiological stress. West Indian elders have offered many wise sayings, such as the following:

- "Empty barrel make a lot of noise" means that people who are not knowledgeable tend to talk too much.
- "Quiet river run deep" means that quiet people are usually deep thinkers.
- "Man smart, woman smarter" is clearly understood.
- "Never trouble trouble, til trouble trouble you" means leave things alone that don't bother you.
- "Fool can make money, but it is wise man who spen' it" means that it takes good sense to spend money wisely.
- "It is not for want of tongue why cow don' speak" means that having a tongue is no reason to speak inappropriately. (Brice, 1982; Lassiter, 1987).

Socialization

Generally, West Indian parents have been described as strict disciplinarians who do not believe in "sparing the rod" when dealing with their children. Disruption of family routines can be punishable. The early childhood period is usually a time of strict behavior control, and childrearing is still largely based on the premise that the child is to be seen and not heard.

The older children of the family are expected to set examples and serve as role models for the younger ones. Youngsters are taught the importance of education, to respect their elders, not to talk back, and never to call an older person by his or her first name. Emphasis is placed on obedience, education, and nonassertive behavior for girls. Boys are socialized to be responsible and nonsubservient and to achieve stable professions that offer opportunities for upward mobility.

Child fostering or "child lending" is a common practice among West Indian families. This practice, either voluntary or obligatory, assures child care by kin or friends for various lengths of time when required to facilitate migration or any travel for educational or financial improvement (Brent & Callwood, 1993; Brice, 1982; Lassiter, 1987).

Although lifestyle in the Caribbean is generally slow paced and informal, social interactions tend to be more formalized than is the norm for Americans. Privacy and acceptable distance are important to many West Indians. Familiarity is regarded as inappropriate, and being called by one's first name may be viewed as disrespectful. Getting too close and touching without permission may provoke anger in some West Indians.

Similar to many other immigrant groups that have acculturated to American society, some West Indian families no longer adhere firmly to their traditional behavior patterns, although many West Indian parents are still considered to be relatively strict. Intermarriage with native African Americans and other cultures by many second-, third-, and fourth-generation West Indians has tended to modify the atmosphere of the modern West Indian American family.

NUTRITION

Favorite West Indian foods are similar to those of other Caribbean people, although each island has its specialties. Generally, Caribbean food is spicy with liberal amounts of salt and sugar. Theory has it that the habit of high salt intake may have developed as a physiological response to the hot tropical climate of the West Indies. Because heat causes diaphoresis (sweating) with a consequent loss of salt, the body instinctively replaces the loss with a diet high in salt. Hot weather also is associated with sluggishness and lethargy, causing the body's physiological coping mechanism to stimulate a desire for sweet substances as an energy source. Thus, it is probable that some individuals from the West Indies have developed a taste dependence on salt and sugar, as reflected in their diets (Leonidas & Hyppolite, 1983).

Jamaica

Jamaican cooking is strongly intertwined with African culinary traditions. *Accras* (fritters), traditionally African and popular throughout the West Indies, are called "stamp-and-go" in Jamaica. The most popular Jamaican dish is probably salt fish: salt fish and ackee, salt fish and rice, salt fish fritters, or curried salt fish. Salt fish is usually cod that is soaked overnight to remove the salt. Ackee, a delicate tree vegetable, requires careful and knowledgeable preparation. If ackee is eaten before the fruit opens on the tree or is forced ripe, it can be unsafe to eat. Ackee are boiled, fried, curried, cooked into a rice soup, or used in pudding as an egg substitute. Ackee cakes are often enjoyed with black-eyed peas.

Plantain, another popular vegetable (green or ripe), may be boiled, fried, or roasted. Green plantains are often eaten with salt fish. Other favorite vegetables include *tous-les-mois* (bears every month), or French arrowroot, and cho-cho (flavor similar to apples), used in soups, stews, and puddings.

Among the popular Jamaican dishes are peas and rice, turtle soup, ackee soup, king fish, crayfish, and baked black crabs. Favorite meats include beef, mutton (usually goat), pork, and poultry. Frequently prepared desserts include breadfruit, tapioca or ackee puddings, cashew nuts, avocado, rose apples (seeds are poisonous), guineps, mangoes, and other tropical fruits. Popular Jamaican beverages include tamarind drink (pineapple, chewstick peel, ginger root), ginger beer, chocolate, Jamaican rum, and many herb teas (Sullivan, 1996).

Trinidad and Tobago

The foods of Trinidad and Tobago show a strong East Indian influence. One of the most notable East Indian cooking techniques is the use of curry, that originally contained hot chile peppers. Today curry dishes are milder, but hot pepper sauce is often added at the table. Almost every foodstuff is curried, including mangoes, pumpkins, eggplant, potatoes, green tomatoes, okra, chicken, fish, beef, and goat.

Breads are another hallmark of East Indian influence. The most popular is *roti*, a thin bread (*chapatti*), cooked on griddles or baking stones. The technique of wrapping the thin bread around curried stuffings to form a burrito-like sandwich originated in Trinidad and is called roti. There are many kinds of roti: fish, chicken, liver, goat, beef, shrimp, conch, duck, and potato channa (curried chick peas). Roti has been described by calypso writer Daisann McLane as Trinidad's major contribution to world cuisine. Other bread favorites are *bakes*, a biscuit fried in oil in a skillet, and *doubles*, a sandwich made with fried bara bread with several fillings (usually curried chick peas, hot sauce, and kucheala, a spicy mango pickle).

A signature dish of Trinidad and Tobago is *callaloo*, a spicy soup made of okra and callaloo leaves (also known as taro, dasheen, or tannia) and any meat, ranging from pig's tails to crabmeat. Callaloo is a green vegetable similar to spinach. The dish is usually served in Trinidadian homes on Sundays and special occasions. After callaloo, two other popular soups are cowheel and sancoche (vegetable soup). Sancoche is also a versatile vegetable beef stew that may contain several ingredients, including yams, tannia, tara, cassava, potatoes, pumpkin, and plantains.

A favorite Trinidadian meat dish is *pelau*, caramelized (African practice) chicken or goat. The meat forms a dark brown layer on the bottom of the pot called *bun-bun*, that many enjoy. Pelau contains meat, pigeon peas or black-eyed peas, coconut milk, rice, squash, onions, and spices. Popular also are stewed oxtail, coconut-curried goat, and black pudding (originally made from pig's blood, but now liver is substituted). Seafood is important in island cuisine: shark steaks, snapper, grilled grouper in banana leaves, curried cascadura (Trinidad catfish), and curried crabs and dumplings.

Favorite Trinidadian desserts include cassava pone (any combination of sweet potatoes, yams, or pumpkins with brown sugar, raisins, and spices), coconut rice pudding, mango mousse, and Trinidad black cake. Black cake, very rich in butter, sugar, fruits, nuts, spices, and rum, requires at least two months' preparation and is most frequently served on holidays and special occasions. Mangoes, oranges, grapefruit, and papayas are favorite fruits. Popular beverages of Trinidad and Tobago include passion fruit cocktail, rum punch, pina colada, ginger beer, and various herb teas (DeWitt & Wilan, 1993).

Barbados

Barbadian specialties include pickled finger bananas, pumpkin and spinach fritters, fried chicken, okra and tomatoes, flying fish in green seasoning, mashed breadfruit, fried plantains, roast pork, and coconut pie. Green seasoning is a mixture of herbs and spices similar to Dominican *sazón* or Puerto Rican *sofrito*.

Bajan's Saturday night special is pudding and souse. The pudding, cleaned pig's intestines stuffed with seasoned mashed Bajan sweet potato and West Indian pumpkin, is served with souse, that is, a spicy stew of pig's feet, snouts, tails, and flesh, boiled and pickled in a blend of lime juice, bell peppers, cucumbers, onions, and hot scotch bonnet chilies.

A Bajan Christmas favorite descends from a Scottish dish called *haggis*. The Bajan version, called *jug-jug*, consists of salted meats cooked with millet (guinea corn), green pigeon peas, and seasonings. Chicken may be the most popular single food; fried and stewed with plantains, coconut, breadfruit, and sweet potatoes, or as "fowl-down-in-rice" or just deliciously seasoned fried chicken.

Cou-cou, a cornmeal and okra dish, called *fungi* or *foofoo* on the other islands, is an African recipe that is virtually unchanged over four hundred years. Cou-cou requiring a long cooking time and constant stirring (said to build muscles on the chef), is served with fried salt fish cakes.

The British heritage in Barbados is evident in a British holiday (Guy Fawkes Day) celebration marked by Bajan sweets called *conkies*. Conkies are a mixture of cornmeal, pumpkin, sweet potato, coconut, brown sugar, and spices divided into two-tablespoon portions and steamed in plantain leaves or aluminum foil. Among other popular Bajan foodstuffs are the many tropical vegetables and fruits of the Caribbean area. Beverages include fruit juices and the famous Bajan rum punch (Robertiello, 1995).

RELIGION

West Indian Americans from areas originally colonized by the British are predominantly Protestant, while those from islands having a strong French or Spanish influence are predominantly Roman Catholic. Many of the Christian churches established schools in the Caribbean as well as in the United States. Other influential religious groups are Rastafarians, Moslems, Jews, and folk and tribal religions (Brice, 1982).

Rastafari and Reggae

The Rastafari religion, that began in Jamaica in 1930, professes that Haile Selassie is the true living God. The name, Rastafari, was derived from Haile Selassie's family name, "Ras Tafari." The Rastafari philosophy is based on Garvey's legacy of Ethiopianism, Pan-Africanism, and black consciousness. Rastafari is a religious-cultural movement that focuses on traditional African culture and natural lifestyle. Rastas (members) are generally vegetarians and avoid alcohol, but they consider marijuana a holy and sacramental herb. Rastas believe that the hair is part of the spirit and therefore should never be combed or cut, but worn in "dreadlocks." Rastafari has spread worldwide since the late 1960s, primarily through its medium of reggae music (Klevan, 1990; Mulvaney, 1990; Semaj, 1985).

Many claim that the word *reggae* means "raggedy," "everyday," or "from the people." Reggae is a type of pop music influenced by rock and roll, rhythm and blues, soul, Latin American music, traditional Jamaican religious and secular music, and African musical themes. Reggae is characterized by its slow tempo, its unique rhythmic structure (in 4/4 time) in which beats two and four are accentuated rather than beats one and three, and its chant-like vocals. When associated with Rastafari, socially, politically, and religiously critical lyrics serve as a form of protest. Reggae, now the most popular form of Caribbean music, is frequently enjoyed in concerts, dance halls, parades, and parties. Its esteemed performer, the Rastafarians' most prominent spokeperson, was Bob Marley, who died in 1981 (Klevan, 1990; Mulvaney, 1990).

Obeah

Obeah, a religious system prevalent in the West Indies, reflects aspects of African Ashanti religious practices and Protestant beliefs. Obeah, invokes the supernatural, to cause good or evil by influencing people's lives with special "powers." Believers hold that Obeah, led by its shamans (Obeah men and women), can cause or cure most physical and mental conditions.

Obeah is based on the belief that spirits (*Jumbies*) are able to inhabit and possess humans. An Obeah man or woman usually works with a client to cure an illness, to cast spells on others, or to counteract spells cast by other Obeah practitioners. Some West Indians believe that the practice helps to structure and control intangible forces that can act on humans; thus, Obeah may serve as a method of coping with stressful situations (Brent & Callwood, 1993; Lassiter, 1994; Leftley & Bestman, 1977).

HEALTH

West Indians tend to view health as a combination of West African holistic and modern germ-theory philosophies. The germ theory is upheld more by some middle-class and better-educated West Indians. Others may define the illness as a product of unnatural influences and seek help from a shaman. Generally, West Indians believe that most illnesses can be caused by "cold," "gas" or "wind," "heat," "bile," blood imbalances, or germs. Cold is the result of "catching a first draft" or getting wet. Gas or wind in the body may manifest as pain in the back, joints, or stomach, possibly precipitated by changes in the weather, overexertion, poor eating habits, or the aging process. Despite comments about West Indians' lack of confidence in scientific medicine, it was noted that West Indian Americans consult general practitioners more regularly than many other ethnic groups (Balarajan, Yuen, & Soni, 1989; Lassiter, 1994; Mitchell, 1983).

West Indian folk remedies may include a variety of substances, for example:

- To relieve fevers: bush bath with lime leaf (liquorice bush) or teas made of fever grass, ackee leaves, soursop, cowfoot, sage, jack-in the-bush.
- To treat a cold: several "bush" teas including calabash and wild sage teas.
- For sore throat: boiled goongoo leaves.
- For indigestion, liver ailments, diarrhea: ginger tea or bitter bush tea.
- To cure rheumatism: marenga root steeped in rum applied to the area.

• To ward off evil: baths, such as indigo blue dye water and lotions like Florida water mixed with amber and rose oil, and/or special items to be worn, for example, bags of herbs, treated amulets, chains, or medallions.

Common Health Conditions

The most frequent conditions encountered in West Indian Americans are obesity, diabetes in older people, hypertension, and heart disease. Because of their African heritage, small numbers may present with sickle cell anemia (discussed in Chapter 1).

REFERENCES

Anthony, S. (1989). *West Indies: Places and peoples of the world.* New York: Chelsea House.

Balarajan, R., Yuen, P., & Soni, R. V. (1989). Ethnic differences in general practitioner consultations. *British Medical Journal, 299*(6705), 958–60.

Brent, J. E., & Callwood, G. B. (1993). Culturally relevant psychiatric care: The West Indian client. *Journal of Black Psychology, 19*(3), 290–302.

Brice, J. (1982). West Indian families. In M. McGoldrick, J. K. Pearce, & J. Giordano (Eds.), *Ethnicity and family therapy* (pp. 123–33). New York: Guilford Press.

Chaney, E. M. (1987). The context of Caribbean migration. In C. R. Sutton & E. M. Chaney (Eds.), *Caribbean life in New York City: Sociocultural dimensions* (pp. 3–14). New York: Center for Migration Studies of New York.

Chisholm, S. (1970). *Shirley Chisholm: Unbought and unbossed.* New York: Avon Books.

Collier's encyclopedia: Vol. 23. (1996). West Indies (pp. 412–19). New York: Collier's.

Dewitt, D., & Wilan, M. J. (1993). *Callaloo, calypso, and carnival: The cuisines of Trinidad and Tobago.* Freedom, Calif.: Crossing Press.

Foner, N. (1987). West Indians in New York and London: A comparative analysis. In C. R. Sutton & E. M. Chaney (Eds.), *Caribbean life in New York City: Sociocultural dimensions* (pp. 117–30). New York: Center for Migration Studies of New York.

Gordon, M. (1981). Caribbean migration: A perspective on women. In D. M. Mortimer & R. S. Bryce-Laporte (Eds.), *Female immigrants to the United States: Caribbean, Latin, and African experiences* (pp. 14–55). Washington, D.C.: Smithsonian Institution.

Halliburton, W. J. (1994). *Coming to America: The West Indian American experience.* Brookfield, Conn.: Millbrook Press.

Hunter, B. (1996–1997). *The Statesman's Year-Book: A statistical, political and economic account of the states of the world for the year 1996–1997* (133rd ed.). New York: St. Martin's Press.

Klevan, M. (1990). *The West Indian Americans.* New York: Chelsea House.

Lassiter, S. M. (1987). Coping as a function of culture and socioeconomic status for Afro-Americans and Afro-West Indians. *Journal of the New York State Nurses Association*, 18(3), 18–30.

Lassiter, S. M. (1994). Black is a color, not a culture: Implications for health care. *ABNF Journal* (Association of Black Nursing Faculty), 5(1), 4–9.

Leftley, H., & Bestman, E. W. (1977). Psychotherapy in Caribbean cultures. Paper presented at the 85th Annual Convention of the American Psychological Association, San Francisco, California.

Leonidas, J. R., & Hyppolite, N. (1983). West Indian patients: Care in United States a challenge. *New York State Journal of Medicine* 2, 218–20.

Mitchell, M. F. (1983). Popular medical concepts in Jamaica and their impact on drug use. *Western Journal of Medicine*, 139(6), 820–28.

Model, S. (1995). West Indian prosperity: Fact or fiction? *Social Problems*, 42(4), 535–50.

Mulvaney, R. M. (1990). *Rastafari and reggae: A dictionary and sourcebook*. Westport, Conn.: Greenwood Press.

Palmer, R. W. (1995). *Pilgrims from the sun: West Indian migration to America*. New York: Twayne Publishers.

Robertiello, J. (1995). Food: Barbados boasts Bajan bounty. *Americas*, 47(3), 58–59.

Semaj, L. T. (1985, December). Rastafari: From religion to social theory. *Caribbean Quarterly*, 21–31.

Sullivan, C. (1996). *Classic Jamaican cooking: Traditional recipes and herbal remedies*. London: Serif.

Sutton, C. R. (1987). The Caribbeanization of New York City and the emergence of a transnational socio-cultural system. In C. R. Sutton & E. M. Chaney (Eds.), *Caribbean life in New York City: Sociocultural dimensions* (pp. 15–30). New York: Center for Migration Studies of New York.

Sutton, C. R., & Makiesky-Barrow, S. (1987). Migration and West Indian racial and ethnic consciousness. In D. M. Mortimer & R. S. Bryce Laporte (Eds.), *Female immigrants to the United States: Caribbean, Latin and African experiences* (pp. 92–116). Washington, D.C.: Smithsonian Institution.

U.S. Bureau of the Census. (1990). *Statistical abstracts of the United States*. Washington, D.C.: U.S. Government Printing Office.

Index

About the Author

SYBIL M. LASSITER is a retired professor of nursing from East Tennessee State University and Adelphi University. Her various positions have included Public Health Nurse for the New York City Department of Health, consultant for the New York State Health and Education Department, and examiner for the Regents External Degree Program in Nursing.